CONTENTS

Acknowledgments

There are various people who have helped me in writing this book and whom I wish to thank. They include all those editors and publishers who have allowed me to quote from their publications, named in the text, and the Copyright Department of the British Broadcasting Corporation.

Mr. Greene himself has been very helpful and so has his secretary, Mrs. D. R. Young. It is very difficult picking out names from amongst the others but I would especially like to mention Mrs. Margaret Knight, Dr. J. A. Hadfield, Dr. Bernard Raymund, Miss Helen May Stewart and Mr. A. R. Redway, whose bibliography will unfortunately appear too late for me to make use of it.

Above all, however, I am indebted to Mr. Leon Drucker, who appeared out of the blue to offer me his assistance. I have exploited his willingness most shamelessly and hope that this acknowledgment will express in small part my gratitude.

J.A.

Preface to Second Edition

THE author is in a vulnerable position because reviewers can do what they like to him and his own letters to the press are not always printed. This was my own experience, with the publication of this book, because it aroused the ire of the Greene claque.

One wrote (referring to my treatment of *Stamboul Train*): Had I never met a female journalist? The answer is yes, often. I've also met white mercenaries, whoremongers and pimps. But I didn't know that such acquaintance should be regarded as literary criteria. On the other hand, I thought it my job to criticise GG's early tendency to snigger at (oh!) SEX. As I made it clear that the mature GG is one of the most interesting writers we have on the subject of sex, it seemed worth while stressing that development had taken place. But adolescence lurks in every corner and literary adolescence insists on being portentously thrilled by (oh!) SEX.

This type of criticism is typical of the pettiness that one encounters far too often in the weeklies these days. The nineteenth century reviewers used to be long-winded and at times boring, but they knew their stuff and they usually dealt with essentials. Fundamentally the kind of criticism I have quoted is a good example of the irrelevant treatment of one of the novel's main concerns: characterisation. Compare the characterisation of Mabel Warren in *Stamboul Train* with what was to come later in *Heart of the Matter* and *End of the Affair*, and ask yourself: Why do so-called critics expose themselves in this way? The answer lies in a pathetic prurience that is a sickly expression of erotic frankness. And the youth shouts I'M REALLY WITH IT. The very expression is outmoded before it reaches print.

Now we come to a criticism that is not more serious but is more seriously put: Mr Atkins has no point of view. I should hope not. Are we never to progress? Bentham, Marx and Spengler are sound examples of critics who not only had a point of view but had very little else.[1] Do we regard them as the culture heroes of our time? Since then we've had J. C. Powys, I'll even chance it and add Henry Miller, crazy though he may be as a thinker, to at least suggest a way of getting out of our monomania. To hear people prating of point-of-view in artistic matters, after the Cubists have broken with the rules of perspective and the physicists have begun to express their theories in four dimensions, is to experience a quiet despair. But perhaps these chaps don't understand, perhaps they really don't understand what the modern debate is all about! I'm afraid one is compelled to confess that the synthetic approach to experience has come largely from the scientists. The humanist critics have not surmounted their personal barriers. They have not yet caught up. I think my publisher ought to bring out a special edition of J. C. Powys, if he can get the rights. An inkling of what we might do, of the next step we might take, is there.

Then there was exception taken to my apostrophes to GG on pages 219 and 222 of the first edition. For the last dozen years I've lived in the land of apostrophe, and perhaps it's catching. Clearly, this is a form of mockery. Either there is something wrong with expressing mockery in this way, or you mustn't mock GG. Well, of course, so far as the acolytes are concerned it is the second interpretation. But there is also a strong movement, stemming from the English Honours Schools, I fancy, to straitjacket the way you say a thing. There is an insistence today on a kind of Tomtiddler's Rules of criticism that serves no purpose but to drain such work of humanity, humour, jollity and ultimately vitality. The rules of criticism taught in our modern universities remind me of the rules of morality censorship tries to impose.

I tried to give a picture of Greene as a tough-minded writer who is greatly impressed by the power of accident and misinterpretation. Like many other writers, he does not necessarily understand what makes him the way he is. He happens to attribute most of his principles and prejudices to his Catholic faith. Far too willingly the critics accepted him as a Catholic novelist, confusing the essence with the mask. Greene himself encourages the reader to put the

[1] This sounds rash. I had better say they allowed a point of view to dominate other excellent qualities.

Catholic cart before the creative horse. The central preoccupations of the novels might very well have been expressed without any recourse to theology. But now Greene, wearied by the mindless process he helped to set in motion, protests in his Epitaph to *Carving a Statue*. I must be very careful to explain exactly what I mean and not take it for granted that everyone will seize my meaning without the kind of emphasis one usually hopes one can avoid. Greene has often written about Catholics and he has made Catholic belief the arbiter of much of his work. No-one could possibly deny this. But this does not mean that criticism of Greene's work should therefore reduce itself to an essay in moral theology. By no means. The greater part of discussion on Greene's fiction still belongs to this genre, however. We will never see Greene straight and clear until we look behind his own protestations. Greene says that a knowledge of good and evil is an essential part of the novelist's equipment. I discuss this view in Chapter XVIII of this book. What I want to stress here is that, except when he is self-conscious, Greene's equip-ment is part of the common property of the humanist English novelist, and should be viewed as such. Critical principles and stan-dards should never be varied to suit the subject; the unchangingness of standards is the very thing that allows differences to be seen clearly. Greene has suffered greatly from this kind of critical feckless-ness.

It is quite obvious that although I admire Greene's skill I don't care for his slant. This is where point-of-view comes in. Undoubtedly Greene's personal taste for the pessimistic side of experience finds a ready response from many of his readers. We are really concerned with two types of people, as fully contrasted as introvert and extro-vert, classical and romantic. For you may admire the tree and legiti-mately dislike the fruit; you may enjoy the fruit and care little for the tree; but to suck the fruit, spit it out in distaste, and exclaim 'God, how marvellous!' suggests either dishonesty or a pathetic lack of adjustment to anything that brings order to a disordered world. We are up against a new spirit in criticism, which has managed to winkle literature out of the area of permitted enjoyments. Pompous, sterile and joyless, it mopes under the cloud of the Eng. Hons. schools up and down the country. The banner is the disastrous

B

Pelican volume entitled *The Modern Age*, intended (I quote) 'for those many thousands of general readers who accept with genuine respect what is known as our "literary heritage" '. The respect they are taught reminds me of the respect Pavlov's dogs felt when they heard the bell. In keeping with this are the letters I get from young fellows who (often very matily) tell me it's not enough to approve or disapprove, you've got to analyse. The truth is that there is a time for analysis as there is for enthusiasm. Without initial enthusiasm, analysis is about as fruitful as peeling potatoes for someone who likes them in their jackets. The aridity of so much modern criticism comes from the fact that it is passionless. It's a job. When recently I read a thesis for a Master's degree (which was awarded by a British university) that was so inept, so lacking not merely in judgment but in any attempt at judgment, that showed such a weary lack of passionate concern for its subject, that was so drearily and incontrovertibly a piece of writing that had been undertaken merely to get a higher degree—then I realised that this particular part of the academic process has passed beyond redemption.

This edition is substantially the same as the first except that a pun in French, which was not appreciated, has been removed. I find that if I make puns in English I am left in peace, but if I make one in French or Arabic dozens of people hasten to point out the other meaning. No wonder so many writers turn to other callings.

According to a recent publication twenty books and dissertations have so far appeared on Greene. Approximately another twenty deal with him as part of a larger problem—note how I accept, *pro tem*, this classification of a prominent writer as a problem and not a human being, an *objet d'art* or a source of entertainment. Periodical articles on Greene are legion—I have seen a 'select' list of one hundred and eleven. I have read very few of these but should like to make a few comments on one or two I have read.

In the Pelican *The Modern Age*, to which I have already made an unfavourable reference, there is an example of a writer striving manfully to get out of his straitjacket. All honour to him. This is Graham Martin whose contribution is entitled 'Novelists of Three Decades: Evelyn Waugh, Graham Greene, C. P. Snow'. Critical honesty compels Mr Martin to resist his academic training and the literary climate with sufficient power to write this: 'Novels can be more socially conscious than novelists, and this is the case here (*Brighton Rock*) and with a number of Greene's novels; Pinkie's condition is socially meaningful . . . ' Later he makes another percipient comment: 'What, of course, makes it hard to identify the social consciousness of Greene's novels is either the exclusion in the early ones of any explicit comment or, in the later ones, the insistence of the theology'. Perhaps I did not state this clearly enough in my study but in fact it is implied throughout. Greene's work is valuable as social commentary and much more as individual (including personal) revelation, but least of all as theological argument. The theology is on the surface, planted there rather weightily in many cases by Greene himself, but it is a surface growth. Even where, in two or three novels, Greene works hard to suggest that the dilemmas he describes grow organically out of religious doctrine, he is cheating. I do not mean this in any objectionable sense; we all cheat. It is the duty of the critic to know when his author is cheating. In the case of Greene, and from the early days of his career, the critics have been bamboozled. What is sad is to see that many of them are still blinking through the wool (of the Lamb) pulled over their eyes by an author whom they have erected into something as magical as the True Cross. There is no better example of theological cheating than in *The Power and the Glory*, as Mr Martin has noted. The policeman and his arguments are a parody of what they are in life, and the priest gets his strength not through his arguments but through his experiences.

David Pryce-Jones, author of the book on Graham Greene in the Oliver & Boyd series, 'Writers and Critics', missed his opportunity and produced a study of a religious man who had tried to write novels. It is not meant as an insult, one can be sure of that, for Greene is treated with the greatest apparent reverence, but it is in fact insulting, though perhaps to literature rather than to Greene. And yet he goes so near. He compares the manoeuvring of characters in some of Greene's fiction to the progress of a game of chess. This should have given him a clue—but no, he goes from here to call *The Power and the Glory* his 'most powerful novel', in other words, puts his finger on the faulty connection but doesn't feel the shock. For it is in the power of this novel that its true weakness resides, the power that is really expressed by its lack of humanity (terrifying, one would have thought), its abstraction of a world made by priests and politicians for their own dubious purposes. In this novel Greene trundles around a corpse (as he liked to do occasionally in his early stories, but without the symbolic trappings) and apparently hoodwinked the majority of his readers into believing the man was alive. There's black magic for you.

The most ambitious work on Greene during the last few years has come from the University of Kentucky: *Graham Greene: Some Critical Considerations*, edited by Robert O. Evans. Most of the contributors are Americans, but they include Miriam Allott and myself. Mr Evans was kind enough to ask me to write a Reconsideration of *The Power and the Glory*, an assignment I accepted with alacrity. Before I finish this preface I should like to pick out some of the points made by various contributors which I feel can assist in our understanding of this slippery author.

Francis L. Kunkel, in 'The Theme of Sin and Grace', states the real objection to Greene's theology:

> Not only are the Catholic characters greater sinners, but they are frequently less happy in the state of grace than they are in the state of sin. Sarah Miles, for instance, is a carefree relaxed sinner before her conversion and life of virtue plunge her into woe. The nearer she approaches to God, the less joy she takes from the created world and human love. Pascal describes the wretchedness of man without God; Greene describes the wretchedness of man with God.

A little later Mr Kunkel says that Greene does not glorify sin, he glorifies humility. This may well have been his intention but how often is such intention obtrusive enough to be noticed? And is it always humility? Humilty is, I imagine, the most difficult of the virtues, or conversely, it is the most effective mask for a host of less pleasant qualities. One often feels that there is a definite pride in, a wallowing in sin, especially the sinfulness of sin, which is its intellectual aspect. Again, *The Power and the Glory* represents the summit of this aspect. When Mr Kunkel refers to the misery of the converted Sarah he scores a bull. One's instincts cry out that this is wrong. One's instincts cry out that there ought to be no argument on the matter. If faith in God decreases Sarah's sum of happiness, what more need for discussion? Certainly I will be accused of old-fashioned utilitarianism, but this brand of utilitarianism has never been adequately disposed of. In *Brighton Rock* Greene tried to relegate the idea of 'wrong' to a level lower than that of 'evil'. This is one of the arguments that I challenged in this book and still do. I do not challenge the author's right to claim anything he pleases, but I do maintain that a critic's function is to examine terms, assertions and ideologies, to see exactly how much reality they possess.

If you follow Greene's story as a human drama you will keep your feet on solid ground and you will know where you are. If you surrender to the allurement of a theological interpretation (including any he himself provides for us) you will soon be lost in a never-never land of assumptions that you may be tempted to accept simply because they are strange and at times outrageous. (Of course, anyone has the right to read Greene in the spirit that one reads science fiction, but readers of science fiction do not assess it according to the weird ologies they encounter in this form. I once wrote a book on science fiction in which I solemnly accepted all the conventions on which this form is based, but the whole thing was a spoof). Greene's theology, when stripped of the skill with which it is presented, is really little more than a complicated metaphorical structure. There are terrifying moments when one feels it exists merely to ward off the truth.

Mary McCarthy accused Greene of introducing 'words with churchly connotations' to awaken in the reader religious sentiments having no justification in the action of the novel. I feel that some of the authors of the Kentucky University book have (as have so many reviewers and critics before them) come to rest with the religious sentiments and lost sight of the life behind them. David H. Hesla, writing on 'Theological Ambiguity in the "Catholic Novels" ', was compelled to do this by his choice of subject. My complaint is that this subject is too freely chosen. Kai Laitinen, a Finn, writing on 'The Heart of the Novel: the Turning Point in *The Heart of the Matter*', does not do this but cuts right through the candy-floss to something that belongs to all of us. It should not be required of a critic that he be a theologian to discuss a novel that is hung with theology; if we do accept such a requirement, then the general critic (and the best critic must always be general) will be compelled to retire in the face of any cosy little expertise the author wishes to confound him with. The critic must take a direct look at the theology, or the campanology, or philately, or whatever it is that gives the novel a special tone or starting point, and try to answer the question: is this a recognisable picture of our world? It may be unbalanced, it may be a caricature, but it can still be recognisable. Then to what extent is it recognisable? And how is it done? We touch on theology and we expect restraint—from the critic. The only excuse for criticism is its purity.

Greene comes out of the test brilliantly. His work is recognisable. He portrays life and people with a personal slant that helps to stimulate the reader. We can discount the prejudice and the idiosyncrasy. What we should not forgive is the emphasis laid by some critics on subsidiary matters. And if you want to discover how Greene gets his effect you could not do better than read Dominick P. Consolo in the Kentucky book, writing on 'Style and Stylistics in Five Novels'. It is a relief from moralising.

Finally, in addition to this rather jolly Preface you will find a new chapter at the other end of the book, dealing with the books Greene has published since this work first appeared.

                                                           J. A.

Khartoum
March, 1965

I

APPRENTICESHIP

Nineteen Twenty-Five to Nine
'Babbling April', 'The Man Within'

I SHOULD like to treat Graham Greene as an island newly discovered on 2nd October, 1904. Charles Henry Greene, Headmaster
of Berkhamsted School, was primarily responsible for the dis-
covery. Whyte Melville and Robert Louis Stevenson lay in the
background, like ships anchored offshore or even consigned to the
breaker's yard. It is always a vexed question, deciding whether
specific capacities can be handed on from father to son—or, to maintain my analogy, to what extent one culture can be essentially
affected by another. But no analogy retains its usefulness for long
and it is time I dropped this one. It will be enough to say that
Graham attended his father's school and then went on to Balliol.
The school had a powerful influence on him, which I shall refer to in
due course. While there, however, Graham was still known only to
his friends and relations and I shall continue to regard him as *terra
incognita*. Balliol and Oxford made little impression on him, and he
even less on them. He was not a scholar by temperament, although
his changeable, mercurial character sometimes yearned for scholastic
success. He took a second in modern history. He also met Vivien
Dayrell-Browning, an attractive Roman Catholic.

It should be remembered that this young man was not one of the
Great in embryo. He was to become a talented and successful author,
something much subtler and more interesting than the Great Man
with his sledgehammer impact on society. Graham was not even a
prefect at school. He must certainly have been a boy of considerable
gifts, though they were gifts which required maturity for their full
expression. He was not the kind of person whom schoolmasters
automatically set over others; neither presence nor authority nor
bluff were his. Later, in a book by Hugh Kingsmill and Hesketh

9

Pearson, we get glimpses of a man whom others, particularly the hearty, pipe-smoking type, tend to patronize. It is probable that Graham never impressed anyone immediately, and that he possessed a subtlety and understanding that were so removed from the ordinary clubman's comprehension that he was regarded as being rather funny. Other men thought Milton effeminate, although he wasn't, and similar misapprehensions were current concerning Keats and Shelley.

After Oxford this young man showed a desire to go East—not unusual in the middle-class society of the time. The East promised adventure, money and sex. He took a job with a tobacco company because it offered the prospect of three years in China, but it never came to anything. He appears to have considered the consular ser-vice and the Nigerian Navy, a force which I imagined at one time he had invented. He tutored a small boy for a few weeks but without enthusiasm: 'I don't particularly like small boys and I had forgotten all my Latin.' As we get to know him better we understand that the reference to small boys was almost certainly an understatement, and yet we must associate it with a tendency to weep over the small boy's corruption. From the small boy he rebounded to Vivien, proposing to her. Next came a job with the Nottingham *Journal* without pay, 'just for the experience'. At this time he became friendly with a Catholic priest, Father Trollope, and after three months of discus-sion he was received into the Catholic Church (February 1926). The same priest married him to Vivien in October 1927 and later a son and daughter were born. After some years of happiness relations cooled and Mr Greene now lives apart from his wife, although on friendly terms. This study is to be of Graham Greene as seen through his writings—after all, it is his writings that make him interesting to the world at large. His domestic life is undoubtedly important as a fund of experience, but it is not something over which I wish to linger. I prefer to return to the year 1925, when he produced his first book, *Babbling April*.

Having compared Graham with an island I now propose to liken him to an onion. An onion is a vegetable peeled by housewives, and as the operation is frequently attended by tears it has served as a valuable image for generations of critics. One peels off layer after layer to get to the true, basic onion. But let us reverse the process and imagine the true, basic onion (which we can never know, it being the divine spark) being clothed and fattened. This volume of poems, produced when the author was twenty-one, may be regarded as the first layer. It was dedicated to his father and mother; it took a sour look at life's dinginess, and it spoke knowingly (as do so many books by very young men) of death. If Wordsworth was right, a young man of twenty is closer to death (his last death) than an older man of thirty, and is therefore justified in laying emphasis on it. As for the title, it came from a poem by Edna St Vincent Millay—

> It is not enough that yearly, down this hill,
> April
> Comes like an idiot, babbling and strewing flowers—

and appears to have little relevance to the contents, except that it probably pleased Graham to call April names.

The Death label, or wrapping, had more reality than is usual in work of this type. The first and last poems in the book refer to an occasion, or occasions, when Graham actually contemplated suicide and went some way to meet it. I prefer, however, to leave consideration of this event until a later page, when I deal with the essay complementary to these two poems. With them removed, the references to death are as tiresome and seemingly pretentious as others of that genre—which tempts me to ask whether we are justified in dismissing so coolly the anguish of youth and its habit of extreme expression. In 'Après Vous' Graham tells his girl he will follow her quickly if she departs from life, but would prefer not to go first as he is shy in new company. In other words, she is to be a heavenly ice-breaker. He advises her to tell Michael not to let him talk to God 'of the superiority of Hell's constitution'. In another poem he tells her that he will be happy when she's gone—like a stone, and repeats it in 'If You Were Dead' by stating that he would have rest. Wry humour enters into 'Death and Cosmetics': death being near, he (or she) makes up, to 'snatch a brief handicap before decay'. This sort of verse only impresses young men and women who are trapped by the death-wish. As I have said, the wish may have been more intense than we are apt to suspect, but I have my doubts, as I will explain in due course.

The most successful poem in the collection (largely in the light of the later prose) is called '1930' and hence qualifies for an anthology of writing about the future. Graham's anticipated future was, to say the least, seedy.

> Eating a Lyons' chop in nineteen thirty,
> And staring through the heavy-lidded pane,
> Wondering why they keep their plates so dirty,
> And why there's dust in a London April rain,
> I shall see out of the sick swim of faces,
> Huddled beneath umbrellas in the Strand,
> Dim reminiscence of those better places,
> Where my rich cargo drove upon the sand.
>
> Then through the crumbling of some bread I'll ponder,
> I'll ponder through the scraping of a plate,
> How love which should have been a blaze of wonder,
> Has been a dusty and untended grate,
> With crooked, grimy bars twisted asunder,
> Because its servant rose from sleep too late.

There we have one note which was to become familiar: the obsession with failure, only it would have to be other people's failures, for he was doomed to succeed. And here we have another touch, equally characteristic, the astonishing custom the sun has of shining on chamber pots, the vital relationship noted in a song that used to be sung by amateur footballers on the way home: [1]

> Star of the evening,
> Beautiful evening star,
> Star of the evening,
> Shining on the shithouse door.

Graham's outstanding contribution, though written without any élan whatsoever, to this mode is called 'The Banbury Road, 12 p.m.':

> Two men, chasmed by twenty feet,
> Half-turned to each other;
> Black overcoats like cloaks outthrown;
> A cigar-end—the point of an unsheathed sword;
> The lustre of night and the star-dazzled sky—

I listened so hard for the cry,
'Three counts and engage at the handerkchief's fall'.
Did the challenge come first at the ball,
(Minuette and Gavotte)
With over that ear a rose
And the night was so hot,
And no-one can see in the dark,
And a rent in the Spanish shawl.
I was drunk, so I came up close.
Two men, like dogs, were using a garden wall.

The world was a cheat and life was not worth living. His elders, tradition, poetry, perhaps even some of his instincts, told him that life was enjoyable—

> All nature's mine, they say, and I agree—
> And yet, God knows, I am dissatisfied.

And then an outburst of anger, entitled 'On A Walking Tour', fury at the suspicion that the best things would come in age, that it was necessary to wait, that life was a fraud because the fruit of promise was frustration.

> Oh damn you, bird, what do you want up there?
> I'm dirty, and I know it, and I'm tired,
> But need you speak,
> You in your old grey wisdom of the years,
> Of fires that flicker in an open hearth,
> And little sparks that like a troop of horse,
> Charge on to die upon the chimney back?
> I tramp because I like it, you damned owl,
> You pedagogue, you crazy-hug-the-hearth.
> Why should I let you whisper in my ear,
> When I am tired, but young, and cold, but very young,
> That age is best, that age is always best?

There is an endearing yet pathetic note here. His youth mocks him. He wants to know the secrets of maturity—and that was a very encouraging thing in a country where immaturity had ruled the literary roosts for so long. One can imagine the grimace that accompanied the strident 'I tramp because I like it'. It is quite obvious that he had been told about the delights of walking, and here he was, loathing every minute and mile of it. And how different from that other hike, through Liberia, which he undertook because he knew it would be hateful.[1] One cannot help comparing the angry life-hatred of it all with Wordsworth—

> (Dear Child! dear Girl! that walkest with me here,
> If thou appear untouched by solemn thought,
> Thy nature is not therefore less divine)—

and at the same time welcoming it with a touch of excitement, for although Wordsworth was a poet of direct vision his 'appetite', as he called it, has been watered down and served up in the form of Wayside Pulpit pieties. There was an interesting voice in *Babbling April*. But youthful interesting voices are common enough, and no-one took much notice. Persistence is of equal importance in literary affairs.

I know nothing of the spiritual conflict that caused Graham to turn to the Catholic Church, and he has told me in a letter that he wouldn't discuss it anyhow. Having read the poems it is possible for me to say that he was intensely dissatisfied—'adrift' is the popular word in this context—and the Catholic faith offered him anchorage. Turning to more mundane matters, we find that the journalistic experience in Nottingham led to *The Times*, for in 1926 he became sub-editor in the letters department—a department to which he has been a frequent and lively contributor in later years. It seems likely that someone on that newspaper had said to him, 'Get some provincial experience, old man, then try again in three months' time'. As I have no intention of writing a formal biography, with chronological order intact, I will take the opportunity to state that Graham (or Mr Greene perhaps I should call him, seeing that he is now on *The Times*) remained in journalism until first the war and then literary success allowed him to escape. He remained a sub-editor of *The*

---

[1] He seemed to suffer from a tramping compulsion. He covered practically the whole of his journey through Liberia on foot, where others would have been carried in a hammock.

Times until 1930, served first as film critic (1935–9) and then as Literary Editor (1940–1) on the *Spectator*, and then joined the Foreign Office in 1941, staying there until the end of the war.

Before the appearance of his first published novel, *The Man Within*, Greene wrote two novels and began a third which he did not complete. He has left strict orders in his will that they should never be published in extract or any other form. This provides us with one of those little mysteries which tend to cluster about Mr Greene, for one might expect him to destroy the typescripts. But apparently he cannot bring himself to do this, and so shelters in his drawer material for posthumous betrayal. (It is a test that literary men are prone to set. Orwell presented his executors with similar temptations.) I have not been allowed to see these novels but Mr Greene tells me that the first 'dealt with the birth of a black child to white parents—a throw-back to some forgotten great-grandparent!' This is posthumous betrayal with a vengeance! The third story (detective) centred round a murder committed by a child of ten, 'and the clues left behind were therefore completely confusing to the police as they were all connected with the age of the child'.

But it is the second of the two unpublished novels which is of especial interest. It concerned 'the Carlist activities of Spanish exiles living round Leicester Square in London at the time when Carlyle wrote his life of John Sterling', Mr Greene told me. It is not much to go upon, but the episode in Sterling's life which is naturally brought to mind was a gift to a young man who felt a compulsion to write about failure. In 1823 a number of Spanish exiles, driven out by Charles X and now under the leadership of General Torrijos, used to leave their lodgings in Somers Town daily to parade Euston Square and around St Pancras church. Six years later they were still there, but by now Torrijos and his wife were friendly with Sterling, who had just come down from the University and had rooms in Regent Street. The defeated, well-nigh hopeless exiles looked to Torrijos as their only means of salvation. They were prepared, in their desperation, to risk anything on an invasion of Spain; they were able to persuade themselves that a few men with a few thousand pounds could drive out the tyrant. Such a scheme must have appealed to Greene, not for its heroism but for its certainty of failure. In the following year Sterling's cousin, Lt Robert Boyd, late of the Indian Army, was persuaded to finance the expedition. (He was a genuine romantic and needed little persuading.) There followed various movements which were calculated to excite the young and inexperienced and exasperate their elders—and us who look back. A letter from Sterling to his friend Charles Barton is fearfully conspiratorial and obvious in the naive way of romantic amateurs. Sterling visits Barton's sister to say good-bye, she weeps, he proposes —and his part in the expedition is at an end! The Spanish Envoy gets wind of what is happening, there is a police attempt to arrest the conspirators who make their ways individually to Gibraltar. There the invasion force assembles: Boyd and a few 'Regent Street democrats', as Carlyle calls them, Torrijos and fifty 'picked Spaniards'. They have no arms. The irony of that word 'picked' is superb, as though they had battalions to choose from. They were picked for plucking, anyway.

It is delicious comedy, ending in pathetic and futile tragedy. The Spanish population did not rise to join them—Torrijos, with the egoism of an exiled leader, had promised this. They hung about in Gibraltar for eighteen months, watched by the British authorities and awaited by the Spaniards. The Regent Street democrats, clutching their identification papers, toured the south of Spain, then returned home to the Reform Bill. The Governor of Gibraltar, aware that he was harbouring men who considered themselves desperate, offered them passports and protection to any country in the world—except Spain. Nothing could have been calculated to stiffen romantic pride more effectively. On 30th November, 1831 the invasion force left Gibraltar in two small boats and sailed for Malaga. They landed, barricaded themselves in a farmhouse, were refused treaty, were taken prisoner and shot.

I don't know what elements Greene selected from these events, but this is the story as given by Carlyle. It contained certain features that naturally appealed to him—folly, defeat and, it may seem strange to us now, romance. The youthful Greene was romantic at heart, but he suffered from the conviction that romance would always fail. Perhaps this shows greater wisdom than a starry-eyed faith in romance, but it implies a continuing pain and frustration.

After all, few people mistake two men relieving themselves against a wall for duellists—but when they do they are likely to enjoy the conceit and not destroy it with a withering reference to dogs. It is interesting to note that the original vision is Chestertonian, and that Chesterton was quite incapable of the deflation. And against the romance we must set the betrayal. After the death of Boyd (who did not desert), Sterling wrote: 'I hear the sound of that musketry; it is as if the bullets were tearing my own brain!' It would be an overstatement to say that these words tore Greene's brain, but they wormed their way in and were warmly received.

His first published novel was about a betrayal, and it was set against a background of sceptical romance. In this and the next two books Greene experimented with romance, and then dropped it. It was not for him. He became aware that a romance that is not based on faith is a hybrid that satisfies no-one, and so he turned to one of romance's distorted reflections, realism. The title of *The Man Within* was taken from Sir Thomas Browne's 'There's another man within me that's angry with me'. Again we can note the appeal of this sentiment to something already wrapped round our onion. In a poem called 'Selfdom' he had said that he wouldn't put himself out to please a girl (romantic stuff!) but he'd do anything to please 'my only God, to win from critic Self but one approving nod'. In a prefatory note to the reprint in the Uniform Edition Greene calls it 'embarrassingly romantic' and 'derivative'—but redeemed by its youthfulness. The re-issue was a sentimental gesture towards his past, 'the period of ambition and hope'.

The Man Within has a psychological subtlety in the part of its chief character, Andrews, that distinguishes it from others of its kind. Apart from that, however, it was 'prentice work and Greene might even be considered lucky to have had it published. As his first two novels had been rejected it is interesting to speculate on what might have happened had this one shared the same fate. However, Greene was fortunate in his publishers, Messrs Heinemann, who subsidised him for three years. The next two novels were inferior work, the fourth was an improvement but by no means impressive, and it was not until 1935 and his sixth novel that he really justified the faith that had been put in him. Success in the literary world depends on many accidents, and Graham Greene certainly owes much to the patience and shrewdness of his publisher. But even if *The Man Within* was not a great novel it found a public and was reprinted four times before going into the Uniform Edition. There is of course a large public for romantic dream-literature of the *Rogue Herries-Jalna* type, and no doubt many of Greene's early readers belonged to this class. And yet they must have felt rather uncomfortable in the presence of Andrews's constant self-examination, a practice that is unfamiliar in the world of romance.

The novel was partly redeemed by having a coward for the main character, instead of the usual swashbuckling hero. Here lies its strangeness, especially in the contrast of easy sexual victory (but this emanated more from the author's attitude than from the incidents narrated) with insufficiency of courage—for courage and sexual conquest normally go together in this branch of literature. The heart-searching of Andrews after the trial lifts the book out of the rut prepared for it by easy virtue and hotel beds. The symbolism of the second half makes it more than just a good yarn, though it is that as well, with almost unbearable suspense and a very affecting love story. The result is baffling. Here is an important new writer, one might be tempted to say, and yet . . .

But without the central figure of Andrews the story sags. Even if he doesn't understand himself, at least he realizes that there is a mystery of self, and that takes us far beyond the normal historical novel of excitement and action. (It is presumably set in the eighteenth century, and is concerned with smugglers.) The weakness shows up most clearly when Andrews, neither knowing or understanding other people, pretends to do both. Only it is the author who is guilty of the pretence. He knows one person thoroughly (it is hard to resist the conclusion that Andrews is himself) and is baffled by everyone else. The result is therefore like a Hollywood essay into depth psychology. We have, for instance, the man who moodily dips into his Bible and goes for long walks by himself because he has sinned, and is aware of it. When he discovers that the Bible condones his sin he is satisfied. Bible-reading and walks cease. He even begins to feel the prickling of sexual desire. It is like a dynamo being switched on and off. It reminds me of a film I saw many years ago, in which an uncouth man looks greedily at a book entitled *Works of Oscar Wilde*. His grubby finger slides beneath the line, 'Men always kill the thing they love'. He then lurches into the next room where a beautiful ward is waiting to be killed. But it is interesting to note the written word moving the hand and silencing the guilt.

There are certain aspects of this novel which are of particular interest in view of the author's later development, despite the failure of the whole. There is no doubt, for instance, that he is possessed of a powerful sexual drive, which frequently bursts through the bonds of the narrative to assert itself where the demands of art would be opposed to it. On the second page Andrews is tearing a way through brambles, whose twigs 'plucked at him and tried to hold him with small endearments'—and once this conceit has been introduced Greene cannot resist it but has to follow it to its logical end. Soon the thorns are 'sharp, pointed nails', they accost him with words, he replies 'Another day'. The effect is ridiculous. When Andrews meets the girl he acknowledges her with an 'automatic leer'. A little later he is insulting her 'in a brief, physiological sentence'. When he gets to town he is irritated by the passionate idiocies of lovers—wherever he goes, Greene always sees them and overhears them. It is a strange thing that lovers, who try so hard to find privacy, can never escape him. One gets the impression that he is maddened by his own urge. He loves and he hates, and he is already laying the foundation for an assault that will bring him notoriety.

Secondly, Andrews despises himself, not only because he is a coward—that is clear-cut and a respectable object of self-hatred—but also because he is an actor and, by implication, insincere. He makes impressive phrases and repeats them, although he knows they are meaningless: 'engaged in the favourite process of dramatizing his actions'. He exclaims histrionically to the girl, 'For the love of God', and the author explains that 'he had picked that expression from the stage, but the girl could not be expected to know it'. His whole being is a drama instead of a unity. The angry man thunders at the coward, and the coward whines. 'It was only to suit his own ends or his own self-pity that he allowed himself the pleasure of melodrama.' His character was built of superficial dreams, sentimentality, cowardice, and yet he was constantly made aware beneath all these of an uncomfortable questioning critic. There is a brief reference to what was almost certainly a fact from Greene's own childhood, which I have already inferred: the sense of being left out, slightly victimized, not quite treated as one of the gang. 'There was a game which he had played at school, where one boy, *too often himself*, stood with back turned counting ten, while the other boys advanced to touch his back.' (My italics.) But the angry man, the critic, would say, 'This isn't *me*, it's not the real *me*—the real *I* will prove myself one day'. Andrews and Greene were both tortured by their awareness of the patronage of others, and yet they were both ultimately convinced of their personal sufficiency. But mere conviction was not enough.

It is interesting to note that Greene's major preoccupation in later days, the sense of sin, does not make itself felt in this novel until near the end. Andrews has betrayed his friend and leader, Carlyon, but will not admit he has sinned. He blames himself for cowardice, but cowardice is a quality, not an act, and therefore not easily ascribable to sin. The word 'sin' is first mentioned in connection with his seduction by Merriman's mistress. (The seduction is in the true tradition of romance; the anguish that accompanied it and the sense of sin that followed it belong to the psychological novel of our time. Henry James miscegenates with Stevenson, or even the mature Stevenson with the youthful one.) Lust and its natural consequence, adultery, are the living embodiments of sin. Greene is modern and strangely puritanical in his attitude. Although a Catholic, he had been brought up in the English Protestant tradition, and the sexual impulse had always borne the hallmark of impurity. His soul-searchings on the theme of sin in this book are, as one might expect from a young man in his early twenties, naive. He tended to equate shame with purity. 'How could he ever keep clean if the sense of shame was so short-lived?' Then he considers Life: 'if it were barren of desire and of the need of any action how sweet life would be'. He believed in the exact opposite, of course. But this is the kind of conflict that the sexual impulse sets up in the mind trained to inhibition. And this conflict was to be the central one in Greene's life and literary career, bringing forth his most tortured work, his most passionate intensities and his most reprehensible falsities. But at this stage none of them could be foreseen. Andrews has merely come fresh from a

harlot's bed—not so fresh, come to think of it—he has feelings of
love for a girl who is not a harlot, and is young enough to let such
a label dictate his judgment. Twenty-five years later he published a
story which destroyed any virtue that might once have belonged to
that particular label.

Technically the novel has many faults, as we might expect.
Greene adopts the stream-of-consciousness technique for denoting
weariness, but he is not happy with it. Even if a man is utterly fagged
out, while pushing his way through trees, it is not easy to accept the
following 'stream' as genuine: 'What's this wood doing? Why a
wood? Hansel and Gretel. There should be a cottage soon with a
witch in it, and the cottage should be made of sugar.' Like Greene's
fictional dreams, which I shall refer to later at some length, this line
of association is forced and unnatural. It comes not from the unconscious, as it should, but from the head. He was occasionally
guilty of verbal abuse; after scratching himself on a bramble, 'his
wrist was sending stab after stab of pain up his arm, and the edge of
an approaching mist touched his consciousness'. The first clause reminds one of some of Carlyle's violences, such as 'words like
Austerlitz battles', and it is possible that Greene picked up more than
a story from Carlyle and later had to lose it, as any sensible writer
must. The second clause gives a hint of that mingling of concrete
and abstract that Greene was later to develop into a characteristic
imagery of impressive effect.

Here and there the centuries clash together like cymbals. 'God,
you're respectable!' says Andrews to the girl, and for a moment the
eighteenth century cottage is snatched away and replaced by a group
of twentieth century undergraduates gabbling anti-bourgeois sentiments. The reader is frequently irritated by just noticeable depart-
ures from truth in characterization and the description of human
behaviour. When, during the Lewes episode, romance is given its
head we step into yet a third world or atmosphere—one where
women are gained merely by wanting them, and where wonderful
bargains can be struck. And so the novel comes to its close, incom-
plete, naive and crude and yet marked here and there by touches of
subtlety which did not fully redeem it by any means but which gave
a hint of what might come.

II

THE REJECTED NOVELS

Nineteen Thirty to Thirty-One
'The Name of Action', 'Rumour at Nightfall'

SHORT stories were also beginning to appear. In the same year as *The Man Within* there were two which he later put into his collected stories. One of these, 'The Second Death', is pretty pointless except for its evidence of religious feelings at work. It is rather strange that although Greene did not become a Catholic until 1926, and then presumably passed through a critical phase at that time, spiritually speaking, there is practically no evidence of it in his early writing. It was to be much later, some time after the war, in fact, before any kind of spiritual conflict or even enthusiasm began to show in his work. (*Brighton Rock* is cold, artificial stuff compared with *The Heart of the Matter*.) This story, which treats of a man who recovers from death, in the course of which he meets God, seems to be as far as Greene was prepared to go in this field at the time. It is mentioned that a miracle-worker had been in the district, but the sceptical attitude prevails that one doesn't really believe in such things these days. There is also an obscure reference to Christ at the end. One gets the impression that Greene feels some compulsion to adopt a religious outlook, but that the compulsion is a relatively mild one. What is far more interesting is his attitude to death. It is scarcely an English one, and is not touched by the familiar Protestant fears and obsessions. It is not enough to retort that Greene was a Catholic; he was an *English* Catholic, and a late convert at that, and his attitudes had been moulded by a Protestant childhood. Even the most rationalist Englishman, although he may have excellent reasons for not treating death with undue seriousness, nevertheless does so in nine cases out of ten. But Greene, who a few years before had been obsessed with death, even inviting it, was now able to write a story where a man jokes to his dying friend that he is for once alone in bed. This is horrifying to the puritan and a civilized manner of opening a conversation to the pagan. Chesterton had already made it perfectly clear that a pagan is closer to the possibility of salvation than a Protestant.

In the other story, 'The End of the Party', the subject is childhood fear. To a very real extent Greene's later life and his literary production have been governed by fears experienced in childhood, which embedded themselves deep in his psyche. Twin brothers go to a birthday party, where they play hide-and-seek in the dark. Francis is of a nervous disposition, and Peter tries to protect and comfort him—yet the unexpected touch of Peter's hand in the dark kills Francis with shock. As a story, the effect is muffled—it should be sharp and clear. Is there in it, as in the title, a hint of what was to be developed into *The End of the Affair*—the stark truth that too much loving can kill as effectively as too much hating? In the novel Sarah was to die of a disease, but there is a strong suggestion throughout that the unassuageable love between her and Bendrix will certainly overpower one or other of them eventually. This story ends with Peter clutching his brother's dead fingers in puzzled grief. 'His brain, too young to realize the full paradox, yet wondered with an obscure self-pity why it was that the pulse of his brother's fear went on and on, when Francis was now where he had always been told there was no more terror and no more darkness.' If this means anything it is that Francis is still in communication, although from beyond death. But there is neither passion nor conviction in the story, merely a small boy's fear worked up with too much rationalization. But in death there would be 'no more terror'. Greene's parents had obviously brought the boy up on modern lines. We can now see that the death-wish of the poetry was not, as it so often is, a case of hypnotism. If anything it came from its opposite, a genuine desire to visit that attractive land of light and happiness. Francis's fear was a new and disturbing note.

In the following year there are two more stories worth a mention before I return to the novels. 'I Spy' is an exciting foretaste of what was to come, of the glimpses we get of the enormous gap between child and adult which was to be so skilfully explored in 'The Basement Room'. The child only half understands what is happening, and has no understanding at all of the reasons. In this example of the genre a boy creeps downstairs at night to his father's tobacconist shop, to smoke his first cigarette. While there he is surprised by his father and two men. He overhears their conversation from his hiding-place. It is clear that his father is leaving, and that the men have some power over him. The boy can understand nothing in his innocence. We suspect that the men are police, but actually know little more than the boy. The great difference between us and him, however, lies in our knowledge that such things do happen. For the boy it might be an exercise in magic for all the meaning it has for him.

The fourth story from these early years, 'Proof Positive', is also concerned with death. It is very unGreenelike in its matter, yet it foreshadowed a later preoccupation. A speaker, addressing a Psychical Society, tries to supply 'proof positive' that the spirit outlives the body, but except for a few flashes he utters nonsense. He falls back dead. On examination it is discovered that his body has been dead a week, that the spirit has been animating the body which has had no organic life of its own. This was the 'proof positive'. Greene's comment was that all the speaker revealed was that, without the body's aid, the spirit decayed into whispered nonsense. At the time it seemed hardly worth saying, and yet *The Heart of the Matter* seems to give the story significance. Greene had become filled with wonder at the eucharist, a wonder which appeared greatly intensified during the years after the war, a sense of awed grace at the privilege of taking God's body in his mouth. At the height of his crisis Scobie dreamt he was drifting in a boat down an underground river, accompanied by a dead body on a stretcher. 'The smell of decay was already in his nostrils. Then, sitting there guiding the boat down the mid-stream, he realized that it was not the dead body that smelt but his own living one.' He woke up and his wife told him that it was time to go to Communion. And Scobie went, and took the wafer, the living body, in his mouth, and all the time he knew that his dream had given him 'proof positive' of his own corruption.

The Name of Action takes its title from *Hamlet* and is dedicated to Greene's wife, who has now become Vivienne. It retains the high romantic background of *The Man Within* without the latter's psychological interest. The romance is not in the Meade Falkner-Smuggler vein but in the Anthony Hope-Ruritania. There has been a revolution in Trier and a dictator is in control. Oliver Chant, a rich young man, goes to help the freedom forces, almost on an impulse. He falls in love with the beautiful wife of the dictator. She plays with him but shows interest—Greene's women in these early novels are much kinder to strange young men than are their organic counterparts. There is a chase, with the attention to detail that we now regard as particularly Greenesque: the pursued doubles back, creeps into shadow, hides in doorways, torches shine on cats and the actual number of yards separating fugitive and police are meticulously recorded. Greene exhibits his power of imagery but it is inflated and made incongruous by the romantic fervour that bullies the style: 'a revolver drooped like a parched flower to the pavement'.

The dictator is a youthful Catholic's idea of a puritanical Protestant. He forbids music, closes the brothels and has never consummated his own marriage. He is certainly a possible human being but, like everyone and everything else in the novel, he is drawn larger than life. His inhumanity is not matched by the buried strains of humanity that we know must exist in even the most extreme cases—Kant's crystallized fruits and Hitler's flaxen Rhinemaidens. And yet Greene, while striving to protect the simple human pleasures against their destroyers, also tries to retain an aspect of cynical wisdom—an act of creative juggling that he was not to manage successfully for several years, not until the hard-bitten (but soft underneath) Maurice Bendrix was compelled to accept that Sarah was not only a sexually attractive person but also a good woman.[1] After Kapper and Chant had murdered the policeman (Kapper is a typical Catholic projection of the godless intellect run wild), they return home and send the lugubrious Mrs Kapper to cover the bloodstains with raw meat. Laughter is heard from the flat above. On one level it was Greene's better self but on another it was a gentleman known as Adolph. 'He wakes often in the night and thinks of something funny', says Kapper. 'He is a very happy man. But his jokes are bad.'

While many novelists go from bad to worse it must be said for Mr Greene that he has gone from bad to better. In 1930 he was capable of writing, 'It was incredible that there, a few nights before,

[1] *The End of the Affair.*

he had held Anne-Marie Demassener in his arms'. No-one in his senses would deny that a man can feel like that, but the skilled novelist avoids the cliché. Only a few words need be altered and today Mr Greene would carry out the surgery successfully. But some of the embarrassment lay in the incident, not in its description. Chant once threw his revolver away. 'I won't live', he shouted. 'I don't want to live, let them shoot.' (The death-obsession was still strong.) He flung himself into the road, his body lit by the head-lamps of an approaching car, 'with arms held out to clasp death and have done'. He thought it was the police but it was the woman he loved. She stopped in time, too. The forces that sought the author's death also stopped, as we know. But in the midst of this palpitating body of fantasy there keep intruding keen gusts of something much more cynical though not necessarily more true. How could he have gone on living if she had died, asked Chant. 'Of course you would have lived', she replied, 'none of us have integrity like that.' After the unreality that preceded this statement one is liable to be stam-peded into admiration. Nevertheless, Anne-Marie very properly knocked the stuffing out of Chant's facile idealism.

There are occasional references to the Catholic faith which sur-prise by their uncommittedness, in view of what was to come. Once again, Greene's religious fervour appears when least expected, and is absent when we have reason to look for it. This is one of many paradoxes which point to stresses and tensions felt by the social man and prodding the spiritual. One of the conspirators in this novel says of the local people that they are all good Catholics, 'as though he held some standard that had nothing to do with elementary schools or priests or even attendance at mass'. This is probably the first approving hint of Catholic mystery to be found in his work. He was not yet using Catholic heroes and Chant is quite untroubled by his adultery. (Not that any of Greene's characters appear to worry themselves about the casual sexual encounter. 'Thou shalt not commit divorce' appears to be regarded as a much more serious injunction than 'Thou shalt not commit adultery'.) Anne-Marie's fault is a minor one for, although she is a Catholic, her marriage had not been consummated and was therefore annullable. Chant dis-covered that he wanted 'a good wife and a good Catholic', but the desire had not yet been darkened by its intensity. Finally, the twins of betrayal and failure are prominent. Chant betrays Anne-Marie— but unwittingly, like the girl who betrayed Raven in *A Gun for Sale*. Anne-Marie had already betrayed her husband. The Englishman going to the assistance of the revolutionaries is the Sterling story transferred—but the political move is unexpectedly a success. However, the personal aims are not accomplished and Chant returns to England where he can mourn the lost lover. She is not dead, like Andrews's Elizabeth or Bendrix's Sarah, but she is equally out of reach.

In the following year came *Rumour at Nightfall*, prefaced by these lines by Thomas Traherne:

> O ye that stand upon the brink
> When I so near me through the chink
> With wonder see: What faces there,
> Whose feet, whose bodies, do ye wear?
> > I my companions see
> > In you, another me.
> They seemed others, but are we;
> Our second selves those shadows be.

Again the suggestion of split personality. At the third time of asking we begin to discern the formula that Greene was following in these early novels—and fortunately discarded. One of the two heroes (Englishmen in a Spain torn by the Carlist wars, one of Greene's early obsessions) bears the symbolical name of Chase. The other, Crane, desires his enemy's woman. The melodrama is pitched even higher than in the previous book, and Heinemann must have been worried by the steady decline in the quality of their new author's work. *The Name of Action* was at least in an acceptable tradition, but *Rumour at Nightfall* was a hybrid between Hope and Conrad. Its total effect was crude, because in emphasising his characters' sensitivity the author loses his own. Here is an example. Crane goes to find a woman Chase is looking for, locates her house but does not go in. Crane asks him why. ' "What do I always fear?" Crane bursts out with a nervous gesture of the hands and eyes that begged to be reassured. "Danger, pain." He hesitated and added "Death" softly, his eyes no longer seeking another's response but clouding with thought.' It was perhaps with thought that the youthful Graham's eyes clouded as he mused on death, but here it clouds the character- ization with the pomposity of a Hollywood epic. There is a sim- plicity of vision that would delight Erroll Flynn. Greene's Spaniards reiterate with tedious monotony their view that all a man wants at night is a woman, a culmination of the familiar Anglo-Saxon view that all Spaniards are passionate, and that passionate men are only passionate about women. It wouldn't matter so much if it were not stated so coyly. The women are as bad, only their lasciviousness is more direct and carnal. A strange woman loses no time in telling Chase about the hardness of a baby's gums on her breast.

Altogether there is a rather owlish solemnity about the style. Crane and Chase are indistinguishable, and preposterous bores. The story is sluggish. This is the sort of picture we get of Crane. 'Behind him was childhood and the womb and the first terror of birth. Somewhere in front was what he hoped and believed to be the last terror of death. Every peak must be passed before he reached it and peace. There was no short cut and no halt was possible or even desirable, for what comfort would it be to stay in the eternal com- panionship of the same present fear?' Crane might be seen as a reincarnation of Andrews, the coward, but he uses more violent terminology and is to that extent less interesting. The differences between Chase and Crane are stated but never worked into their characterization: they are dummies who take on qualities as and when required, then drop them. But it is worth noting that Chase, who works for an English paper, says, 'My position is in a No- Man's-Land. I want news, that's all', while Crane says, 'One must always take sides'. These attitudes scarcely have any importance in the novel but anticipate a time when Greene was to become vocal on the subject of being committed. In *The Quiet American* (1955) we are presented with the two opposing powers of Communism and Colonialism, East and West, Materialism and Catholicism—for they are, finally, the terms in which Greene sees the conflict. There is considerable discussion about the necessity to take sides or to remain neutral.

Crane, like Oliver Chant, was not a Catholic, but also like Chant he met his Catholic lover in a Catholic church. Greene does not thrust his religion either at us or at his heretical heroes in these early days, but he undoubtedly hopes they will be infected. Crane cannot resist the atmosphere (not so much of holiness as of rightness), and he and Eulelia confess to each other soberly and religiously. God is left out. Crane confesses 'cowardice, lust, poverty'. His marriage is resented by Chase as a betrayal—another necessary ingredient, and leading to the complication of Chase identifying himself with the common enemy, Caveda, who is betrayed by his former lover Eulelia. In some mystical way Caveda appears to be Chase's second self. Thus the betrayals fall into a circular track, which may have seemed more profound to their author than a simple betrayal, but which does not hold the attention of the reader, unless he be concerned with understanding the mind of the man who later wrote *The Heart of the Matter*. The Spaniards receive another pat on the back when Chase says, 'They don't betray each other, these Spaniards'. Senor de Madariaga would be surprised.

The novel is also marked by its confusions of identity, as in a dream. But even worse is the confusion of feeling, which never allows the reader to adopt a defined attitude towards characters or events, and this is unforgivable. Senora Monti sees in Chase a future husband for Eulelia. It is Crane who marries her, betraying Chase. Chase draws close in feeling to Caveda, the enemy, and even wishes to warn him of his danger. He himself is mistaken for Caveda (who dominates the novel, but is never seen), and in the subsequent fighting Crane is killed. Chase now feels guilt of his old friend's death. Eulelia also claims responsibility. The book ends with an orgy of self-recrimination, something like a communist guilt-session, and yet there is an insistence that everyone is happy, that solutions have been solved in some mystical fashion. We are told that Crane died in happiness and that one can be happy if one suffers, among other untested but noble affirmations of a youthful inexperienced novelist. The truth is that wisdom may be found through suffering, and perhaps Greene dimly perceived this. In a later novel it was to become an important part of his faith. But on the whole *Rumour at Nightfall* has the misty, phantasmagorical atmosphere of a dream, like so many of the later books, and yet fails to justify its earnest and plodding self-importance.

III

GOING EAST

Nineteen Thirty-Two
'Stamboul Train'

THIS was a better novel than the preceding ones but still not a very impressive one. Prefaced with a quotation from George Santayana ('Everything in nature is lyrical in its ideal essence; tragic in its fate, and comic in its existence'), it was dubbed an Entertainment by the author. The division of his fiction into Novels (serious works) and Entertainments (pot-boilers) has been retained by him, but its usefulness is doubtful. One of his more important books, *Brighton Rock*, originally a novel, was published in America and re-issued here as a Penguin under the label of Entertainment, but reappears in the list of novels supplied in the Uniform Edition. *The Quiet American*, which lacks the sense of wholeness to be found in the preceding novels, is nevertheless ascribed to that category. It was unwise of Greene to label his fiction in that way. It smacks of lecturing the reader, attempting to control his responses, when in fact the essential product of an author's mind should be indivisible, regardless of its superficial lightness or gravity.[1] Once again Greene's wistful desire to be thought an intellectual, linked with his sense of personal insufficiency, peeps out. *Stamboul Train* is not more sensational than *It's A Battlefield*, the novel that followed it, nor is its psychological penetration less ambitious. The fact is, Greene can only write well in one way, and this is the first novel in which he finds his personal style. By pretending that some of his books are intentionally more 'popular' than the others he is in fact admitting that the others are rather more strained than the some.

The sense of guilt which appeared towards the end of *Rumour*

[1] It should also be borne in mind that books such as *The Incredible Adventures of Professor Branestawm* and *The Inimitable Jeeves* are much superior artistically than the more pretentious *Forsyte Saga* and *Family Reunion*.

At Nightfall reappears and is emphasized. There is nothing remarkable about its prevalence in our disrupted society but it is noteworthy
how early it appears in Greene's work, when he was so young.
'Guilt' is perhaps a loaded word at this stage; 'shame' would be
better, more adapted to youthful feeling, less religious in its connotations. A sense of guilt is normally the product of failure—we
have an example of it in this novel in the person of Czinner. It is
strange to find a young man, especially one who appears to be
succeeding in his chosen career, feeling failure so acutely. But it
should be remembered that at this stage Greene had not really tasted
success; in fact, a run of three indifferent novels was not encouraging.
There is also another factor which we can neither measure nor
account for, and that is his early death-wish which was not a pose
and cannot be attributed to any known incident without probing
deeply and intimately into his past. It is useless to exclaim, Why
should Greene brood on failure? What does he know of failure? as
though such a preoccupation is an insincerity. Certain facts have to
be accepted and cannot be swept away by indignation or distaste.
What we are compelled to do is to accept the preoccupation and
relate it to other factors existing within the same framework. At this
stage the other dominant in his work is a rather unpleasant attitude
towards sex, a prying into its more sordid aspects, a concentration on
the squalor rather than the ecstasy. One is tempted to ask if the
obsession with failure may be related to sexual disgust? Everyone
else seems to think sex is marvellous, to feel romantic about it, we
can imagine the author saying. What is wrong with me that I should
feel differently? Again one is struck by a strong implication of
personal insufficiency, capable of leading to desperation at times.
One might also notice that Green's self-hatred is given an objective
expression by concentrating it on an author, who is easily the most
unpleasant character on the train. This anticipates his later full-
blooded assault on his own feelings and even his own character,
through the medium of a fictional author, in *The End of the
Affair*.

I have already drawn attention to the intensified drive of Greene's
sexual urge, which might reasonably be called his demon. It is well
to bear these two precocities in mind, the sexual and the failing

confidence, and to realize that they may well be connected.[1] In our
world lovers are always embracing, usually unseen. In Greene's they
can never escape his roving eye. As the Orient Express roars on its
way our attention is directed to the lovers lying entangled on the
bank. The sexual relationship is put starkly and simply, a few words
of warning handed down by 'old dry women of experience: "There's
only one thing a man wants." "Don't take presents from a stranger."
It was the size of the present she had been always told that made the
danger. Chocolates and a ride, even in the dark, after a theatre,
entailed no more than kisses on the mouth and neck, a little tearing
of a dress. A girl was expected to repay, that was the point of all
advice; one never got anything for nothing. Novelists like Ruby M.
Ayres might say that chastity was worth more than rubies, but the
truth was it was priced at a fur coat or thereabouts. One couldn't
accept a fur coat without sleeping with a man. If you did, all the
older women would tell you the man had a grievance.' Greene was
fascinated by tarts. He wanted badly to know what they got up to
in bed, especially with each other. His libido could compel him to
make a false step in characterization, as when the respectable Mrs
Peters told Coral Musker that she belonged to Arbuckle Avenue.
This was the name given by taxi-drivers to a row of one-night
hotels near Paddington Station, and it made such a deep impression
on Greene that he referred to them again in a later novel. Kingsmill
and Pearson, in *Talking of Dick Whittington*, describe how Greene
came to them at their club and told them with a sigh that nothing
had hurt him more in the London blitz than the partial disappearance
of Arbuckle Avenue. And yet at this stage Greene knew there was a
gentler side to love. Even the old women admitted that, if a girl were
loved, she had the 'right to take and never give'. But he did not
retain such illusions for long.

There was already a conflict in Greene's mind, even if only the
echoes of conflict, between the cheerful and the seedy. A cheerful
outlook never stood much chance with him but it was worth
knocking down. This act was performed through the medium of
Mr Quin Savory, a popular author. Greene loathes him. He is a

[1] Perhaps I should explain that these characteristics had been precocities.
By the time of *Stamboul Train*, of course, they could no longer be called such.

cheery, cheeky cockney who has done well with romantic novels and is unbearably extrovert. When asked what he considered might be his contribution to English literature he replies, 'Surely that's for somebody else to state. But one 'opes, one 'opes, that it's something of this sort, to bring back cheerfulness and 'ealth to modern fiction. There's been too much of this introspection, too much gloom. After all, the world is a fine adventurous place.' It might be Mr J. B. Priestley, whom Mr Greene does not care for. Miss Warren, the newspaper correspondent, cables back a flattering yet ironical story about Savory. Greene (who often chooses, whether consciously or unconsciously, names that carry significance or a comment) piles insult on Savory. When the train reaches Stamboul Janet Pardoe, whom he had got to know on the train and whom he believed he had impressed deeply, casually drops him and attaches herself to someone else without a scruple. The same kind of contempt which Greene loads on Savory is also poured upon a muscular Anglican parson.

But who is Savory? There is no doubt that Greene had made a fairly prolonged attempt to become a flattened version of him. He had written three romantic novels, and even now he was still aiming at a popular success. *Stamboul Train* is, after all, on the author's confession, an Entertainment. The squalor is becoming marked but it may well be the squalor of failure. Supposing the Ruritanian adventure had had a bigger sale and Greene had ventured further along a false track—who knows what agonies he might have suffered, loathing Savory yet succumbing to him? The advantage of the existing situation was that he was in no position to succumb to Savory. Some years later, in *The Third Man*, he could consider the popular writer with greater detachment, and the result involved less venom. Rollo Martins was not a rival to be envied and therefore hated. His popularity was that of the adventure writer, not the man with a cheery message. By then Greene himself was a popular author, and yet something more—he was admired by the intellectuals. A new Conrad had arrived. He could afford to look at the writer of Westerns, patronize him slightly and at the same time treat him like a human being.

Savory is allowed to make one statement which is not entirely fatuous. It was something Greene wished to say but could not put in anyone else's mouth. Savory said he was the penitent, going before the public. 'In so far as the novel is founded on the author's experience, the novelist is making a confession to the public. This puts the public in the position of the priest and the analyst.' The public does not care to perform this function, of course; it is taken over by the critic. More than the work of any other contemporary novelist, Greene's fiction is a running confession. Like all novelists he is compelled to rationalize and sublimate, but no-one else carries out these tasks with so little concealment of the psychological tangles they utilize. The tide of guilt is beginning to wash through his work as a whole. The chief spokesman of this mood in this novel is Dr Czinner, the failed revolutionary. The guilt is traced directly to the failure. He feels he is no longer a doctor, certainly not a believer, not even anyone's son; he is simply a Socialist, but his efforts have come to nothing. He is aware of his personal deficiencies, his vanity, his meanness, even his snobbery and love of comfort. His motives were always mixed, and he knew that the purity of his faith had been smirched by these faults and made failure ultimately inevitable. As his desperation increases, as his enemies close in and his chances of escape evaporate, he remembers the religion he was brought up in and which he had rejected. There was no-one now of whom he could ask forgiveness. He certainly could not expect the Party Secretary or the third-class passengers to listen to him and then forgive him. He longed for the comfort of God. This incident is the first occasion in the fiction where Greene's motives for becoming a Catholic are suggested. Like Dr Czinner, although at a much less mature age, he had looked for comfort. He had been subject to a mental depression that rarely lifted and he had never felt capable of dispelling it unaided. He had even tried to run away but he had sufficient insight, rare among the young, to know that mental states cannot be annihilated by physical action. It is worth noting that when Czinner decided he would like to return to God he did so hesitantly; he was not certain but he had tried the alternative and it had failed him. We can only speculate whether Greene's conversion carried any more permanent conviction.

Associated with guilt, like an obvious image, is the squalor which is emphasized for the first time in this novel. It is only a minor foretaste of the notorious Greene seediness, but it lacks nothing in intensity. Andrews and Lucy in *The Man Within* had been sordid in essence but agreeable in action. When Josef Grünlich visits his mistress in *Stamboul Train*, we are given a picture of Anna that would have graced Arbuckle Avenue. 'She shared his age, but not his experience, standing lean and flustered and excited by the window; her black skirt lay across the bed, but she still wore her black blouse, her white domestic collar, and she held a towel before her legs to hide them.' She has uneven and discoloured teeth; Josef wags a finger at her playfully and asks what Anna has got now; 'A great big man? Oh, now he will rumple you'; with 'horrible middle-aged coquetry' she comes to him, 'with the thin tread of a bird, in her black cotton stockings.' There is not much of it, but what there is must have delighted readers who demanded what some critics call Realism.

But the sordidness is as much an element in the author's mind as in the world about him. It is always a difficult point to decide to what extent an author may spotlight the less pleasant characteristics of his world, without being suspected of delighting in them for their own sake. This was the first occasion on which Greene seemed to be going out of his way to emphasize the scabrous and the scatological. The book turned out to be his greatest success to date, so perhaps he drew his own conclusions. It might be objected, of course, that a particular theme calls for a particular type of character, one who thinks, feels and talks smut, for instance. In *Stamboul Train* it is Mabel Warren, and she is responsible for most of the passages to which objection could be raised. When she cables her newspaper she spells out the word Kamnetz: 'K for Kaiser, A for Arse, M for Mule, N for Naval, no not that kind. It doesn't matter; it's the same letter. E for Erotic, T for Tart, Z for Zebra.' In a later cable, about Savory, she says, 'He has a curt (don't be funny. I said curt. C.U.R.T.) manner which, etc.' But Mr Greene enjoys it all too much to allow us to attribute the frequency of such passages to the sacred cause of characterization. What is truly surprising is that this propensity to snigger had not appeared in the earlier books, as though his critical censor had warned him not to indulge it. But now

c

it breaks through and, again, it seems to pay. That is putting the affair at its lowest level, but what other level can it be treated on? Neither artistically not psychologically do his books gain from this failure to control the adolescent. As I have said, he was highly charged sexually and young men who suffer in that way are lucky to avoid the need to express themselves salaciously. Something petty and immature still clung to him (after all, he was only twenty-seven, and a man's maturity at that age is mostly façade). He had showed a taste for psychological subtlety and he was obviously a master of narrative, but he had not the bigness of character necessary to restrain him from gloating over man's less attractive features. A writer such as Aldous Huxley, less creative but nobler minded, may be appalled by them and may react vengefully, but he does not titter.

Fundamentally the same outlook is eventually expressed by Coral Musker, for whom this journey is a kind of graduation ceremony. She cannot take recourse to smut to give reality to her newly discovered hatred and distrust of life, so she resorts to more respectable abstractions. I'm tired of being decent, of doing the right thing, she thinks. This is a state of mind to which many of us are driven at some time or other; decency seems to get you nowhere. If you love people you lose them, either through unforeseen circumstances or betrayal. And if you try to love them on a grander scale you come up against indifference, power, vested interest. Life's lesson, thought Coral as she crouched over Czinner's dead body, is not to fuss, to let things slide. And there is an element of truth in this providing you *don't* fuss and *do* let events take their course, instead of letting this attitude conceal your inner desire to avoid the good and discover, thankfully, the bad. When Coral Musker decides, when she is barely out of her 'teens, that reality is dreary and ugly and depressing, she is making an affirmation on behalf of her author. For in this novel Graham Greene had thrown Romance aside and adopted Realism.

Literary categories are misleading. Realism, for instance, should be an attempt to portray reality in the human condition, and it will include bowls of flowers as well as chamber pots, babies' bottles as well as french letters, ecstasy as well as bitterness. It is an historical accident, to a very large extent traceable to the success of Zola, I believe, that realism has come to denote the less pleasant and less hopeful aspects of life. Greene with his prurient interest in tarts' bedrooms is as real as Trollope with his arid interest in bishops' drawing rooms—a comparison that should appeal particularly to Greene, who is (or was) fascinated by Trollope. (I nearly wrote 'enjoys Trollope' but prevented myself in time; Greene has read a lot of Trollope, which may be an entirely different matter.) But he is not more real, and similarly his excursions into the sordid are not more real than Trollope's enquiry into Victorian hollowness. Trollope was considered a realist in his time, for each age sets up an image which it finds pleasing and calls real. The Victorians admired successful and inhibited men, whereas we admire the failures who can afford to set civilization aside. I cannot accept the term 'realism' in its current usage, and propose to replace it with 'sordidism', which will also allow me the use of an aptly abominable adjective, 'sordidist'.

Looking back, we know now that Greene's best books have been set in foreign lands. There is a satisfying symbolism, therefore, in *Stamboul Train* which takes its chorus girl and popular novelist, Lesbian journalist and socialist revolutionary, currant merchant and suburban couple, to the East. As frontier succeeds frontier and Teuton is replaced by Slav, the standard of living falls, uniforms become thicker and coarser, the position of women declines and silk stockings give way to robust peasant legs. As a boy and as a young man Greene had looked East—for the lands of mystery and delight, whatever the map may say, are always East of Suez. Money, adventure, women; and later, when God declared himself a Catholic the red parts were scarcely satisfactory. Stamboul was only a stopping place on the way to Saigon.

IV

OUR VACANCY, WHICH ART IN HEAVEN

Nineteen Thirty-Four
'It's a Battlefield', 'The Old School'

THE title of this novel is taken from Kinglake. The battlefield consisted of a number of circlets, such as the mist would allow, without shape or depth, in which the soldiers fought in utter ignorance of what happened around them. It is an image of life. The novel is a considerable advance on the previous one, in its writing, its understanding of personal relationships and its depth of enquiry. From it there comes a strong sense of meaninglessness. In its slighter way it recalls *Point Counter Point*, which had appeared in 1928, but the worlds are different, only meeting once, glancingly and briefly, at Caroline Bury's lunch table. Huxley gave a positive attempt to suggest a possible meaning in, among others, the person of Everard Webley, the Fascist; Greene's positive thrust came from the Communists, but there was no individual character who could be compared with Webley. Greene's Communists do not believe either in themselves or in their theories. They are like rats behind the wainscoting. The only man who can believe in anything is the Assistant Commissioner, whose name we do not know, but it might well be Scobie. He believes only in his work. When he arrests a murderer who affects to be a religious man, we find that the latter is merely playing with belief like a toy shield. Occasionally the Assistant Commissioner envied younger men who might be serving something worthy of their allegiance. Throughout the book runs the question, What can you believe? There is not an ounce of encouragement. Not even the Catholic faith is trotted out with its consolations. The characters either admit vacancy or fall back on pretences. Conder, the Red journalist, pretends to have a family life. His activities become so involved he begins to wonder what is real and what is not. He confuses reality with his dreams. He has a strong

38

conviction that he is being followed, until he discovers that his shadower has run away because he thinks Conder is following him! If your major criterion of fiction is a moral one this is a very bad novel. If it is artistic, then it is a fair one.

Conrad Drover had never had much to believe in, but at least it seemed clear enough: a System, comprising Law, Justice, Police, Jury, Civil Servants, etc. But they had all collapsed now. *They* had decided that his brother Jim was a murderer. Either they were wrong or a murderer was nothing very terrible—certainly not the kind of person to instil horror and loathing, as Conrad had previously believed. The Assistant Commissioner, who served the paraphernalia of law and justice, was as aware as Conrad of their hollowness. He had long ago ceased to believe in any great directing purpose. All he knew was a sense of waste, of people dying and suffering uselessly; 'these were not spare parts which could be matched again'. A man had to lose himself in something, and the Assistant Commissioner devoted himself to his work. He rejected values. His friend, Caroline Bury, felt the waste and aimlessness of existence as keenly as he, and chose a different way out. She affirmed 'faith', but in what it was impossible to say. She surrounded herself with all the objects that have come to be associated with faith—incense, idols, ikons—and hoped for a solution that would be almost mechanical. She was cleverer than the Assistant Commissioner, who was on most counts a dull and stupid man, yet her solution was, if anything, more idiotic than his. Anyone with imagination was bound to suffer from the guilt of shame, lust or social failure—Conrad Drover was a case in point. You could only overcome shame temporarily by surrendering to its cause, just as you could only eliminate hate by indulging it. *It's a Battlefield* leads naturally to *The End of the Affair*. The later novel is more personal and intense. The question that arises about the first one, and which cannot be answered with certitude, is: Does this represent Greene's mood at the time or is it intended as a warning? For the complete absence of some kind of spiritual consolation, however slight, is noteworthy.

At the end of this disturbing novel the chaplain says, 'I can't stand human justice any longer. Its arbitrariness. Its incomprehensibility.' The Assistant Commissioner replies that this makes it

sound very like divine justice. The chaplain, who must have read
Dostoievski, says, 'Perhaps. But one can't hand in a resignation to
God'. The attack on human justice pervades the whole book. Injustice 'was as much a part of the body as age and inevitable disease.
There was no such thing as justice in the air we breathed, for it was
those who hated and envied and married for money or convenience
who were happy'. Coral Musker's newly formed opinions were now
being transformed into a system. When Milly Drover visited Mrs
Coney, the dead policeman's widow, to ask her to intercede for Jim's
life, she realized that the grim and rigid ceremonial of taking a life
to pay for a life was not the 'justice' of ordinary people but of kings
and lawyers and gentlefolk, who incidentally filled their pockets
during the process. Decisions were not made by people who cared
but by those who neither knew nor wanted to know the victims of
their justice. This note is repeated so often that it becomes one of the
dominants of the novel; off-setting the general mood of despair is a
vein of intense social sympathy, never to be repeated so forcefully.

One can make nothing of life, it is a thing of whim and chance.
Conder knew it only too well. 'They hanged this man and pardoned
that; one embezzler was in prison, but other men of the same kind
were sent to Parliament.'[1] You could not even speak of the situation
as 'injustice' because it was not systematic enough. Priests and
teachers tried to convince themselves and others that godliness and
cleanliness could be accepted as testimonials, but the Assistant
Commissioner knew that one would cut a throat while calling on
Jesus and another would wash to the waist before poisoning his wife.
The traditional attitudes were utterly false. They served to entrench
their possessions against shame or retribution, but they had no
moral validity.

If justice is undermined, so is love. We have, of course, been
prepared for this. Love received rough treatment on the train to
Stamboul and in this novel the assault is continued. In the general
collapse of his world, Conrad feels there is nothing he can do but
lash out against his environment. He had been fond of his brother,
now he felt he hated him. At least, he hated something or somebody,

[1] If Mr Greene had written these words in 1957 he would have been called
to the bar of that self-conscious assembly.

and one couldn't hate such a bloodless entity as the law. Unknown to him, desire for his brother's wife Milly was rising within him and upsetting his normal standards. Milly begs him to be 'reasonable', a word that so often denotes nothing: 'Hating doesn't get you any-where, any more than loving does. A bed in a hospital, that's about where both get you.' When Milly gives way to Conrad, his love for her is warped by his hatred of Jim, of his employer's nephew, of two strangers in Piccadilly who had chanced to offend him. And in the next room lay Kay, smiling in the fulfilment of her lust. It was inevitable that Conrad should first protest against and then accept with bitterness what seemed to him a proven fact—that happiness came from the lust that preachers and teachers decried, while love, which received their benedictions, brought misery. And his new partner in bed, who had been crying when he woke up in the night, had discovered a similar falsity about goodness. Mrs Coney had been good to her when she had gone to plead for her husband. Mrs Coney had been sympathetic and made her tea, and yet it would lead to nothing positive. The kindness, the natural goodness, would evaporate in the face of facts. They were entirely relative. And then, to complete the darkness of the picture, the only light goes out. Kay is not happy after all. She has her man, it is true. They are young, he has even received a small legacy, they go out for the day and book a room for the night on the strength of it. But there is a flaw, there is always a flaw: Jules's sexual performance was not even worthy of a perfunctory encounter in the park. The older men knew all this. Mr Bernay, for instance, had once believed that to be a woman's lover would armour anyone against shame, 'when there had seemed promise of infinite confidence in one short movement.' Sex was the big cheat and love did not transcend it. Only time could protect a man. And time was habit.

The book is heavy with individual misery. Greene's sense of insecurity, insufficiency and failure, with the possible addition of sexual maladjustment, come to a head here for the first time. There is no question of the mood being faked. It is also accompanied by a social conscience that later disappears. In the first chapter, for in-stance, the Assistant Commissioner is appalled to discover that the Government sees Jim Drover as a mere pawn in the political game.

Will the workers be more stimulated by his execution or by his pardon? If they strike it will cost the country fifty million, taxes would go up, and the next election might be lost. Greene seems anxious to show here (as elsewhere) that it is not always those who talk most about humanity who have the greatest charity. His bitterness against privilege and corruption follows in the direct line of Chesterton and Belloc, two famous Catholic champions of the poor against their exploiters and their socialist allies, whom they considered mechanist and insincere. Greene's picture of Conrad and Milly is of two babes in the metropolitan wood, where wires vibrate with the voices of generals and politicians, bishops and schoolmasters, where everyone who counts for anything has a cousin, an uncle, a nephew, a niece, while 'Milly's face was lost among the harsh confident cultured faces'. Again, there was no justice, but there was plenty of influence.

There is no reason to doubt Greene's sincerity. The year was 1934. By 1948, shall we say, I believe he had ceased to care, or rather only cared when something reminded him that he ought to care. (It is almost impossible to pass judgment on anyone without immediately qualifying it.) It was fashionable at the time to call oneself a Marxist and to join a left wing party. Some of Greene's contemporaries were anticipating revolution. This would never happen, said the Assistant Commissioner, and it was probably Greene's opinion also. 'The truth is, nobody cares about anything but his own troubles. Everybody's too busy fighting his own little battle to think of me, the next man.' It was a pretty shrewd assessment of the British people, lulled by prosperity in the past, poisoned by a hundred years' injection of false values, and only stimulated by the World War to stand together, sunburnt shoulder from the Riviera to emaciated shoulder from Jarrow. There is this to be said for Greene: he was the chronicler of the little people who were rubbing their noses in their own dirt instead of filling their hearts with irreproachably progressive emotions, as some of the left-wingers imagined.

The novel that springs to mind while reading *It's a Battlefield* is Conrad's *The Secret Agent*. The same sordidness, the same bitterness and dark intensity run through both of them, there is the same sense of defeat, of hopelessness, despite the occasional expressions or implications of hope. And, despite the pace that Greene can command, there is the same massiveness, even sluggishness, when writing of working class characters, or of people who are rooted in their environment, who virtually never move and who have a kind of tree-like strength because of it. Greene's idle rich, on the other hand, carry no conviction. Even Hardy did better. We should also note the name of Conrad Drover. He felt selfconscious because of it, it was not the kind of name that ordinary people have, and it had always cut him off from others, both at school and in the office. He had been named after a seaman, a merchant officer who had once lodged in his parents' house! Joseph Conrad was one of the three modern novelists whom Greene revered above all others.

There are also traces here and there of the influence of *Brave New World*, which had created an enormous impression on its appearance two years before. The description of the factory where Kay Rimmer worked is obviously to be related to that of the prison where her brother-in-law was awaiting execution. In each case there is movement from Block A to Block B and on to Block C; prisoners and proletarians moved in regiments like the embryos in Huxley's famous Hatchery. But even more suggestive of Huxley is the use of the very unGreenesque name of Surrogate for a character. The people in Greene's novels usually have commonplace names (so far, Andrews, Chant, Crane, Warren, Myatt, Drover) and when they are not commonplace they tend to be vaguely romantic, like Carlyon and Caveda. They frequently have significance, but it is usually an unconscious significance, as in the case of Chase and possibly Conrad. But a name like Surrogate is an invention, and therefore suggests intentional symbolism. The word is scarcely used today, except in ecclesiastical circles and in the writings of Aldous Huxley, who uses it throughout his work as a synonym for 'substitute'. In the same way we would know that a novelist who named one of his characters D. Gringolade must have been under the spell of H. G. Wells, and that a humorist who centred his stories on a character named Denny Gration was secretly an admirer of Aneurin Bevan.

In *Brave New World* few things were left unchanged or 'unimproved'. Substitutes (or surrogates) had been found for most natural products. The embryos in the Hatchery and Conditioning Centre, for instance, fed on blood-surrogate. Blood-surrogate lay at the basis of the new civilization. Its regulation and control were therefore of the first importance. And then there were surrogates for all the other things that we consider necessary for a satisfying life: love, poetry, drama, even tragedy. Mr Surrogate in *It's a Battlefield* is a wealthy Communist. He demands change, but he has no real significance at all. He is an empty vessel. There is real need of a revolutionary leader, but Mr Surrogate is only a poor substitute. He issues works of a politically violent character from a comfortable Bloomsbury address, and he deals fiercely yet lovingly with abstractions and shudders away from personalities. He would seduce a healthy young proletarian but found any other form of intercourse intolerable. One wonders why Greene chose such a Huxleyan name. I believe he regarded this novel, very partially, as a reply to the kind of thinking that produced *Brave New World*. I do not wish to labour this point, because it could only be incidental, but in effect Greene was saying: Yes, I can see the processes you mention but I don't believe they'll ever come to the end you foresee. People are too undependable, they have insufficient constancy of purpose, to make such a world. They can never see a thing whole.[1]

Technically this book marks a considerable step forward. The vintage Greene, the cinematic Greene, the Greene who frequently subordinates his characters to their environment instead of allowing them to dominate it, makes his first emphatic appearance. 'He saw the private secretary detach himself from two women. Tall, with round smooth features and ashen hair, he shone with publicity; he had the glamour and consciousness of innumerable photographs. His face was like the plate-glass window of an expensive shop. One could see, very clearly and to the best effect, a few selected objects: a silver casket, a volume of Voltaire exquisitely bound, a self-portrait by an advanced and fashionable Czecho-Slovakian.' It is clear-cut, sharply portrayed. Each image stands by itself, yet in their totality

[1] Another echo of *Brave New World* is to be found in the name of Janet Crowle, a murder-victim. (Names provide a fruitful field of enquiry in Greene's works.) One is reminded of Fanny and Lenina Crowne. N and L are easily interchangeable.

they create an unambiguous sensation. Greene has adopted the clarity of Conrad (who always set down what he *saw*, including a 'headless body' if he couldn't see the head, despite the shock to the reader) and fused it with something of his own, the concrete object producing its own mood. The phrase 'he shone with publicity' has no meaning syntactically yet it has its own peculiar sharp evocation. It was this trick that first caused readers to take note of Greene, and not any view he had of man or nature. He had perfected a new, if rather glossy, method of communication.

Both character and atmosphere are evoked by a cross-sample of manipulating imagery. Greene was the Mass Observer's ideal novelist. 'Milly noticed everywhere the signs of a fussing and incompetent woman, a woman who drives the dust from one room to settle in another, who buys Danish eggs for economy and leaves the gas burning.' His picture of the vibrant London streets is nervous and restless, comprised of carefully selected snapshots fitted together to make not so much a pattern as an aggregation, but a living one. 'The man who tears paper patterns and the male soprano were performing before the pit queues, the shutters of the shops had all gone up, the prostitutes had come on the second time at the super-cinemas, and the taxi ranks were melting and reforming.' And so on, noting the man at the counter of the Café Français selling 'Weights', the Battersea match factory working overtime, the cars in the Oxford Street fun-fairs, and the last edition of the evening papers, with news of rape and murder, Mr MacDonald and disarmament, the Special Service for footballers. And then, like a pebble dropped cleanly on its target: 'At each station on the Outer Circle a train stopped every two minutes.'

Some of the old faults were still there. Conder leans against a shop front and one of Greene's Harpies inevitably appears, 'with ravaged restored face', and says, 'What's the hurry dear?' She went hopelessly on, not because Conder was a hopeless client (although he was) but because Greene's Harpies are denied hope as a condition of their being. His streets sometimes look like Ealing Studios' remarkable visions of Soho, before Ealing Studios were famous. Another new dodge, not quite so successful as the cross-sample method and never used again so insistently, was the selection of recurring images which play the part of leitmotifs. At times of stress Conrad's mind always reverted to memories that were rooted in his childhood—the smell of anthracite, the sound of drills, pictures of starved, naked children on a screen. In this crisis of his life he convicted himself of cowardice, lust, incompetence and ingratitude, and with each failure he associated a childhood memory which tended to be transformed into a childhood terror. Each memory, innocent at the time, seemed in retrospect to be a prevision of a later failure.

The secret of Greene's personality lies in his childhood, as he would be the first to admit, and for that reason is partially hidden from us. Throughout his work there are frequent references to childhood events which later appeared to possess a relationship, perhaps a formative one, with the adult personality. It is not surprising to find Greene editing an enquiry into the Old School. Childhood was beginning to take on for him the character of a primitive land from which the tribe had emerged, only partly freed of its totems and tabus. One of the major criticisms made of the public schools during the nineteen-thirties (Greene's was Berkhamsted, where his father was an admirably progressive headmaster) was that they warped the sexual instinct. Greene was wholeheartedly in agreement. No matter how sincerely the headmaster wished to adapt progressive ideas to education and the organization of a boarding school, he was himself inhibited from any contact with new ideas by his insulated life, graduating from school to university and so back to school. As a result, even the best headmasters still believed in their hearts that sex was dirty and acted on that assumption. They were guilty in the main of two misconceptions: that sex could never be pleasant or amusing, and that marriage is always sacred.

This is a very interesting comment. It is quite clear from Greene's statement that he approved of neither of these beliefs and yet his fiction often underlines them. I suggest that in the first case it does so naturally and in the second unwillingly. It would be difficult to imagine any better illustration of Greene's thesis that childhood experience dominates the adult mind, whatever intellect or self-interest might prefer. None of Greene's lovers enjoy their embraces (the newly-weds in *Brighton Rock* and *Loser Takes All* are pathetic) and, much as he loathes the marriage-bond, an ironical fate has induced him to adopt a faith which demands that it be honoured!

The schoolmaster's hatred of sex led to a bar on privacy. 'I cannot believe that my own school, so progressive in many ways, was peculiar in its mistrust, the attitude that privacy could only be misused, the attitude of the divorce courts. Lavatories in my house had no locks, so that even that opportunity for a little quiet reading or writing was denied.' All work was done in an atmosphere of clamour and smells, and the excessive sexual purity of his house vented itself in the crudest of scatological jokes. What did the masters imagine would go on behind locked doors, he wondered. 'One is alternately amazed at the unworldly innocence of the pedagogic mind and its tortuous obscenity.' The choice of the word 'unworldly' is admirable, for the people responsible would have been hard put to it to have discovered activities that could not equally well have been undertaken in the dormitory or the countryside. Solitary walks were also forbidden, and a walking rota arranged, with consequent mental agony for the boy with few friends. I have already suggested that Greene is probably not a 'clubbable' person and he probably suffered the agony referred to. (Once one is famous, of course, it is perfectly easy to be clubbable because people want to be seen talking to you.)

Some critics have suggested that coeducation is the answer to this unsavoury sexual situation in our schools, but Greene was against it. It would only produce another, even worse, monstrosity. 'There is no advantage in educating boys and girls together if an unnaturally "safe" tone is preserved by laughing at any sentimental relationship. A "comradely" no-nonsense-about-sex attitude between men and women is peculiarly repellent. There is an air of unreality about the whole business of coeducation in England, a combination of rather conscious daring and rather secret prurience.' It was the 'unreality' of the system as a whole that aroused Greene's antagonism, but his view of reality was a peculiar one. He wanted schoolboys to be literally young men, i.e., young adults. He didn't want them to snigger about sex but did not trouble to consider the fact that sniggering goes on until its place is taken by sexual intercourse. It was all very well to criticize the habit of urging boys to 'own up' ('who in later life owns up to all his petty illegalities?') but it would be even more futile to plunge boys into adult society without first of all breaking the shock. The real difficulty, from Greene's point of view, was that he happened to be one of the few emotionally mature writers in modern English literature. His models, James, Conrad and Ford, were of the same calibre; apart from them he enjoyed the works of overgrown boys like Anthony Hope, John Buchan and Rider Haggard. But for the mass of underdeveloped English fiction-writers, victims of a repressive society which did not give their feelings full play, from Thackeray and Anthony Trollope through R. L. Stevenson and John Galsworthy to J. B. Priestley and John Masefield, he could develop little or no positive enthusiasm. (This is certainly not to deny interest.) When he had done a little coaching he discovered that he didn't like little boys. It is probable that he never had liked them, had developed emotionally at a very early stage, and chafed under school restrictions and the normally accepted mythos of boyhood. That is to say, he had been boy enough to want to discover gold in Africa but not sufficiently to find girls a kind of natural joke, as were the lower classes for the *Punch* subscribers of that day.

In *The Fallen Idol* Greene was later to develop the idea that a single event in childhood could leave its mark for life. In *It's a Battlefield* we are given another instance of the lasting, ineradicable impression, this time made not during childhood but during a moment of emotional susceptibility akin to the plastic nature of immaturity. Early in the book the Assistant Commissioner is suddenly struck by a strange phrase that comes to him out of the crowd at Piccadilly: 'a pram on a taxi'. He asked his companion if he knew what the phrase could have meant. His companion laughed so loudly as to attract attention, and he repeated the phrase wonderingly: 'A pram—on a taxi—how can I tell?' A young clerk halted and stared at them, convinced that he would never forget this meaningless joke: 'A pram—on a taxi.' He recognized the Assistant Commissioner, whom he had seen such a short time ago in court at his brother's trial. When, driven almost insane by the senselessness suddenly revealed to him, he set out to shoot the Assistant Commissioner and eventually stood before him with a revolver clasped in his shaking hand, it was this memory that dominated all others in Conrad's mind: the joker outside the Berkeley, 'a pram on a taxi'. Whatever else might happen to him, that phrase was burnt into his mind, as were the sight of the housekeeper's crumpled body in Philip's mind in *The Fallen Idol*, and the green baize door and the witch at the corner of the nursery passage in Greene's own mind. And as Greene's conviction grows that the real power of creation derives from the persistent pressure of childhood fears and misgivings, and as he learns to draw on them more easily, so his fiction improves and its intensity deepens.

V

PAIN, BE THOU MY PLEASURE

Nineteen Thirty-Five
'England Made Me', 'The Bear Fell Free'

AFTER a dedication to Vivien, with ten years' love, and a quotation from Walt Disney, 'All the world owes me a living', this novel, easily his best until *The Power and the Glory*, starts with a perfectly evoked mood of waiting, looking for someone who is not there. 'She might have been waiting for her lover', we are told. We feel certain he will never turn up. There is no sense of anticipation, only hopelessness. The tone is set for the novel, we know it will be an excursion into failure, not because it is by Graham Greene but because the manipulation of word and phrase is perfect. There will be no more false starts. The mechanism is in superb working order. In the end Anthony, her brother, actually does turn up but we feel it would have been better if he had not. He carried failure with him wherever he went. We recognize him at once, his round face which always looked as if it had only just lost its freshness, like a worn child's, 'the bonhomie which even a stranger would not trust'. And Kate knew that he could not open his mouth without lying. Greene's writing has by now become so expert that it gives the impression that deception is impossible. The author cannot be deceived. This only adds to the sense of hopelessness, for normally we hope to escape through our dishonesties as through windows from reality. It is impossible to persuade a fully-rounded Greene character (there are several in this book, Anthony and Minty being perfect specimens) that you are better off, better educated or better provided for than you really are. Anthony liked to pretend that he was entitled to wear a Harrow tie, but Minty knew he wasn't and Anthony knew Minty knew he wasn't. It didn't matter. Both of them had lived for too long on pretence to expect anything different. People will always see through you but that is no reason, although the moralists like to claim that it is, to go about naked. Kate knew the game as well as he did and played it unconsciously. Their meeting is a masterpiece of description, of two intimates who love each other in their way yet would not dream of trusting each other. 'He beamed at her; he rested both hands (she noticed his gloves needed cleaning) on the top of his umbrella, leant back against the counter and beamed at her. Congratulate me, he seemed to be saying, and his humorous friendly shifty eyes raked her like the headlamps of a second-hand car which had been painted and polished to deceive.'

Anthony was, in fact, pain, fear, despair, disgrace. He objectified these qualities for his sister, who was only slightly superior to him, and even then her superiority was not really moral but technical. She had gifts which were easier to turn to account. She had been successful and he had failed. She knew that he was 'conceited with failure', a brilliant perception that only a fully mature novelist could have. He was no stock figure, entirely bad or entirely 'weak', in the manner of the lesser novelist who wishes to avoid the charge of making his characterization too clear-cut yet has not the ability to reproduce living paradox. There is plenty of paradox in Anthony. He was a rogue, of course, but he was also responsible and conventional and well-meaning. He would certainly vote Tory but he would have sold secrets to Hitler if the chance had presented itself; he could have been trusted to give up his seat to an old lady (though Anthony was not the type of person one normally meets on a bus), yet necessity might have caused him to cheat her in a financial transaction. (He wouldn't have filched her handbag for that would have been vulgar.) Intellectually he was soft and sentimental—Kate's hard-headedness shocked him. Women, in his view, ought to marry for love and bear children, and they certainly shouldn't get 'squiffy'. He could never quite accept Kate's status as Krogh's mistress. His morality centred round the sweet angel figure of womanhood and he was perfectly prepared to blackmail Krogh and he regarded his Harrow tie as a legitimate piece of plunder.

There are few decent acts in *England Made Me* and hardly any of them are performed by Anthony. This may upset the moralists but anything else would have upset just as severely the balance of truth in the story, which was fairly obviously inspired by the career and social implications of Kreuger, the match-millionaire. Again there is evidence of social conscience (the theme would lose much of its impact if there were none) although it is less strong and intrusive than in the previous novel. And yet it is at that very point that Anthony tries to perform an act of goodwill which in fact marks the turning-point in his brief association with Krogh. Andersen, a workers' leader, declares a strike which may well topple over Krogh's precarious empire. Krogh manages to persuade the old man to cancel the strike, and then cynically sacks him. Andersen's son, bewildered and angry, decides to call on Krogh and finds him at a restaurant. By this time Andersen is wet through and half exhausted, and it is his condition that appeals to Anthony. (He has been down and out himself, and experiences an unexpected sense of solidarity with the young workman.) Krogh feels guilty and refuses to see him. Anthony for once wants to help another person without consulting his own interests, and will not send him away. In the end Hall has to do it.

Hall is a character of considerable significance, both in this novel and for a full appreciation of Greene's genius. He is an Englishman who shared Krogh's early hardships, who is incapable of Krogh's creative brilliance, and yet is absolutely devoted to his old companion. Hall is Krogh's shield, the common man with almost inexhaustible powers of endurance, who will protect the other man who is incomparably superior and yet is subject to moments of weakness. The odd thing is that both Hall and Anthony are right in their treatment of young Andersen. Anthony feels the other's wetness and misery and also, with a flash of insight, realizes that it would do Krogh good to meet one of his workmen in a human rather than an industrial relationship. When Anthony fails he knows he is on a dirty job. His whole life previously had been devoted to dirty jobs, but always without the troublesome responsibility of knowing (or admitting) it. The girl he had seduced, so casually yet so disappointingly, had told him his job was not respectable, and he had laughed, yet now he knew she was right, though in a much profounder way than she had imagined. As for Hall, he had treated Andersen brutally because he had to protect Krogh. It was Krogh he was thinking of, not himself. In that distressing, unpleasant scene when Andersen had been bundled out, there had been a lesser display of selfishness than was normal in that society. Another paradox, of course. Hall, who had come from England at Krogh's request because things were not quite as they should be, saw at a glance that Anthony and the rest of the company (even Kate, while her brother was there) were simply sponging on his old friend. Everything they did must be wrong, it was as simple as that. And Hall would do anything to keep Krogh safe. Even kill.

Krogh, on the other hand, represented success. In his large modern office building of steel and glass, with the fountains splashing beneath the concealed lights, surrounded by dividends and new flotations, he represented man's conquest of matter. His credit stood a point higher than that of the French Government. It was like a testimonial, proving anything. Yet success was never more than partial. The more convinced Krogh was of his financial power and astuteness, the less confident he became of his judgment in other matters. It irritated him to think that he could not appreciate the statue that formed the fountain. He had no feelings for it at all, and it was this absence that caused the uneasiness. He would have liked something traditional, a marble goddess or naked child, and instead, with his power and all his money, he had got a green shape, which he neither liked nor disliked. But he told himself it must be good, it was by one of Sweden's leading sculptors—money gave him that power, he could buy what he knew to be good. Money judged for him. Going down in the lift the liftman was rash enough to call it 'a bit odd', and Krogh nearly bit his head off, reminding him that the statue was the work of Sweden's greatest sculptor and that it was not the business of a door-keeper to understand such things. With shame Krogh realized he had forgotten the sculptor's name. There is just a suggestion in Krogh's reprimand of the doorman, of Greene's criticism of Krogh—that is to say, of Greene wanting to admire the *avant garde* in art yet not really appreciating it. And then, hey presto, he attains power as a respected novelist, and his opinion on a vast number of subjects is sought, even by intellectuals. The intellectual fears are being conquered but so far they are by no means quiescent.

Here, then, we have the two extremes of human experience. Anthony is the more vital character because he has the attraction (for his creator) of seediness.[1] Greene cannot make himself sufficiently interested in success to do much with Krogh. He remains something of a stick. Even twenty years later, when Greene tries to portray another successful financier in *Loser Takes All*, the character stubbornly refuses to come to life. The author has learnt some tricks in the meantime and does his best to animate the old man, but he never becomes more than a zombie, like the hero of 'Proof Positive'. Greene liked to catalogue a man's possessions, he liked to define him by his possession, but not such a man as Krogh. His possessions were too ordered, they lacked intimacy, in most cases they had been transmuted into currency and then again into figures in a ledger. It is quite different with Anthony. What few possessions he has are his and very much his. It is a joy to watch him unpack, to see the crumpled and battered articles coming out of his bag for the umpteenth time 'as if he were re-affirming his belief that certain things were inevitable, that certain things were past, that you had to take life as you found it, success and ignorance, failure and the stranger in the bed'. And out tumbled the torn photograph of Annette, the ties, pants, vests and socks, *The Four Just Men* in a Tauchnitz edition, a copy of *Film Fun*, the pencil, the half-crown fountain pen, and the rest of it. I can remember being shown a similar collection, half shamefacedly and half lovingly, by another Anthony, in one of London's tiny bed-sitters. The sociological truth of this character is almost terrifying. He cannot possibly become serious or pompous about life. Erik Krogh was only a poor bloody foreigner who didn't know how to dress, but he had the tin and he had, incredibly it seemed, offered some of it to Anthony. 'The whole damned thing is luck,' he told himself as he must have told himself a hundred times before. 'What a laugh. Look after number one.'

Poor young Andersen believed in justice. 'He had seen it working, the idle man dismissed, the industrious rewarded. His own wages had been raised two years ago.' Anthony hadn't seen it working. Conrad Drover stood between these two, but he could never have become an Anthony Farrant. Barriers of class and education

---

[1] Anthony fascinated Greene. His abandoned novel, 'The Other Side of the Border', is about an Anthony-type character named Hands. Greene believes that one reason why he did not continue it was because of this repetition.

stood between them, and would never be crossed. Anthony had had better chances, on the face of it, but on the other hand he had been in a position to see through the social fake at a time when Conrad was still stuck fast in Sunday School pieties. Anthony, like Minty, was an exile. Minty was a genuine remittance man. Anthony would have been if there had been anyone who thought him worth a remittance. But there was only Kate, who loved him and wanted to possess him, hold on to him, not send him away. He was always running away (as he had done from school, as had Graham Greene himself), and then coming back to sister Kate. For men like Anthony and Minty the world really offered little more than a series of work-houses strung out across the globe—Shanghai, Aden, Singapore, even unexpected places like Stockholm. 'They were not fresh enough, optimistic enough, to believe in peace, co-operation, the dignity of labour, or if they believed in them, they were not young enough to work for them. They were neither one thing nor the other; they were really only happy when they were together: in the clubs of foreign capitals, in pensions, at old boys' dinners, moment-arily convinced by the wine they couldn't afford that they believed in something: in the old country, in the king, in "shoot the bloody Bolsheviks", in the comradeship of the trenches: "My old batman", I said, "Don't I know your face? I believe you were at Ypres in '15".'

Anthony can't keep off the women, of course. For one thing, his type couldn't, and they all believed in their type. They liked to think of themselves as individuals but secretly it was the gang they revered. And then, Anthony was Greene's *alter ego*. He was such a lovable failure, he had done all the dubious things his creator wanted to do, he had gone much further East than Stamboul. He liked his women common. I don't know how Greene likes *his* women, and it would be indelicate to ask, but he is only successful in portraying common ones. (In the same year he brought out a story about people who weren't common and it didn't come alive.) It is true, Minty didn't like girls (and this fact gives Greene the chance to bring out a few superlative phrases: 'he didn't like girls, he couldn't have said it in words more plainly; tawdry little crea-tures, other people's sisters, their hats blocking the view at Lord's'). But there was something not quite right about Minty, despite

Harrow—and that was another paradox, that a man who came from
Harrow should not be good enough for this other institution, the
International Exiles. The slick phrases which drop so appropriately
from the lips of Anthony and Minty become embarrassments when
Kate uses them. All she wants from life is the companionship of her
brother, and she is always on the point of losing it. 'You're my
Ladies Bar, Anthony, my beastly port.' Only the strongest emotion
could have wrung such bathos from her and it is her last defence
against breakdown into the deepest pits of sentiment. And she knew
Anthony well enough to realize that sentiment would drive him
away. She would have to suffer the agony of a sentimentality she
knew was false. In fact, their relationship borders on incest. One
feels that Kate could easily surrender to physical love with Anthony.
He, of course, could not even have imagined such a thing. There
were doubtless few acts he would not have performed with a
strange woman in Shanghai or Saigon or Coventry, but with Kate
even the most orthodox sexual act would have been unthinkable.

Anthony is conquered not by love but by the temporary,
spasmodic itch (the lech or yen, as Greene likes to call it, and it is as
well to give it a name. Reviewing *The End of the Affair* Evelyn Waugh
regretted the paucity of the English language for some of the
commonest human actions and organs). The itch is nothing compared with love, yet it destroys the other by its occasional savagery.
His indifference almost drives Kate mad. Her liaison with Krogh
means nothing to her, it is a mere convenience like the School
Certificate, and yet Anthony's reply to her declaration of love was a
mocking, 'Brother and sister!' It wasn't simply that he didn't understand her feeling, it was that he was incapable of understanding.
Kate was doomed to suffer the worst pangs of unrequited love. For
him Loo was a 'recurring itch of the flesh; this was thirty years in
common; but the itch when it was there, he knew, would always be
stronger. Kate was for his satisfied moments; when you were satisfied you could turn to a sister, to family love'. And as if the itch
weren't strong enough in itself, it enlisted self-pity. He would have
to leave Kate and rush off to Coventry where a certain fuck awaited
him.

As I have said, this was his best book so far. He had always been a writer of pace, yet in the previous books it had been intermittent, checked at intervals by moments of reflection. The reflection is still here—a good book cannot do without it—but it is absorbed into the narrative and does not affect the tempo. It has a vitality of its own which keeps up with the narrative, and there is none of the stopping and starting that marred *It's A Battlefield* and *Stamboul Train*. But this was a height he had attained yet could not for the time being maintain. A short story called 'A Day Saved', published in the same year, is one of the worst things he has ever written. I believe it was specially written for broadcasting and perhaps he was too conscious of writing for a different medium. (One feels—and there is also quite clear evidence—that he does not allow such consciousness to impede his film writing, which is full of entirely literary images and even the occasional dream which is not ostensibly film material at all.) The story is a mysterious, pretentious one of a type popular during the 'thirties. One man follows another. The pursuer does not know who his prey is, nor why he is following him. (There is an echo of Conder and his supposed shadower here. It is a symbol improperly realized.) 'He carried something I dearly, despairingly wanted', but what it was he didn't know. It is rather on the level of Sam Beckett and Ionesco and Canetti and the new Paris-Irish-Italian drama: surface oddity, without deriving the oddity from life, as did Pirandello and Kafka. As for the apparent significance, the futility of 'saving time', nothing could be triter. Even John Gordon would take the point. The paraphernalia is far too elaborate.

But experiment was in the air. Greene was still young enough to be unsure of where he was going, and still energetic enough to want to go in several directions at once. *Ulysses* was still regarded by the *avant garde* as one of the major literary works of all time, and the surrealists were providing stimuli for all those people who were sick of traditionalism. Greene wasn't quite sure whether he approved of the past or not. His religion urged him to be sceptical of modernism, and his main literary models were classicists, but the artistic climate is always difficult to resist, especially for the young. The result of all this ferment, in Greene's case, was *The Bear Fell Free*, a story published in a limited edition of 285 copies and prefaced with a line from Weyl: 'Events do not happen; we come across them.'

It was an attempt to impress the intellectuals. The time sequence jigs back and forth like a rocking horse, never very far, never as violently as in Huxley's *Eyeless in Gaza*, for instance, yet less systematically and more confusingly. (It appears to be a technique that attracts Greene, for he returned to it in *The End of the Affair*, where once again he handled it badly.) Apart from that, the main novelty lies in his use of the stream-of-consciousness method, which he had already used in *The Man Within* and also, to a limited extent, in *England Made Me*. But the prose is intelligible, which is more than can be said for much of the experimental writing of the period. (*Petron*, by Hugh Sykes Davies, published in the same year, is worth a comparison: there is no actual failure of intelligibility and there is a weird beauty about the writing, yet the author's intention is not fully divulged. Greene's is, but it is doubtful whether it was worth the effort.)

At a dinner party Farrell says he will fly the Atlantic. (This feat had enormous symbolic value for the middle class of the day. Henry Williamson's *The Gold Falcon* had appeared only two years before.) Carter, the ex-war hero, admires him. Baron, serious and political, is angered by the waste. Baron dies in his bath. Farrell crashes and only the teddy bear, put in by his wife, is recovered. She sleeps with Carter. They are all recognizable Greene figures but they have been raised a social notch to mark the occasion. Farrell fails, but his failure is of the type, like Dunkirk, that all men admire. The characters are middle-class, but well-to-do, not seedy. They are obviously members of golf clubs and do not keep shops or sponge on one another. In fact, it says nothing that has not been said much better by Greene before, but the failure is partially obscured by the verbal *mêlée* of the concluding pages, where everything merges with everything else, and images are forced into intimacy without benefit of form or grammar. '. . . poor Carter, feet out of the mud, Davis dead, Farrell dead, war hero, trench comradeship, belief in reunions, Toc H and Tubby Clayton, feeling a heavy guilt going downstairs from Jane's flat, taking things seriously, guilt all down the street, guilt as he wept, guilt in Talbot House lighting lamps of remembrance, guilt on the service revolver, etc. etc.' It could be a confession by the author. Farrell might be Farrant in slightly happier circumstances. Tubby Clayton amused the intellectuals of the time and was to the same extent revered by all good clubmen. Auden and MacNeice, in their 'Last Will and Testament', left him some ginger-pop.

Here is Greene's attempt to distil significance out of this rather slight affair. 'The plane met the water at a hundred and twenty miles an hour: the wheel smashed upwards at Farrell's head, screwed his neck, broke it without killing; the side of the cockpit caved in and cut through his skull to the brain, his knees were struck upwards, the broken bones jabbed through the broken neck.

Birth and death simultaneously tainted with each other. Guilt and suicide in the maternity ward, guilt and suicide in the trenches, in Jane's flat guilt and suicide. Patient serious Baron, tasting from the first of the final soapsud, soapsuds in settlements, soapsuds in Parliament, soapsuds in Buckingham Palace. Money for nothing wrenched from Mrs Farrell's womb, sherry circulating through the broken neck, etc. etc.'

Not all the soapsuds in the world will cleanse the stables. The teddy bear, the cuckold's teddy bear presented by an unfaithful wife, alone survives. To guilt we can add triviality. It is amusing to realize what never seemed to be noticed in those days; for the ordinary public the message can be presented with restraint and subtlety, but for the *avant garde* it had to be hammered and thumped: guilt, guilt, guilt . . .

VI

AFRICA, ALMA MATER

Nineteen Thirty-Six
'Journey Without Maps', 'A Gun For Sale'

GREENE'S account of his visit to Liberia is prefaced with quotations from W. H. Auden (appearing to cast doubt on the idea that anyone can ever really find his way anywhere) and from Oliver Wendell Holmes (asserting that one's life has a plan but many of the pieces will not fit until late in the game). Greene was certainly looking for something when he set sail from Liverpool. He was aware of a deep feeling of dissatisfaction and, instead of trying to establish his motives by rational process, he wisely associated what appeared to be two dominant aspects of his psychology, and waited for their off-spring. The two aspects were childhood fears and his love of seediness. As a kind of sub-department of the latter he was able to include his fascination with failure. Liberia might well precipitate a solution. It was primitive and it was very down-at-heel. 'There seemed to be a seediness about the place you couldn't get to the same extent elsewhere, and seediness has a very deep appeal: even the seediness of civilization, of the sky-signs in Leicester Square, the "tarts" in Bond Street, the smell of the cooking greens off Tottenham Court Road, the motor salesmen in Great Portland Street.' (These are permanent staff in Greene's human comedy.)

He didn't want the Africa of the white settler; he was looking for 'a quality of darkness', the inexplicable. He hoped that the call of his personal mastodons would be answered in the jungle. Once he was there he realized that his search was based partly on fear. He looked for the primitive because he was half afraid of what he would find. Once he got to Duogobmai his fears vanished; he couldn't sink lower into the heart of mystery. Again we find Greene clarifying for us the modern neurosis. Orwell did the same when he sought humiliation in French kitchens and English spikes. It was necessary to 'go deep', to disappear from the sight of civilization, beyond restraint, get back to the youth of man. In Duogobmai he found rats, leprosy, yaws and smallpox, and he was happy. The theme is muted at first but gathers momentum as the book proceeds, which is as it should be, because Greene did not know at first what he would find. When he returned it was with the conviction that the line separating Duogobmai from Leicester Square was a very thin one. It was a consoling thought. If we could only start again . . . 'If one could get back to this bareness, simplicity, instinctive friendliness, feeling rather than thought'. The lines of development diverged *after* Duogobmai. Our civilization did not create seediness, it only gave it a new character.

Greene attributes a similar longing to others. They might not be thoroughly aware of it but it was part of the modern human condition. He compared Mungo Park and Livingstone with Freud—they only chose different, more costly and less easy methods of return. The writers, such as Rimbaud and Conrad, were aware of what pulled them; the explorers may not have been. When the child suddenly cries, without apparent reason, it is because he still possesses the ancestral fear; the devil dances in his sleep, he longs for Africa. Dreams play an important part in Greene's work, and I shall discuss them at length in a later chapter, but in *Journey Without Maps* he devotes a brief section to them. When he got to Africa he recognized his earliest, recurrent dreams: someone waiting to come in, the witch at the corner of the nursery passage. All these dream figures were beings who controlled power. The Princess of Time used to haunt his sleep when he was sixteen. She was not evil. Evil was introduced later in the form of civilization. He decided on certain equations, such as that the supernatural world of Africa (or the dream world) is Power, and civilization is Evil. He then persuaded himself that his journey was an investigation into Power, original, protean Power, and a flight from Evil. He managed to symbolize the process at one point, when he found himself in a strangely English-looking landscape but saw a file of men crossing the stream, naked except for their loin-cloths, carrying bows and steel-tipped arrows. 'It was like the world of Miss Nesbit, where odd savage people appear in country lanes; they might have been coming through the Amulet

out of the African forest into an English park. We passed them
going ourselves into Africa, while they with their bows and arrows,
their naked cicatrized bodies, went on into the park, towards the
great house and the butler's pantry.' Here and there we meet people
who straddle both worlds: the American gangster, the European
conspirator, the Gold Coast Oxford graduate, the Americanized
Liberian lawyer.

Conrad had said that Africa might take the form of an 'un-
explained brutality'; Céline called it 'a sense of despair'. Greene
quoted from Kurt Heuser's novel, *The Inner Journey:* 'The interior:
that might signify the heart of the continent, but also the heart of
things, the mystery: and finally, the comprehension of himself in
nature and in Time'. But linked with this interpretation was the fact
of failure, and it might be failure that proved the stimulus to this
return to the starting point. On the communal level it might be,
Why is civilization thus? But on the personal level it might be,
Why am I as I am? To complete the picture in literary terms Greene
sent a failure to Africa on a kind of last-chance mission. 'A Chance
For Mr Lever' appeared in the same year as *Journey Without Maps.*
Lever had never sunk as low as this before; for thirty years he had
sold heavy machinery in Europe and the States, but now he sat surrounded by black faces and banana trees and impenetrable forest
with Eastbourne only a dream. 'He could hear his filter dripping in
the hut, and somewhere somebody was playing something (he was
so lost he hadn't got the simplest terms to his hand), something
monotonous, melancholy, superficial, a twanging of palm fibres
which seemed to convey that you weren't happy, but it didn't
matter much, everything would always be the same.'

Greene's mind was still full of the taste of failure. Lever dwelt
miserably on his own hard lot. It wasn't fair that after thirty years'
hard travelling a man should have to go from door to door begging
for a job. He had been a good traveller, yet somehow he had been
left behind. People talked about men being thrown on the dustheap
—*he* had been pitched into the jungle! And again, in the same year,
Mr Chalfont was aware of the same bitter sense of insufficiency. He
did not even venture out for the Jubilee but stayed in his bed-sitting
room eating ham rolls and heating the iron on the stove ('Jubilee').

He was separated from Mr Lever by a chasm of respectability and 'honest purpose'. Mr Chalfont never whined about his good intentions coming to nothing. He had always lived on bad intentions. When he met a vulgar, breezy woman named Amy who had made £5000 by opening brothels for the Jubilee, he was made to realize his reduced status. She pitied him and offered him money; his pretence no longer worked. Chalfont was a Minty who had chosen to be a gigolo rather than a newsman. It might have been Anthony if he had lived. This story straddles a moment of transition in Greene's development, for in addition to the backward glance we also have a prevision of *Brighton Rock's* Ida Arnold in the being of the amiable Amy. And that was to be a new element altogether.

To return to Mr Lever, then, and his despairing visit to Liberia to find a man with whose help he could make a lot of money and achieve his Mecca, Eastbourne. He had to get to the bottom before he could get out of the mess. But at the bottom he found only death and squalor, and there was no return. At last, but too late, Mr Lever flared into rebellion. He saw the old clichés for the cheats they were. 'The Solemnity of Death: death wasn't solemn; it was lemon-yellow skin and black vomit. Honesty is the Best Policy: he saw quite suddenly how false that was.' At the end he recognized only one personal relationship, his affection for Emily, his wife. This is thoroughly in keeping with Greene's normal outlook, although hasty reading has caused many critics to miss it in favour of an overwhelming cynicism. In his fiction most values are discovered to be hollow but there is always someone's love that remains sound: Rose's in *Brighton Rock*, Scobie's in *The Heart of the Matter*, and Bendrix's in *The End of the Affair*—or, looking backwards, Kate's in *England Made Me*. The love is usually battered, even warped (as was Bendrix's) but it was still recognizably love. And Mr Lever, in his humble way, made the same affirmation. He felt that all pettiness had left him, that he had been released from the psychological compulsion of counting costs and shrinking from the so-called dishonesties. (Here was a very useful escape hole that Greene was to use to its full extent in *Brighton Rock*, the conviction that if wrongdoing is petty when set against a cosmic background, then there can really be little of evil in such wrongdoing.) In the last paragraph Greene threw his story to the winds and announced that a kindly God would give Mr Lever three days of happiness (triumph, we might call it) before taking him with yellow fever. And all around was that drab, empty forest, that Greene himself had got to know so well, with its absence of spiritual life, of anything except dying and shrivelling vegetation. He made exactly the same comment about it that Aldous Huxley had made several years before, that this Nature, this untamed tropical Nature, could not be possessed as Wordsworth and A. E. Housman had believed. But he also compared it with the objectivity of child-hood, when the moments of extraordinary happiness had been counter-balanced by boredom. This was before one had learned the fatal trick of transferring emotion. Mr Lever recovered objectivity, and died. The story ends inconclusively: there are two opinions about everything, as Mr Lever himself was fond of saying. Either he laughed successfully at God or God punished him.

The third story of this year was the famous 'The Basement Room', written on a cargo vessel returning from West Africa. (It was reissued as *The Fallen Idol* in 1950 after it had been filmed. In a preface Greene pointed out that the new title was meaningless, and had been chosen by the distributors.) Africa is still one of the leading characters and was, of course, to agitate Greene's consciousness for some years to come. Once again it was linked with childhood—to Baines, the housekeeper, the boy Philip resembled his lost Africa. No time is lost telling us that Africa is still in the front of his mind, that Old Coasters rank as the élite of mankind. The day with Mrs Baines went badly. Philip sensed it and Baines, momentarily restored to his state of African freshness and primitiveness, knew it too. Philip knew nothing of love but he could share disappointment. The boredom of childhood, which had driven Greene to thoughts of suicide, began to cloud this promising day, spoilt by Mrs Baines, adult and civilized. The grown-up was the witch of the dream, so frequently alluded to, trying to snatch the child away into another world. And yet the attraction of Baines was partly his distance, the fact that he led the man's life, had a revolver, acknowledged responsibilities. He lived behind barriers, good to witness but not to share. And when these barriers were torn down Philip wanted to die. Mrs Baines came home unexpectedly, knowing that her husband was 'carrying on', and she questioned Philip and dragged him into their horrifying world. 'It wasn't fair, the walls were down again between his world and theirs; but this time it was something worse than merriment that the grown people made him share; a passion moved in the house he recognized but could not understand.' Their passions even flooded the night nursery.

This story equals de la Mare's 'An Ideal Craftsman' in its intensity and successful coupling of two distinct worlds. It is a lamentation for 'the lost childhood', a phrase which Greene took from a poem by AE and later used as a title for his book of essays. The conviction that one emotionally charged incident in childhood can leave its mark on the whole of later development is the moral basis of the story. Greene has applied the notion to others, ranging from Beatrix Potter to Henry James, and there is little doubt that we could apply it to him if we knew enough. (He is hampered in the same way; childhoods are so easily lost he is reduced to looking for the formative influence in adolescence or even later life. It is unsatisfactory, but it is all that can be done until case histories are spread out for the critic's use. It is the final reason why the biographical types of criticism, as favoured by men like Hugh Kingsmill, can lead to uncharitable falsities as well as geniune perceptions.) But with Philip we have all the evidence. We know that certain things happened on that day that were to condition him for the rest of his life. One of them was the sight of Mr Baines, sitting in the tea-shop with the girl. When he was dying, sixty years later, he asked, 'Who is she?' (Welles took the tip in *Citizen Kane*. It was Greene who actualized a Freudian possibility.) When Mrs Baines tricked him into telling her that Baines had been with the girl, she promised him a 2A Meccano set. It stopped his life. 'He never opened his Meccano set again, never built anything, never created anything, died, the old dilettante, sixty years later with nothing to show rather than preserve the memory of Mrs Baines's malicious voice saying good night, her soft determined footfalls on the stairs to the basement, going down, going down.'

The writing of this period illustrates a mood felt by Greene when preparing to set sail for Africa. 'I find myself always torn between two beliefs', he wrote. 'The belief that life should be better than it is

and the belief that when it appears better it is really worse.' Sitting in
the huge hotel lounge at Liverpool, he felt at home. His surround-
ings aimed at so much and achieved so little. All the morally doubtful areas of existence, retired Majors making appointments at
brothels, broken-down Old Etonians taking the air in the park, were
close to some vague beginning, were not so very far from the
central darkness. 'Like Monrovia its building has begun wrong, but
at least it has only begun; it hasn't reached so far away as the smart,
the new, the chic, the cerebral', he wrote of seediness in general. And
in this way he traces the unexpected link between the broken-down
and the corrupt on the one hand and childhood on the other. For
most of us these two extremes are terrifying, or at least alien, for our
childhood is lost. We get to love what we know, whether it is good
or not. When his pilgrimage was over and he returned to an outpost
of civilization he was glad, for it meant iced beer and the Empire
programme from Daventry. He knew that these were coarser tastes
and pleasures than the ones he had been experiencing, and they also
brought a coarser terror in their wake.

Unhappiness, he remarked, was always happening all the time
everywhere. He accepted it as a fact yet remained fascinated by it. He
told himself that you don't weep unless you've been happy first.
'Tears always mean something enviable.' Tears meant a failure—the
failure of a previous happiness. His obsession with failure could take
a neurotic shape as when he discovered that the film of one of his
books had been a failure. Again one is tempted to ask, is this affec-
tation? I think not, although the rationalization is. He said that failure
hadn't the shamelessness of success; 'it might be vulgar, but it wasn't
successfully vulgar'. But that wasn't the reason, and I doubt if he
would press it now. The reason lies in the intensity which causes us
to accept his attitude as sincere. We would have to trace it to some
stupendous event in his past, such as an attempt at suicide, or the
pretence of such an attempt, followed by remorse—and I will consider this possibility later. All I can do at this stage is state, and reiterate, the fact of Greene's inner contradiction, like two live charges
crossing each other—perhaps evidence of a personal version of
Newman's 'aboriginal catastrophe' which may very well have prepared Greene for his religious conversion. Perhaps it was precipitated

by his first memory, a dead dog at the bottom of his pram. It had been run over and his nurse had picked it up and put it in. There was no emotion attached to the sight. Then there was the man who rushed out of a cottage with a knife in his hand, threatening to kill himself. Later, at fourteen, he used to hang about waiting for a girl he wished 'to do things to'. He thought of pain as something desirable, not to be dreaded. 'It was as if I had discovered that the way to enjoy life was to appreciate pain.'

Like the little boy in 'The End of the Party' he had always believed that death was desirable. It was only when he caught fever in Liberia that he realized that he loved life and wanted to hang on. Few people these days believe (as many used to) that death is the entrance to a more desirable state of being, yet there is always the possibility of the odd child who takes to the idea naturally, just as the odd child finds he can play the violin with scarcely any tuition. It is well known that it is almost impossible to reverse a belief held firmly in childhood. Greene may have come to agree intellectually with others that death was the failure of the great good, life ,yet emotionally he would never accept it. Later he would try to find justification for his undoubted taste for darkness. Darkness; Africa; a girl crying in Leicester Square; there is a strange, subterranean linkage which irritates his intelligence and finds outlet in his fiction. It occurs to him that Africa has the rough shape of the human heart, and the image seems stupendously significant. The last entry in the journal which he kept on his return to West Africa in 1942 (published in *The Mint*) suddenly sparkles with the joy of fulfilment as he smells the smoke drifting across from Freetown. 'It will always be to me the smell of Africa, and Africa will always be the Africa of the Victorian atlas, the blank unexplored continent the shape of the human heart.'

The sex thrill is scarcely restrained, although the Liberian women did not excite him. He was still free to think of the prostitutes he had once seen in Riga. They were dreadfully *passé*. To Greene Riga was a city of 'Whispers, giggles from hidden seats, excited rustles in the bushes', yet, lest you imagine that it was a kind of Oriental Paris, all gaiety and glitter, he hastened to explain that whatever else it was, it certainly wasn't 'new, lovely and happy'. On this journey he felt the same old compulsion to emphasise the sexual aspect ('a

D

girl's nipples bulged against the back in front, her buttocks were
pressed by the girl behind') nor do I think there can be any honest
objection to this. In Africa a European realizes how starved his eyes
have been of breasts. But immediately Greene follows up with the
deflationary pay-off; it appears to hurt him to consider that the
squeezing of these breasts and the pinching of these buttocks is an
old, old story. 'There is not so much virginity in the world that
one can afford not to love it when one finds it.' And then there are
the occasions when the sexual intensity achieves a literary triumph,
as when he wrote of a German artist and his wife on board his ship,
'All the time, in the cabin, at dinner, at a café table, they gave the
impression of having only just risen from bed'. One sees them immediately, blowsy and sensual. The image is so apt, so well-chosen,
so evocative it is guaranteed to disturb the emotions of a person
whose own sexual instincts are normally healthy.[1]

Greene has not yet become a propagandist for his adopted religion, but he makes a statement which strikes one as ingenuous, to
say the least. 'I am a Catholic with an intellectual if not an emotional
belief in Catholic dogma.' Later in the book he writes, 'I had not
been converted to a religious faith. I had been convinced by specific
arguments in the probability of its creed'. These are strange statements because they are the reverse of those normally made by
Catholic converts. Their usual argument runs, 'I know the credal
side is logically unacceptable but I happen to believe emotionally'.
One cannot help feeling that Greene is trying to be clever, that he
has been urged to express himself thus by his nagging sense of intellectual insufficiency. Moreover, it makes it easy for him to justify
the attitude towards humble right and wrong that he adopted later
in *Brighton Rock*. He realized, he says here, that it was sinful to miss
a Mass on Sunday, but he could not feel very guilty about breaking
a solemn oath. 'These contradictions in human psychology I find of
peculiar interest', he writes airily. There is one other aspect to note.
An allegiance based on intellectual grounds would be likely to find

---

[1] There are intriguing references to a cousin who accompanied Greene on
this journey. Both person and relationship are undefined and the personal
pronoun is never used, except on one occasion when it is slipped in casually and
yet, one feels, meaningfully. It appears that the cousin was a female.

its defence a much more difficult task, if attacks became severe, than one based on emotional grounds. And the tests were to be almost unbearable, judging by *The Heart of the Matter*.

There is a suggestion that the Catholic faith provided him with a refuge from tawdry, Protestant if not agnostic, England towards which his feelings were markedly ambivalent. While waiting for the priests to come from Benediction at the mission near Bolahun he felt how much better a civilization their Latin represented than the tin shacks of the English port. The priests were American Episcopalians, but Greene was not thinking of America. It was the Latin that warmed him with its suggestion of the culture that had not gone wrong. Despite his intellectual pretences, Greene's attachment to his religion is almost entirely emotional, the nostalgic longing of an adult for the simple, intimately known home where it was always warm and each day was a week long. It was when you got to a place like Liberia that you realized how well Christianity compared with the commercial civilization that engulfed it. You realized that Christianity was still the revolutionary force, still appealed to the vigour of youth rather than the weariness of age. It did not whisper to its devotees: 'Come to me all ye who are heavy laden and I will give you commercial privileges and will whisper for you in the ear of a Minister of State'. He constantly returns to the contrast between the missionaries, living outside the limits of European protection, in dignity and gentleness, and 'the English in Freetown who had electric light and refrigerators and frequent leave, who despised the natives and pitied themselves'. There was only danger from men in the coastal areas, whose civilization had taught the natives to steal and lie and kill. That was what it had fashioned out of the primitive, the childhood of the race, which in this particular part of the world lay within a day's call.

The social conscience displayed in *It's A Battlefield* had plenty to feed on here. Because Greene is a Catholic a forgetful public assumes that he will automatically be politically reactionary. The fact is that he disclosed himself to be as critical of Imperialist reality as the most assertive Left Winger and one has to take his criticisms more seriously than many from the professional propagandists (as one comes to respect Father Huddleston rather more than, say, Mr

Fenner Brockway M.P.) because he has no compulsive axe to grind
and is not associated with any revolutionary or even reformist
group. The real rulers in Freetown, he said, were men who came
out for a few years, had a long leave every eighteen months, gave
garden parties, and let it be known that they were there for the good
of the ruled. They were the people responsible for the wages of the
platelayers on the narrow-gauge line running to Pendembu: six-
pence a day, from which they bought their food, and from which
one day's pay a month was docked during the depression. This was
the 'meanest economy among the many mean economies which
assisted Sierra Leone through the depression', he wrote—and the
depression was caused by Levers showing a preference for whale oil
over palm oil. Civilization in Sierra Leone was exploitation. The
natives' lot had hardly been improved and we had introduced new
diseases and weakened their resistance to the old. The I.L.P. and the
Communist Party carried on their verbal warfare against imperial-
ism, yet neither had ever urged a strike in England to draw attention
to the plight of the Sierra Leonese platelayers.

There was another way in which Greene had not reacted like
other children to the pressures of his environment. Most of us have
grown up with an unquestioning attitude of superiority towards
missionaries, whom we tend to laugh at as people who insist on putting contented black nudes into trousers. But it was not the missionary who impressed Greene with his ridiculous scoundrelism, like
Mr Davidson in Somerset Maugham's *Rain* or the picture of Father
Damien that Stevenson was moved to attack and destroy in his *Open
Letter;* what impressed Greene were the pictures of starving, pot-
bellied children shown on slides by thin tired men who scarcely had
the energy to be rascals. And these pictures had marked Greene's
mind very deeply, as we may see from *It's A Battlefield*, where they
from a part of Conrad Drover's mental background. The other
children could not understand, they were an easy prey for the anti-
missionary animus, and it was left to Conrad to feel an almost unbearable responsibility for the native children. At this level all
sectarianism is put on one side. If there is a hero in *Journey Without
Maps* it is Dr Harley, a Methodist medical missionary, who had
spent more than twenty years at Ganta, Liberia, by 1946. (We are

told this in a footnote in the Uniform Edition.) He was worn thread-bare, body and nerves, and he went on cutting the pus from swollen genitals, injecting for yaws, anointing for craw-craw and treating two hundred natives a week for venereal disease. This account is followed by a discreditable story about a Catholic priest, whose activities taught the District Commissioner that white men were hypocritical and crooked.

Before leaving this book, it is worth while noting a slight air of ballyhoo which we have come to expect from Greene. His Enter-tainments are blown up fantastically, and even this, on the whole sober, account does not entirely escape the virus. It comes from the atmosphere of pioneering which Greene deliberately imparted. He was not the first Englishman to follow that particular route but he was certainly the most articulate, and he makes good use of his opportunities. (I have already referred to the explorers who would probably have been amazed to hear the psychological reasons ad-vanced for their expeditions.) On the other hand, it should be ac-knowledged that Greene covered practically the whole distance on foot, only using the hammock when sick. The depressing know-alls on the Coast, boasting of their superiority to the native porter, would never have attempted such a feat. Greene's determination to be different may have caused him difficulties many years later. In this book he wrote, 'If there were anything to hide in the Republic I wanted to surprise it. Luckily the Secretary of the Interior had suggested a route for me to follow, and it would be quite easy for me to avoid it'. In September 1956 he wanted to visit the Naga Hills in India and complained that the Indian Government refused to give him permission. In a letter to *The Times* the Public Relations Officer at India House stated that the Government was reluctant to take avoidable risks during the emergency (the tribesmen were in revolt). It is just possible that the P.R.O. had read and remembered *Journey Without Maps*.

'There was cruelty enough in the interior', he wrote, 'but had we done wisely exchanging the supernatural cruelty for our own?' Brutality seems to be one of the marks of our age, and there is a touch of nostalgia in the pleasure we take in gangster novels. In some ways these submen, hurling their bombs and handling their automatics with easy familiarity, are closer to the often religious brutality of the African innocents than the rest of us. We may even learn from them the point of divergence, the moment of going astray. Their cruelty has lost its spiritual sanction, has become hard and selfish and superficial, and yet there are occasions when it seems to be lit up with a brief yet intense significance. This is perhaps the best approach to *A Gun For Sale*, although it is not written with any such set purpose. It is the first book that is obviously written to gain an effect, to stimulate a thrill, to invoke disgust and other of the less agreeable emotions. It is an excursion into the kind of civilized hideousness that Greene felt had broken its moorings. There is nothing fine, nothing noble, nothing attractive in it, unless we except the moments of love that struggle for expression—and unexpectedly asexual ones for Greene. The 'good' men are out, mechanically and soullessly, to get the 'bad' men; the 'bad' men double-cross each other. The furniture is rickety, the dust lies thick. There is some excuse for distinguishing this as an Entertainment, far more than there was for *Stamboul Train*. Greene has found that sensationalism pays and the inevitable has happened; he begins to parody himself. The parody becomes more and more pronounced as the book proceeds.

The chief character, Raven, has a hare-lip and is despised by women and hated by men. He is possibly a reincarnation of the black child of white parents, left over from an earlier, rejected novel. Raven can also be compared with the boy in 'The Basement Room', for they were both affected by events in childhood that could never be forgotten. Raven's father had been hanged in Wandsworth prison and he had seen his mother after she had cut her throat. Raven anticipates, in this respect, Pinkie of *Brighton Rock* whose hatred of sex derived from his parents' 'Saturday night exercise' in the same room. Greene's idea of following up the career of one of those many children who witness the events, or suffer from the consequences of events, reported in *The News of the World* was thoroughly legitimate, and much more worth the novelist's talent than the more familiar seductions of people who have no apparent background at all. We are also told, quite explicitly, that when Raven threatened Buddy, the medical student, with a revolver, Buddy was similarly affected.

There is something about the irrevocability of certain acts that fascinated Greene at that time. They paralleled certain theological beliefs, such as the irrevocability of marriage. Greene was moving towards this, the major item in his repertoire, and he was approaching it over well prepared ground. And no-one ever realized how Buddy's being had been crushed by this single incident. It is worth while remembering these facts if we are to get the full flavour of *The Heart of the Matter*. If a reader objected to Greene, 'Your religion imposes hideous suffering', he might well reply, 'Yes, it does resemble life, doesn't it?'

Raven said the ugly had no chance. 'They have a good time and what do they mind if someone's born ugly? Three minutes in bed or against a wall, and then a lifetime for the one that's born.' Once again one is tempted to speculate on what happened to Greene at school. (He wasn't born ugly or in poverty, the personal 'aboriginal catastrophe' must have occurred later.) His characters are weighted down by their obsessions. For Andrews (*The Man Within*) it was his own cowardice. Later, in *The Quiet American*, Fowler was to discover his cowardice at the crucial moment. Czinner (*Stamboul Train*) could not escape failure. Conrad Drover (*It's A Battlefield*) was branded by his own awkwardness, convinced of his own guilt. The novel proclaimed loudly that there was no justice. Minty and Anthony (*England Made Me*) saw everything they touched go bad. Everything is settled from the beginning. *Journey Without Maps* had only repeated the same story, with the additional thesis that we leave childhood by the wrong turning and become vicious. And it had been laid down that this man Raven, who could be loved by no-one and in return could only love a kitten ('it had been sublimely unconscious of his ugliness'), should be made by hatred; 'it had constructed him into this thin smoky murderous figure in the rain, haunted and ugly'. He bears an interesting relationship towards Bendrix, in *The End of the Affair*, for Bendrix had had all the benefits of love and yet settled down to write a book about hatred.

The frustration that destroyed what nobility there had been in Bendrix's personality fastened its claws on Raven from the very beginning and would not let him go. Raven is that familiar figure of Western literature, the poor man outside in the cold, looking in at the rich man's banquet. He had not been turned out—he had never even been inside. And he knew that his position was hopeless, that no-one would ever ask him in. He looked bitterly at the Christmas decorations in the shop windows and he shut God out, believing with full sincerity that God had shut *him* out. We are reminded of this in Greene's introduction to *Oliver Twist*, when he points out that Dickens's idea of goodness was summed up in the coloured paper scraps of angels and virgins in small stationers' shops passed on the way to the blacking factory. Dickens had enough self-confidence to accept them. Raven rejected them. Early in the novel there is an incident that could have no other significance than its emphasis on frustration as an important ingredient of living. Mather promises to see Anne off on the train to Nottwich. She arrives with only a few minutes to spare, only finds a seat with difficulty, and then cannot get to the window because a fat man wishes to buy chocolate and pushes her aside. Mather is on the platform and she glimpses him, but is unable to attract his attention. It is, of course, another form of failure—petty but much more irritating than the large-scale defeats, which at least have the virtue of their scale to reduce the suffering.

Claude-Edmonde Magny has pointed out the importance of every single detail in the detective element in Greene's novels. 'In the same way', she goes on, 'every detail counts in the spiritual pattern woven into the lives of his characters.' Artistically this results in the emphatically phantasmagoric character of these stories. They are performed under an all-seeing Eye, such as the Catholics believe in, but such as most people give no hint of recognizing. Even Catholics do not live as their doctrine suggests they should. Greene's novels, especially his Entertainments, present a world where the mysteries and paradoxes of life are not cleared up but are accepted as existing—and the result is a kind of glowing horror, with punishment for hypothetical gain—and the rest of us are thankful that life does not (or does not appear to) conform to this unpleasant style. There is a snobbish value in assuming that one belongs to an elect who know Good and Evil, but the sacrifice of love is a high price.

The message of *A Gun For Sale* is quite clear: it is that everyone will be prepared to betray you. The only reason for not betraying is that it is not worth while making the effort. Raven had always believed this, and for a time was puzzled by Anne's loyalty, but in the end she was true to form. The fact that she betrayed him against her will only made the betrayal seem the more inevitable: if you do not betray willingly circumstances will compel you. And, to make the horror complete, Anne knew that 'in that dead mind she was preserved for ever with the chaplain who had tried to frame him, with the doctor who had telephoned to the police'.

Having described the moral content of the novel, I must now try to substantiate my belief that it is a very poor performance. But first I will make allowances. I will concede Greene's right to make of Nottwich (Nottingham, we can be pretty sure) a city that palpitates cinematically. It even has its attractions and is certainly preferable to the kind of country town described by Miss Thirkell or Miss Young. Greene told me that he used to be particularly interested in towns which verged on the country, what he calls Metroland.[1] (I suppose they all do, but he has in mind those areas of new red-brick villas and unadopted roads cut through yellow clay, and such an estate is in fact described in *A Gun For Sale*.) He referred to a poem of Rilke's which mentions the 'narrow-chested houses' and 'the shepherd leaning on the last lamp-post'. Along with Metroland we have the old sex excitement, bred in a warmer and more anciently infested hive. A prostitute puts her tongue out at two policemen passing in a car. These girls, Greene's Harpies, are dragged on to the page rather as they are dragged off to court in the popular imagination. But it is after all only a quirk, scarcely a sin, and there is something engaging about the action. Greene does not hate his Harpies, he cares much more for them than for the pin-striped and bowler-hatted. What is more disturbing is his obvious relish in describing the vicious and the ugly. He never introduces Acky, the defrocked clergyman, and his wife without dilating on the brutishness and cunning of their faces, hers in particular. There is a subtlety here we must notice. He does not draw comfort from the fact that such ugly people are capable of love and fidelity, but seems to gloat over the association of human love and viciousness, and also makes it impossible to find love and

[1] '. . . in England is depression and a kind of Metroland culture' (prefatory note to the abandoned novel, 'The Other Side of the Border').

fidelity among the other characters. Again, goodness is trapped fast from the start.

Irony is piled on in the most slapdash way. Mather, the policeman, regrets that he cannot be chasing the murderer instead of the burglar, not knowing that the two are one. Nor does he know that his quarry was on the train he saw draw out from Euston. The girl Raven gets entangled with is Anne, the policeman's fiancée. (She is a chorus girl and we immediately think of Coral Musker in *Stamboul Train*. They are, in fact, extremely alike: young and innocent, prepared to take what comes yet without the normal cynicism of such an attitude.) As the story gathers speed, so does its reality dissolve. In a thousand touches we are reminded that we are in a territory that has been dubbed Greeneland, but it is a land that has no conviction of its own. In Kafkaland we accept the unreality because it is all of a piece, but in Greeneland reality and unreality are mixed without any consideration of aptness. For two pages we may follow the characters through the reflection of accepted, daily life, and then comes a sentence which shatters the image. On Nottwich station Raven strikes up an acquaintance with Anne, and suggests some refreshments. 'There's a rich choice', says Anne. 'Bath buns, penny buns, last year's biscuits, ham sandwiches. I'd like a ham sandwich and a cup of coffee. Or will that leave you broke? If so, leave out the coffee.' Now this is not what a girl says to a man she is getting friendly with, not even if she does think he may not be able to afford it. If she had such doubts she would simply order less. The explanation is that at times Greene becomes the plaything of his own symbolism. Raven *is* broke, and this has to be mentioned casually by someone who doesn't know it. It is another example of irony, and it is beginning to pall.

The logic of thrillers easily becomes feverish, and compels their authors to take seriously what at other times they would reject. (Greene cannot escape the charge by pointing to his category of Entertainment; it would merely be a roundabout way of admitting shoddy work. Shoddiness is not related to categories.) Anne starts believing that she and Raven are out to stop an imminent war because babies can't wear gas masks. The dialogue is exactly that of the English thriller *film*: down-to-earth, common, plausible and yet false, just a shade too explanatory, never forgetting the less nimble-witted members of the audience. (The second-rate film, for instance, always has a character who recapitulates past action, instead of allowing it to be implicit in present action.) Sometimes the characters try (in reality, the author tries for them) so desperately to be normal and lifelike that the strain shows in the very phrases they choose and a neurotic tinge is given to the whole performance (as against those *characters* who are legitimately neurotic). This passage, for instance, just misses normality—and I mean the normality of extreme circumstances:

> 'I can't sleep', he said, 'I've been dreaming bad dreams lately.'
> 'We might tell each other stories? It's about the children's hour.'
> 'I don't know any stories.'
> 'Well, I'll tell you one. What kind? A funny one?'
> 'They never seem funny to me.'
> 'The three bears might be suitable.'
> 'I don't want anything financial. I don't want to hear anything about money.'

On the whole, the falsity is a cumulative effect, yet even a passage such as the above strikes a wrong note at least twice. Similarly the conversation between Mather and Anne after Raven had escaped from the shed on the railway sidings is slightly out of true. There are moments of immaturity which burst through and irritate to a degree quite disproportionate to their part in the novel as a whole. Greene had moved a long way since *The Man Within* but the undeveloped young man who wrote that book still lingered, occasionally putting his awkward foot where a defter hand normally moved. One such moment, almost incredible in its literary vulgarity, occurs when Raven threatens Sir Marcus and Mr Davis, and the former's valet says, 'Two to one on the field.' Perhaps Greene was not yet skilled enough to control and guide unerringly to its true conclusion a movement of extreme suspense. The rock-bottom of ineptitude, however, occurs a few pages later, when a good-time girl talks to a restaurant porter about her 'date'. In this passage Greene manages to mingle insensitivity with amateurishness, and were it not for *England Made Me* one might have been tempted to give him up at this stage.

VII

THE CURSE OF THE FILM

THE filmic quality of Greene's fiction has frequently been pointed out and as often praised. In fact, it is his worst work which invites the film comparison. Novels like *A Gun For Sale* could easily be filmed (and were) and remain second-rate literature. Later Greene was to learn that excellence in one particular art depends on an adherence to the rules of that art. It cannot be approached through another.

'Unlike the heroes of classical tragedy', wrote Mlle Marie-Béatrice Mesnet in *Graham Greene and the Heart of the Matter*, 'or at least to a much greater extent than they, Greene's characters need an "aura" of images and sensations to give them reality, to compensate, as it were, for their failure in self-creation. Their personality is not sufficiently developed for them to rise above their "situation" in the world.' This very modern characteristic is exemplified by the demand for a 'gimmick', first of all by 'TV Personalities' (who are usually not personalities as the word was once understood) and subsequently by film 'stars' who cannot act. Fame, popularity and reputation depend not on the essence or being of the person concerned but on some trick or gagline. Greene's characters belong to this world. They are created by their environment. The inevitable result is that they tend to be regarded as inferior to the environment, as emanations of it and therefore illustrations of it. The classical heroes were emphasized by environment. Now the character emphasizes the world he lives in. There is no doubt that the general standards of art have been greatly debased in modern times by press, film and radio. Most serious novelists fight *against* this development. Greene, on the contrary, accepts it and uses it as a background. I have already compared Greeneland with Kafkaland. 'Greene's novels are like Kafka jazzed up', wrote Julian Symons in 'Of Crisis and Dismay: a Study of Writing in the Thirties' (*Focus One*, edited by Rajan and Pearse). But Greene has accepted the contemporary world in its entirety, and eliminated the allegorical element. Yet he cannot avoid distortion because his characters have no powers of self-creation. They are merely the products of their environment, something important is left out. The result is, to quote Mr Symons again, 'a world without faith, where men exist simply as the hunter, strengthened by hardness and emptiness, and the hunted, tragically weakened by a disturbing sense of guilt, where sexual relations are unsatisfactory because they are exclusively carnal (something like Auden's view of love as "wrong") and women exist merely as corollaries to men, helping or hindering some vital masculine action, the whole a compound of violence, terror and a bewildered search for some form of faith.' When Greene attempts to fill the emptiness he has recourse to dogma.

It is not surprising that Greene became a film critic. From 1935 to 1939 he was responsible for weekly reviews in *The Spectator* and during the latter half of 1937 in the short-lived humorous paper, *Night and Day*. He also collaborated with Walter Meade in writing the screen play and dialogue for Galsworthy's *The First and the Last*, which could not have been much to his taste. In 1938 he contributed his views on 'Subjects and Stories' to *Footnotes to the Film*, edited by Charles Davy. He began by taking a text from Chekhov, who said of his fellow novelists: 'The best of them are realistic and paint life as it is, but because every line is permeated, as with a juice, by awareness of a purpose, you feel, besides life as it is, also life as it ought to be, and this captivates you.' I have no doubt that Greene believed he was painting life as it is—he was probably unaware of his distortions. (They were not ungenuine; he was not a Babbitt.) But so far there had been no signs of any vision of life as it ought to be. This was to come later, and as the result of definite intention. Both the stage and the popular novel had ceased to represent life as it is, he went on. They gave us nothing more relevant than a holiday snapshot, and their vision of the future did not go beyond sexual or financial happiness. He then quoted Ford Madox Ford approvingly to the effect that in 1911 the only vitality remaining to the stage was to be found in the music hall. The cinema had killed the music hall. Had it absorbed its virtues or 'the sinister forms of morality' still existing in the theatre?

The cinema must be popular yet it must also serve a critical purpose. There is an element of satire in all dramatic art (life as it is, life as it should be). Searching for a film that adequately performs this role, he rejects the specious though much praised *Man of Aran* and selects Basil Wright's *Song of Ceylon*, in which two distinct ways of life are constrasted in a way that only the film could do. But *Song of Ceylon* was not intended to be popular and never would attract large audiences. And here we come up against the chief challenge to the film: it must be as popular as the drama of Webster and bear-baiting once were, and at the same time it must never relinquish its critical role. 'We have got to accept its popularity as a virtue, not turn away from it as a vice.' So-called popular art today has lost the quality that gave the music hall its vitality, viz., vulgarity. It has become refined, muted, private and soothing. A good, popular film should give the sense of having been made by its spectators, not merely shown to them. Examples are few, and most are farces: *Duck Soup*, the early Chaplins, a few Laurel and Hardys. Serious films of the kind are even rarer: perhaps *Fury*, *The Birth of a Nation*, *Men and Jobs*. Unfortunately the censorship will not allow certain subjects to be treated at all. We in England, for instance, could not treat human justice as truthfully as the Americans did in *I Am A Fugitive From The Chain Gang*. This means we are driven back to the 'blood' and the thriller, which is not altogether a bad thing. But our thrillers have been too polite, too middle-class, too much concerned with Raffles and gentlemen cracksmen. We need to dig deeper—in fact, to uncover the Ravens and even the Anthony Farrants, who shame their class. (Raffles, of course, was applauded—he showed that a gentleman could beat a thug at his own game if he only tried.) And so we are given the recipe for a good film story: it must be popular in the true sense, not mock-popular as are the novels of J. B. Priestley, but of the people, *ex populo*, as are the entertainments of Graham Greene. We must recover the level of *The Spanish Tragedy* and then develop in subtlety and thoughtfulness.

Having summarized his argument it will now be worth our while to consider some of his actual criticism. First of all from *The Spectator*. His method of contrasting the simple if crude honesty of documentary with the pretensions of so many big feature films was illustrated when he wrote of a film called *Abyssinia*: 'It leaves you with a vivid sense of something very old, very dusty, very cruel, but something dignified in its dirt and popular in its tyranny and perhaps more worth preserving than the bright slick streamlined civilization which threatens it. I don't refer particularly to Italy, but to the whole tone of a time whose popular art is on the level of *The Bride of Frankenstein*.' This is familiar enough—Abyssinia replaces Liberia, and the Hollywood monstrosities, real and imaginary, do duty for the gangsters. He was tempted to call *Boys Will Be Boys*, based on a fantasy of Beachcomber's, realistic. The morality of Narkover was only slightly removed from that of the public schools. It bears the same relation to the truth as *Candide*. (Dramatic art will always have an element of satire.)

Greene's power as a critic, both of books and of films, derived almost entirely from his faculty of apprehending the significant symbols. His mind is not an analytical one, and his attempts at intellectual process are never impressive. But he can *feel* his subject more intimately than anyone else writing in England today. His criticism is that of the creative writer's, the sort of thing I came across once before in a slapdash article on Hemingway by John O'Hara. The following perception, for instance, is perfectly obvious once it has been pointed out to you, but it could not possibly come from the analytical mind of a Desmond McCarthy or an Edward Sackville-West: 'There was something about floods which appealed to the Victorian temperament (only Herr Freud could explain why), not the gigantic floods of China or Mississippi, but little domestic floods which gave opportunities for sacrifice and the ringing of church bells and drenched golden hair.' But there was a growing tendency to be irritated by films in general, to criticize shortcomings that might be almost invisible—in fact, to nag. He welcomed Asiatic actors in one film because they didn't express their emotions so garishly as Europeans—a 'faint flicker across the broad rice-white surface' was sufficient to indicate love, pain or tenderness. The film version of *A Midsummer Night's Dream* upset him because it seemed to have been written 'with a grim determination on Shakespeare's part to earn for once a Universal certificate'. And although he was impressed by the colour of *Becky Sharp* he could not help wondering if it would be subtle enough for Greeneland: for 'the machine gun, the cheap striped tie, the battered Buick and the shabby bar . . . the suit that has been worn too long, the oily hat'.

These were the sober, barely noticeable beginnings of a vendetta which Greene came to wage against the American film industry. His fury found expression in attacks on two targets: film actresses and Americanism in general. While reading the film criticism in chronological order one is impressed by the change that develops in his attitude to beautiful actresses. At first he is full of admiration. One of them is 'lovely to watch and to listen to; she has a beautiful humorous ease'. Claudette Colbert is 'always pleasant to look at and in the right part she is an able actress'. He mentions the 'loveliness of Miss Loretta Young, who has never been more lustrously, caressingly photographed'. He tells us that he has seen 'few things more attractive than Miss Neagle in breeches'—which perhaps contains a warning tone of irony. But Graham Greene was a highly-sexed young man. Soldiers who attach their lusts to pin-ups occasionally go berserk. The actresses were beautiful but inaccessible. Slowly the admiration turns to frustration, chagrin replaces delight, and actresses who had once pleased now torture. As most of these actresses were American, or had at least been groomed by the American film industry, they come to play the part of symbols for something towards which Greene was beginning to feel an uncontrollable animosity. America was the absolute antithesis of Liberia. It provided the apotheosis of the kind of existence that fascinated him, and which he loved to write about, exercising his mingled emotions of love and hate. He began to abuse America and all things American, and in return the Americans hit back. The result was a conflict which has only recently been resolved.

Greene's first shot seems to have been fired at Cecil B. DeMille. 'Richard Coeur de Lion, in Mr DeMille's pious and Protestant eyes, closely resembled those honest simple young rowing men who feel that there's something wrong about sex.' Here there is a link between the anti-American animus, Greene's dislike of people who retreat from sex, and his peculiar view of Protestantism (to be developed to an exaggerated degree in *Brighton Rock*). There follows a passage that is worth quoting whole (the film is *The Crusades*): 'Neither of

the two principal players, Miss Loretta Young and Mr Henry
Wilcoxon, really get a chance in this film. The programme says all
there is to be said about them. Mr Wilcoxon is "six feet two inches
tall, weighs 190 pounds. He was nicknamed Biff as a child". Miss
Young is "five feet three and weighs 105 pounds". The information
is not as irrelevant as it sounds, for the acting can roughly be judged
in terms of weight. Mr Wilcoxon leads over the hairy hermit,
played by Mr Aubrey Smith, by six pounds, and Miss Katherine De-
Mille, who has an agreeably medieval face, as Alice of France beats
Miss Young by ten pounds. (To quote the programme again, "She
avoids starches, sugars and fats; eats all greens and only enough meat
to get the necessary proteins.")'

After this, sexual, carnal images begin to erupt in Greene's prose
in such a way as to suggest libidinous agitation. 'The wealthy woman
in pyjamas swaying her munificent hips along the shore in pursuit of
the famous conductor is followed by the camera behind a close-up
frieze of enlarged feet stuck out towards the lens, of fat thighs,
enormous backs, a caricature of ugly humanity exposing pieces of
itself like butchers' joints in the sun.' With *Arms and the Girl* we are
referred back to 'the simple rather adolescent American manner
which seems insolubly linked with high cheekbones, fraternities and
curious shoes'. Then comes a comprehensive attack on the industry,
in which he proposes that certain actors and actresses should be
confined to one annual performance—in the same film, of course, to
get it over and done with. The all-star cast would include Pat
O'Brien, George Arliss, Herbert Marshall, Jack Hulbert, Cicely
Courtneidge, Carl Brisson and Penelope Dudley Ward. 'A nightmare, do you say? But I like to rationalize my nightmares.'

It will be seen from the foregoing list that Greene's growing
irritation with the Americans had not blinded him to the shortcomings of British films. His first review for *Night and Day* was a
withering attack on a British film, and again I propose to give a long
extract which will serve as an illustration of his method: 'The best
line to cheer in *The Frog*, an English thriller, is "I must get John
Bennett's gramophone record if I am to save his life." The dialogue
otherwise goes rather like this: "My name is Bennett—Stella
Bennett." "No, not really? Stella Bennett? What a charming name!

I very much hope we shall meet again one day soon." "Must you really go? Goodbye then." "What, Stella! Are these gentlemen still here?" "We were on the point of leaving, sir." "This is my father, inspector. May I introduce Inspector Elk of Scotland Yard?" "Goodbye, Miss Bennett. Please don't trouble to see us out. Goodbye, sir. Haven't we met somewhere before?" "No. Goodbye." While the well-mannered dialogue drones on, a bomb is touched off Scotland Yard, the voice of the master criminal is trapped on a gramophone disc by a bird watcher, the factory containing the matrix is burnt to the ground, an innocent man is sentenced to death, and the public executioner entering the condemned cell finds his own son there. Badly directed, badly acted, it is like one of those plays produced in country towns by stranded actors: it has an old world charm: Scotland Yard is laid up in lavender.' We must retain our sense of proportion. *A Gun For Sale* is better than that! It is also worth noting that Greene was able to admit that *We From Kronstadt* was undoubtedly the best film in London.

Under the suggestive title'Without Beard or Bed' he claims to have uncovered a 'beard neurosis' in American films. Perhaps it had something to do with the astrakhan coats film financiers wore: 'a kind of whisker weariness.' His characteristic comment on *Parnell* was, 'No illegitimate children, no assignations in seaside hotels under assumed names, no furtive vigils at Waterloo station.' *Call It A Day* (the adaptation of a Dodie Smith play) is fair game for him. '. . . what agreeable titillations and temptations: what a Dodie dream of a world where all the heavy labour and the missed cues of infidelity are eliminated and the two-backed beast is trotted out quaintly, gaily and whimsically like a character in *Winnie the Pooh*.' His dislike of adult innocence and his loathing of concealment are barely under control. Almost weekly he darted out to snarl at the caricatures of men and women behaving like naughty Boy Scouts and sniggering Girl Guides. Reviewing *Saratoga* he mentions a point of documentary interest: 'an amusement car in the Racing Special noisy with the innocent songs of men who in this country would be busy in the third-class carriages with packs of cards.'

Meanwhile, the campaign against the Monstrous Regiment is gathering force. Jean Harlow's technique was the gangster's: 'she toted a breast like a man totes a gun', he wrote wittily and salaciously. But of Irene Dunne singing beside a farm horse he is merely crude: 'Miss Dunne is the one without the white patch on the forehead.' Next it was the turn of Grace Moore, who 'would be more at home among blackboards and the smell of chalk and dusters and the dear children' than singing 'Minnie the Moocher', in trousers. 'If you want to escape from a cinema where Miss Moore is playing—I always do—before the end, you feel impelled to raise a hand and wait for permission to leave the room.'[1] Even Bette Davis comes under the ban, for he had once considered her potentially a great actress, but 'now she plugs the emotions with dreadful abandonment'. Of one film he complains that despite a hint of adultery the characters have little more sex-life than amœbas; of another he is stimulated to proclaim that 'every close-up of Miss Linden Travers drives the sexuality home: a leg in the library, buttocks over the billiard table'. He even discovers that Marlene Dietrich cannot act. 'She lends her too beautiful body; she consents to pose', but acting she leaves to her servants. It is not surprising that, as a change from films, he was given *Eve in the Sunlight* to review, and that his notice appeared under the title, 'The Nudest Book of the Week'. How he loved to debunk the classical attitude towards the human form! His desire and his contempt coalesced to produce a frontal attack on 'these plump slipshod haunches posed among the wild flowers, these bony arms thrown up in suburban ecstasy towards the sky, these Leighton limbs grouped coyly round a rubber ball on a beach. . . .' He quotes a caption: 'Nature's supreme achievement', and comments: 'there the achievement ends: a toothy smile, knees coyly crossed, one hand on a silver birch, rather thick ankles hidden in lush grass.' His critical sense, apparently uppermost, is in fact annihilated, else how could he call invisible ankles 'thick'?

The Road Back, based on Remarque's novel, gave him the opportunity for a full-blooded assault on the Americans. 'It might be funny if it weren't horrifying. This is America seeing the world in its own image. There is a scene in which the returned soldiers all go

---

[1] Grace Moore was not the only film actress he likened to a schoolmarm. Another category was 'colonial visitor': 'Like a colonial visitor, Miss Madeleine Carroll falls heavily about the screen, large and lost and oddly dressed'.

back to their school. Sitting in uniform on the benches they are
addressed by the headmaster; they start their lessons again where
they left off—it may be meant as irony (I'm not sure), but what it
really emphasizes is the eternal adolescence of the American mind, to
which literature means the poetry of Longfellow and morality
means keeping Mothers' Day and looking after the kid sister's purity.
One came daunted out of the cinema and there, strolling up the
Haymarket, dressed up in blue uniforms with little forage caps and
medals clinking, were the American legionaries, arm in arm with
women dressed just the same—all guide books, glasses and military
salutes: caps marked Santa Anna and Minnesota: hair—what there
was of it—grey, but the same adolescent features, plump, smug,
sentimental, ready for the easy tear and the hearty laugh and the
fraternity yell. What use in pretending that with these allies it was
ever possible to fight for civilization? For Mother Day's, yes, for
antivivisection and humanitarianism, the pet dog and the home fire,
for the co-ed college and the campus. Civilization would shock
them: eyes on the guide book for safety, they pass it quickly as if it
were a nude in a national collection.'

The Hollywood film moguls could not have enjoyed all this.
They resent adult criticism at the best of times, but the combination
of ferocity and malice that Greene managed to pack into his notices
must have made them writhe. In a sketch entitled 'Film Lunch'
Greene had even mocked Mr Louis B. Mayer, one of the Great. It
seems probable that they came to a collective if informal decision
that Greene must be stopped. One false step, and they would move
heaven, earth and Hollywood to put an end to it. After his onslaught
on Americans (quoted above) they passed by some questionable
comments on Magda Schreider: 'deep-sunk eyes and porcine
coquetry . . . trim buttocks and battered girlishness . . . mouth wide
open—rather too much gum like a set of false teeth hung up outside
a cheap dentist's'. It was obvious that they could bide their time—he
seemed to be in such a state of frenzy against the whole tribe of
actresses, whose photographed charms mocked his insistent carnality,
that he would certainly go too far, if not next week, then the week
after. And he did. On 28th November, 1937, he reviewed *Wee
Willie Winkie*, starring the child actress, Shirley Temple. It would

probably be unwise of me to quote, for Miss Temple's solicitors may still be anxious to protect their client against insinuations made twenty years ago, although in a much earlier review Greene had already noted that some of Shirley Temple's popularity 'seems to rest on a coquetry quite as mature as Miss Colbert's and on an oddly precocious body as voluptuous in grey flannel trousers as Miss Dietrich's'. Briefly, Greene stated that Miss Temple's audience was elderly and its admiration not entirely centred on her acting ability. In the ensuing lawsuit Miss Temple and her studio were awarded $9,800 and *Night and Day*, which was already in difficulties, ceased publication. Just before the end Greene got in a parting shot. *Marie Walewska* 'has its moments when the Frenchman Boyer and the Swede Garbo are together alone, but the awful ocean of American vulgarity and good taste (they are the same thing) laps them round — soon Marie's brother will bounce in like a great Buchmanite Blue troubled about sex, or her husband will slip through the lath and plaster, honeyed and Harvard and humane, behaving as America thinks the Polish aristocracy behaved—with new-world courtesy.'

VIII

IDA ARNOLD AND THE PROTESTANT WAY

Nineteen Thirty-Eight
'Brighton Rock'

T HE publication of this book brought Greene into the front rank of living English novelists, by reputation if not by performance. It has many faults but owes its popularity to the intensity of mood which Greene was able to invoke so successfully. He was only to rival this intensity once more, in *The End of the Affair*, but on the other hand he was to write at least two other novels which were superior artistically.

There is one curious circumstance about *Brighton Rock* which we may regard as symbolic. On the first page we are told that Hale, who is employed by a newspaper and had once been a petty Brighton mobster, bites his nails. Pinkie bit his, too, and he did so partly because Kite, his predecessor, had done so. Drewitt, the shady lawyer, is another. The tension in this little world is so oppressive, everyone is reduced to gnawing his nails. It is strange to recall that Anthony Farrant had done the same, especially when we consider his social pretences and the care he took with his dress. But the kind of life these men lived demanded a release which turned out to be a form of self-abuse.

There is so much falsity in *Brighton Rock* we find ourselves marvelling during the first hundred pages at the impression it has made on the reading public. (In a broadcast talk on 'Truth and Fiction' on 26th September, 1956, Elizabeth Bowen discussed the qualities of a 'good story' and quoted three novels as instances: one was *Brighton Rock*.) As we get into the book the emotional intensity becomes so strong we suspend disbelief and finish it convinced that we have undergone a remarkable experience. I am entirely opposed to what is called 'reading critically', i.e., keeping alert for structural weaknesses and artistic failings. Normally the only purpose served by such a practice is proof of cleverness, whereas one's first aim in reading a novel should be the experience of aesthetic satisfaction. Nevertheless, however tolerant and friendly one may feel towards *Brighton Rock* it soon becomes apparent that much of it is on a level no higher than *A Gun For Sale*. The conversation between Hale and Pinkie in the pub, and Hale's subsequent meeting with Ida Arnold, are embarassing to read. Greene tries to raise ordinary events above their familiar level, as he must do if the novel is to succeed. This can be done by poetic treatment or by hinting at unexpected significances, but not by sheer verbal mystification or shock treatment. I mention this largely for the sake of *Brighton Rock's* army of admirers. Greene himself certainly does not need telling. The fact that he demoted the book from the rank of Novel to that of Entertainment in the American and Penguin editions is sufficient indication of his own view.

I will mention a few more failures of conviction before going on to another aspect. I noted how, in *A Gun For Sale*, Greene would force his characters into improbable actions or statements because it seemed a convenient way of moving the story on to a new stage that was necessary for its development. It's rather like helping a fat girl over stiles. The effect of this is to make the characters subservient to some story-line which is not created by them but by some power outside them. Of course, it is perfectly legitimate for such a power, destiny or Providence, to exert its influence in this way, but the kind of action I have in mind is not that of a god but of a human being, a novelist, who still has not mastered his craft. Pinkie goes to Snow's restaurant to find the card left by Hale, and he puts his hand under the tablecloth. The waitress, Rose, immediately asks him if he has lost something, and even takes the cloth off. It is true, the cloth had to be changed, but her action is unduly emphasized. One cannot accept this rather pointless concern on Rose's part. If Pinkie had been scrabbling under the table it would have been different. But the story demanded (actually, Greene's knowledge of the story's development, already laid down in his mind, demanded) that Rose should be involved. Her action is pointless from her point of view, immensely significant from the story's—and ours. But we don't like it, it makes us squirm. Just as we squirm when Spicer says, 'There's free speech in this mob, ain't there?' Too often Greene has caught the idiom of his characters ('mob') but not the spirit. Spicer surely wouldn't mention 'free speech'—he was in no mood for irony. He was more likely to have said, 'I can give my opinion, can't I?'

Brighton Rock shows up Greene's gaps in experience. He is a chronicler of the seedy but often his observation is inaccurate. His seediness belongs to the lower middle-class and the shady inter-classes; his working class characters are not impressive. His visual observation is excellent, he can reproduce atmosphere, but there are frequent faults in his dialogue. What he writes is racy, colloquial and apparently true—but often it just misses. It is so near that it is not easy to say where or how it misses. This is because the term 'misses' is literally correct. Greene aims at a target and, although we know he doesn't hit it, it is not so easy to see exactly what he aimed at. There are many things, mostly small ones, that are absent from his dialogue, but they contain the essence of the style he seeks to imitate. The ear knows they are not there. Here is an instance. The working class, lower middle class, seedy and corrupt characters that people his novels never use the phrase, 'Go on'. They should. You cannot be long in such a milieu without hearing it. You may say something surprising, perhaps only faintly surprising, and the reply is, 'Go on'. It was originally said with heat, meaning 'Get away! I don't believe you.' Now it is murmured, a conventional reply, the passionless punctuation of a normal conversation. It means, 'Fancy that!' It is part of English lower-class life, and is as indispensable in the deline-ation of such life as the threadbare coat and the smell of chips soaked in cheap fat.

Another interesting point about *Brighton Rock* is that it is, in-tentionally and thematically, a continuation of *A Gun For Sale*. There are frequent references in *Brighton Rock* to Kite, who had preceded Pinkie as leader of the gang. Kite had been killed by razors. We know that, because when Hale was getting into a panic after his interview with Pinkie, he remembered how Kite had died. Now in *A Gun For Sale* we are actually told who killed Kite. It was Raven. When he was hiding in the shed with Anne he told her how they met him at the station, cut his throat and propped him up as they passed through the barrier in a bunch. Then they dropped him by a bookstall and bolted. Apart from this circumstantial link between the two men, Raven and Pinkie had much in common. Each is convinced that everyone betrays. In other words, each is damned. But each is persuaded, against his better judgment, that there is one particular woman who does not conform to the general pattern—and it is only then that they are betrayed, each by the one and only person he has come to trust. But neither of the betrayals is of the heartless, meaningless kind that these men had originally believed in; Anne betrays Raven because she discovers that he is more evil than she had imagined, and Rose betrays Pinkie because she is frightened and bewildered and believes she is doing the right thing.[1]

The reader is also thrown back on occasion to *It's A Battlefield.* Hale is a new version of Conrad Drover. 'He couldn't help showing his desperation. He could hear the girls laughing at him after he'd gone, at his clothes and the way he talked. There was a deep humility in Hale; his pride was only in his profession, etc.' Like Conrad, he was a poor boy who had got on—not flashily or violently, but steadily and with the help of educational opportunities rather than by what is known as 'one's wits'. He had once sold papers, now he reported for them. There was still a slight undertone of social concern in *Brighton Rock*, although it had faded considerably since 1934. As Pinkie bargains for Rose with her parents he is swept by nausea and the idea occurs to him: 'nobody could say he hadn't done right to get away from this, to commit any crime.' There was no justice, we have already seen that, and Pinkie knew it instinctively. Ironically, it was only clever boys, clever enough to get excited by notions of freedom and justice, fellows like Conrad and probably Hale, who had to *learn* the lesson. In the previous year Greene had published a story with a socio-economic background, one of despair and unemployment ('A Drive in the Country'), and the victim's way out had been suicide. Pinkie, convinced he has found a better way to avoid the general fate, comes to the same end. On this level there seems to be only one conclusion: you can't win.

The sex obsession is as strong as ever but in the case of Pinkie it has been given a new twist. Instead of getting excited by the sight of

[1] The connection between Pinkie and Raven suggests that Greene had an organized make-believe private world of saga to draw on, like the Brontës and Auden and Isherwood.

bare female flesh Pinkie is nauseated. It is interesting that such a character should appear at such a time. Greene's natural sexual drive had possibly spent itself—I don't mean physically, but imaginatively. It is only possible to concentrate the mind on sexual images for a limited period; after that there will come revulsion or perversion. Greene gives Pinkie an attitude to sex that he may have skirted himself by that time, although the routes were vastly different. The old sexual drive still exists in Hale who is deeply affected by Ida's 'magnificent breasts and legs'. Pinkie is of course subject to pricks of desire—when he takes Rose into the country he sees the skin of her thigh for a moment above the artificial silk, and the desire disturbs him 'like a sickness'. But he put it aside. For him love was a dirty act, leading to 'the stuffy room, the wakeful children, the Saturday night movements from the other bed'. He couldn't be deceived by lovely words, he knew there was nothing to be excited about. Pinkie is not only a virgin, he is also a puritan, neither drinking, smoking nor betting. The change between Anthony Farrant and Pinkie is from prurience to disgust.

This disgust is drummed upon so emphatically, the nausea recurs so frequently, that it is certain that Pinkie's attitude is described from a profound level of Greene's consciousness. The intensity of mood that I have referred to on various occasions is closely related to Pinkie's loathing of sexuality. It has about it the vibrance of a thing that has a life of its own. It is no mere fictional creation but a part of the author's being. It came to life again in *The End of the Affair* and on that occasion the author tells us that he is writing about hatred. What is equally obvious is that he writes out of hatred. The most superficial reader cannot help noticing that Greene has an obsession, ranging from mild to fierce, on sex. As one reads his work chronologically one discovers that, after the outer coverings of novelty and sensual appeal are stripped away, his obsession takes on the mask of loathing. Later we shall find that a similar development affects his attitude to his religion. In this novel every crude aspect of every natural function, the grunts and the smells, the coarse, inviting shapelessness of female flesh, the pointless insistence of lechery, the dirty jokes and ribald sniggers of back-alley sex, they all coalesced together and forced themselves upon Pinkie in one hideous ball of filth: it didn't matter what you were or who you were, at the back of you and in front of you and all around lay the one dirty scramble. In *It's A Battlefield* a relatively composed Greene had looked at and disposed of the social scene: there was no justice. But now, in a state of emotional upheaval, he probed the personal level and revealed that the tribal totem was the phallus.[1]

Imposed on this major preoccupation is the theological argument which so impressed the critics (mostly Protestants or agnostics for whom the views expressed were new, exciting and, it proved, overwhelming in many cases). The argument underlying Pinkie's action is meretricious rather than sound, and its relation to the action is often tenuous. Greene himself had already declared his intellectual acceptance of Catholicism, and he models Pinkie's belief on his own. When Rose asks him if he believes he answers, ' "Of course it's true. What else could there be?" he went scornfully on. "Why", he said, "it's the only thing that fits. These atheists, they don't know nothing. Of course there's Hell, Flames and damnation", he said, with his eyes on the dark shifting water and the lighting and the lamps going out above the black streets of the Palace Pier, "torments".' Greene has translated his belief into terms that he thinks apt for Pinkie. For the first time we get the suggestion that the Catholic Church gives its devotees something that is priceless and which cannot be obtained from other Churches. We are led to believe that a bad Catholic, though not morally better than a good Protestant, actually lives on a superior level of being. Pinkie is obviously depraved but he holds a talisman. Ida is, in worldly terms, a thoroughly harmless woman who likes a bit of fun but who is branded by her species. One feels that God cannot be very impressed with her. How much of all this Greene believes it is hard to say. It is always impertinent to question a man's belief, but at the same time belief is not a simple, uncomplicated matter. There are times when, in the midst of his fidelity, Greene appears to be immensely uncomfortable.

[1] One undergoes considerable risk in writing about Greene personally. He likes to insist that he goes to particular trouble to exclude himself from his works. This may put some off the scent but if you have only the most rudimentary idea of the creative process you cannot be deceived. The work of an artist is always undertaken in his own experience, either with or against the grain. No artist ever was a pure observer.

The point which Greene fastened on to this novel (thus erecting Ida Arnold as a kind of modern Astarte) was that the world of man was the ravaged and disputed territory between two eternities. Secular man prated of changing ideas and a progressing world but the priest, in touch with the eternities, knew better. In our world we know right and wrong. In the eternities there are larger issues at war, Good and Evil. Sex is the representation of Evil in the world, and priests are right to shun it. Where the world goes astray is in treating sex as an expression of right ('a bit of fun') and wrong. Such an estimate devalues something that is essentially out of man's comprehension. The Roman, even sinners like Pinkie and Rose, understood this instinctively. Their Church was the inner world and everything else was outside, part of the outer darkness. I think there is little doubt that Greene does believe in this double standard. (It is an immensely flattering doctrine, incidentally. One critic poured scorn on another who could not discern the difference and obviously gained immense comfort from his own undefined understanding.) In his introduction to R. K. Narayan's *The Financial Expert* Greene commented on the financier's career: 'but how innocent is all his crookedness'. This judgment was, I imagine, unpremeditated in the sense that it was not adduced to affirm a theory.

As the story proceeds we get the impression that Greene is both fascinated and horrified by his own religion. These twins of feeling parallel the other pair who accompany the idea of sex. The cannibalism of the Eucharist, in particular, preyed on his mind (and continued to prey for, in *The Heart of the Matter*, it was referred to with such intensity we were almost made to feel the teeth of the sinner crunching God's bones). Pinkie frequently refers to his religion in the same disgusted way as he refers to sex. Again, it is fascination shot with horror, an obsession that sometimes verges on loathing. At times the disgust comes very close to that of the Protestant, the rational man who shrinks from a primitive survival which appeals to the atavist in all of us but terrifies the contemporary.

But despite the horror this novel falters artistically in its propagandist intent. (The horror could also be viewed as exerting a subtle appeal, but perhaps it is unfair to emphasize this.) Ida's decency

and generosity are constantly devalued (when she demands justice
she does it as if ordering a pound of tea) while Pinkie's devotion to
sin and Rose's participation, as part of a bargain, are represented as
acts raised to a higher level by their apparent graduation in some
mystery cult—or immersion in mumbo-jumbo, as others might put
it. Greene tries to win our admiration for this obnoxious youth, he
tries to do for Pinkie what Milton did for Satan, but he fails because
Pinkie never rises above his squalor. His ambition is to change his
own kind of squalor for Colleoni's chromium-plated brand.
Heaven alone would have satisfied Satan.

During this period Greene took every opportunity he could to
review books by another, greatly admired Catholic writer, Ford
Madox Ford, in the *London Mercury*. His attitude to Northern, Protestant, modern civilization is stated clearly on several occasions.
'The world of today, with its Northern barbarians and its cellophaned foods, is a foul place', he wrote. (For him cellophaned foods
make an image as potent and disgusting as bottles of stout for the
puritan. See *The Quiet American*.) He already expresses a loathing for
the implied necessity of choosing between two alternatives only,
capitalist and socialist. 'There must always seem something a little
parvenu in the fierce self-absorption of the two new political
creeds: an atmosphere of popular science, "how wonderful this wire-
less, this electricity, this radium, this twentieth century", to members
of an international organization which has existed for nearly two
thousand years.' Ida Arnold came from the heart of this world. Her
ample breasts are the seat of a massive complacency, her superstitions
are part of her wonder-worship. Her Ouija board and the spirit
messages (not part of orthodox Protestantism, but the shapeless
creed of religious tolerance or indifference) are tawdry and con-
temptible, unlike the rite of the Eucharist. Greene calls the tune and
he has the power to make the one appear silly and the other deeply
significant.

The conversation between Ida and Rose resembled an interview
between a highly bred, imperial pekingese and a doomed mastodon.
Rose can look evil in the eye, the wretched heretic trembles at the
very idea of it. In the last resort Ida proves herself contemptuous of
religion. She appeals to 'human nature', something called 'the

world'. Ineffectual Rose rides on a surge of Catholic arrogance and it is now that we are told explicitly of the two levels, that of Right and Wrong and that of Good and Evil. Rose 'knew by tests as clear as mathematics that Pinkie was evil—what did it matter in that case whether he was right or wrong?' The distinctions have their interest but what relation do they bear to Christianity? Greene's faith seems to be no closer to Christ than Hitler's was to Goethe. Ida Arnold was undoubtedly a very stupid woman who managed to categorize life with capital letters, but it seems to me to be sharp practice to attribute her stupidity to her Protestantism, or variant of it. Greene certainly implies this. She has a wishy-washy sense of virtue which may be a product of her spiritual emptiness—I will not deny that. But on the other hand, it is sheer prejudice and sentimentality to pretend that Pinkie's behaviour is preferable to hers. Greene is saying that anything on the higher level is superior to anything on the lower level, when surely the very usage of these terms suggests that the higher evil is much worse than the lower wrong. At the end the priest tells Rose in the confessional that no-one can conceive the 'strangeness of the mercy of God'. Every believer must accept this and along with it many other matters which Greene quite logically introduces into his work (I am thinking particularly of the 'miracles' in *The End of the Affair*), but it does not require such complex machinery as we have in *Brighton Rock* to reach this conclusion. A very strong objection to so much Catholic propaganda is that it beats about the bush so furiously to produce a platitude. If the platitude is often forgotten one should still avoid the pitfall of drawing attention to it by shrill and spurious argumentation. The use of Ida Arnold as a representative of life in the outer darkness reminds me of a Catholic acquaintance who once told me the Protestants had no theologians! It is easy enough to destroy the Protestants by ignoring their most efficient spokesmen. This again reminds me of a well-known literary critic who set out to illustrate the superiority of Victorian to modern literature by comparing *Bleak House* with James Hilton's *Random Harvest!*

I sometimes suspect that Greene joined the Catholic Church because it is the only respectable organization that isn't beastly to tarts. There could be worse reasons, and it is true that the Catholic

Church sometimes demonstrates a vein of wisdom and under-standing of human weakness denied to its rivals. (And just think of Shaw's views on the origin of tarts!) This is quite a different matter from the implications with which *Brighton Rock* bristles. In *Journey Without Maps* Greene confessed that he avoids religious ideas that he doesn't like, such as 'eternal life and damnation'. The Protestant Churches, when they believed in such doctrines, did so with an unpleasant intensity, lending itself to sadism. Greene can avoid this but, by his unveiled contempt for morality, tends to regard himself and his fellow-Catholics as above the normally accepted standards of decency. The view he adopts in *Brighton Rock* and develops in *The Lawless Roads* is that a society that is untouched by Catholic grace has abandoned charity and has put a spurious morality in its place. What is the truth of this?

It is impossible to measure charity, of course, but not impossible to measure the incidence of crime. It is known that the Roman Catholic population is the most delinquent group in the population of Great Britain. The proportion of Roman Catholics in the country as a whole is about 8 per cent. The proportion in Holloway Gaol was about 26 per cent and in boys' Borstal institutions about 23 per cent (in 1955). In the Army during the war the delinquency rates were approximately twice as high among Catholics as among non-Catholics. In Holland, where everyone states his religion on the census form, the highest proportion of convicted criminals has been found among Catholics for many years past—and, incidentally, the lowest among those describing themselves as of 'no religion'. Economic factors have helped to contribute to the differences in this country, as many of the delinquents come from impoverished Irish stock, but the same tendency has been found in other countries where these factors did not operate. Greene would probably reply, 'What have these figures to do with charity, which is a far loftier virtue than adherence to a man-made code?' In reply I can state that American surveys suggest that Catholics are more likely to be prejudiced against Negroes than are Protestants, and that polls in this country show that Christians in general are more likely to take the 'tough' line in such matters as flogging and capital punishment than non-Christians. But we should guard

against distinguishing too clearly between criminal acts and uncharitable acts. A very high proportion of the acts which lead to
Holloway and Borstal must be of the kind that an unprejudiced
observer would term lacking in charity. Perhaps Catholics perform
more positive acts of goodwill to the poor and aged than do others,
but at the same time it seems likely that they also perform more
positive acts of malice. I have thought it worthwhile to digress at
this length because in my opinion Greene is sometimes guilty of
literary sleight-of-hand. He shuffles off the morality of non-
Catholics and in the process conceals many acts which are
more than merely moral, which are in fact informed with spiritual
grace.

What Neville Braybrooke, himself a Catholic, called a 'partisan
spirit', accompanied by an element of priggishness, spoiled *Brighton
Rock*. Technically, however, it was. a considerable achievement.
Even John Lehmann, when compiling his Pelican, *New Writing in
Europe*, felt compelled to admit Greene to his circle. For one thing,
Greene was obviously better acquainted with the seedier side of life,
which one might expect to be the stock-in-trade of the proletarian
novelists and social realists, than most of Lehmann's contributors.
But Lehmann was able to spot the weakness: 'There is something
artificial about them (his characters) all the same; one is inclined to
think at first that he is faking very skilfully—that he really knows
very little about the world he is describing, particularly the mentality
of his gangsters.' Lehmann attributes this to Greene's stylization of
his theme into a phase in the conflict between good and evil, and
compares it to the Communist writer's cavortings around the party
line. There is something more than this. Greene is still slave to a
habit which is entertaining at first but later is seen to be inadequate;
he still does not describe life, but the paraphernalia of living—the
more intimate paraphernalia, such as chamber pots, belches, dirty
laundry and smeared soap dishes.

Lehmann unaccountably refers to Ida Arnold as the heroine.
This could be adduced as Greene's greatest literary success for
although he loathes Ida he regards her as a respresentative modern
northern barbarian. It is therefore expected that a modern northern
barbarian critic should admire what is despicable. Ida is one of the

devil's most subtle successes. She is vacancy, clothed in goodwill. Reading Greene's journalism of the period I have little doubt as to whom he considered the moral leader of Ida's world. Shaw was the plausible demon who urged men to ignore the eternities, to dismiss sin, salvation and damnation as superstitions, who did not believe in evil, claimed that man alone was responsible for his own fate, that he could be guilty of nothing graver than 'wrong'. It is very likely that Ida Arnold had heard of G.B.S. for he was one of those rare men whose names really are household words, but it is extremely unlikely that she had ever read a word of his or seen one of his plays. His ideas or rather the climate they created, seeped and swirled into the world like fog and enveloped those who lived in lodgings and liked a bit of fun and even called in at bars, for the master's teetotalism was easily detached from the rest. Reviewing *Shaw: George versus Bernard*, by J. P. Hackett, in *The London Mercury*, Greene wrote: 'Mr Sassoon once wrote a poem about the jokes in music halls which "mock the riddled corpses round Bapaume", and when the stalls rock to Mr Shaw's slapstick, there is the same ugly taste in the mouth as when we remember men slain in Italy, Germany, Russia and Spain in order that the Life Force should have a high old time. The trouble is that this unpassionate puritan is disastrously free from that sense of chaos and lunacy which opens dreadfully before most men at periods of moral indiscipline. He has never had to accept constraint for the sake of sanity.

'There was a time, the time of his admirable and angry preface on the subject of public school education, when Mr Shaw seemed the champion of the young against the inhumanities of age. Now that he is old himself we have to look for him in the camp of the physical force men, of Lenin and Mussolini. "Try how wicked you can be; it is precisely the same experiment as trying how good you can be." Only an essentially innocent man, a man quite ignorant of the nature of evil, could write that: a worthy man, an ethical man, of course, but the ethical is much further from the good than evil is.'

Now it stands revealed: Ida Arnold is a Shavian who has fallen away from the true faith. She has abandoned her puritanism but she is as innocent as the new-born babe. (Each is guilty of original sin but does not know it.) G.B.S. is Ida Arnold's godfather, or Life Force father.[1]

The pursuit of truth is not as simple as Protestant simplifiers tell us, nor as superficially complicated as Catholic complicators tell us. We are invited to censure Ida Arnold for her superficiality but we are also invited to praise Pinkie and Scobie and the whiskey priest and Sarah's confessor for their forays into obscurity. But they do not dissipate the obscurity, they breathe it in. What is worse is that they tend to believe they have some understanding of it. The furthest any man has yet gone in his search for truth and understanding is a short return journey. He goes into the mystery and he comes out again, chastened and refined. His later position bears a superficial resemblance to that of the original simpleton that he was, but it is grounded on richer soil, like a plant that has been mulched. He is Picasso come back from the Egyptian temples, Koestler back from prison, Auden rescued from anxiety. We find him in the past, and after deeper forays: Shakespeare after Hamlet, Milton after Satan, Goya after the Disasters.

We do not consider Ida Arnold to be a guide. It is a Catholic misconception that we follow our worst while they follow their best. On the other hand, Pinkie is not their best. It is insulting that he should be presented to us, in all his evil, as our spiritual superior. In some ways the Catholic faith appears to have suffered from arrested development, and one aspect of the Reformation (rarely referred to in the history books) is a dissatisfaction with this state of paralysis. It resembles the mingled admiration and frustration experienced when one reads Blake's *Prophetic Books* or listens to Mahler. There is great penetration but no return. They never go beyond a kind of spiritual adolescence, in which they see visions and enjoy insights, but do not pass them through the filter of intellectual maturity. Part of Greene's discontent arises, I believe, from his awareness of this, for he is a fully matured person. We do not want systems, of course, because we know too little to discover the right one, if such exists; but we do require a humble scale of values fit for

[1] In an essay called 'The Poker-Face', reprinted in *The Lost Childhood*, Greene wrote: 'Most of us would have preferred to be wrong with (Conan) Doyle than right with Shaw.'

man rather than for the gods we have not yet become. Catholics linger among the delightful excruciations of ordinances they proudly do not understand. One hesitates to blaspheme by referring to them as satisfied clubmen. Perhaps there is some merit (I make the suggestion very humbly) in coming away with what we can know instead of settling in the mangroves of mysterious 'certainties'. Greene is not the only person who finds Africa congenial. And Ida Arnold has a right to her place in someone else's novel, but she should not be asked to bear the weight of a world's representation. As a democracy we prefer to provide our own delegates.

IX

THE LAND OF THE SKYSCRAPERS

Nineteen Thirty-Nine
'The Confidential Agent', 'The Lawless Roads'

The Lawless Roads, an account of a visit to Mexico, links *Brighton Rock* with *The Power and the Glory*; it combines the pro-Catholic tone of the former with the locale of the latter. All three are 'Catholic' books but *The Power and the Glory* is superior to the others because doctrine is not thrust at us. Instead, it underlies the theme and if we are impressed by the novel its spiritual personality will also affect us subtly. *Brighton Rock* could only irritate at this level.

But Greene had also produced another Entertainment. It was dedicated to Dorothy Craigie, who was later to illustrate his children's books, and it adopted a superficial austerity that was in keeping with its theme. The main character is known barely as D. This immediately reminds us of Kafka's K and symbolism. D is the agent of a government involved in civil war—it has a strong suggestion of the Spanish Government of that time. He reminds us of Dr Czinner in *Stamboul Train* for he is a revolutionary who thinks nostalgically, though not so yearningly, of his lost religion of childhood. During the Spanish War Greene must have suffered from a conflict of loyalties. Religion and tradition urged him to favour Franco but his sense of social justice must have pulled him in the other direction. And so, once again, Greene writes sympathetically of a Socialist, and again expresses another aspect of the psychological tension that gave such a restless quality to his work.

In addition to D. we have a Mr K., a teacher of the Entrenationo language and D.'s contact in London. The enemy agent is L. The hotel manageress (another agent) is unnamed. It is also noteworthy that D. had previously been a lecturer at the University of Zed. It is only the foreign agents who possess this anonymity. The English characters, who exist in a less shadowy world, have substantial names.

At first sight the foreign agents seem to have the status of spirit visitors from another world. They are engaged in unrelenting conflict, but although they can meet and even converse they cannot harm each other directly. They must act through other beings—human beings or Englishmen, according to the level of analogy. It would be rash to call them good and evil, for neither is sufficiently pure for such labels.

K.'s nails were bitten down to the quicks. It is a sure sign of the fighting line.

Greene's Entertainments have been widely praised as thrillers where the emphasis is on spiritual rather than physical danger. What attitude Greene himself adopts to the thriller may be seen in a review by him of Eric Ambler's *Judgment on Deltchev* (*The Month*, July 1951): 'The thriller is sometimes regarded with patronage by the readers, and even the authors of detective stories, with their twelve suspects and their family gatherings and their deaths in the library, a Heath Robinson apparatus built out of ancient clichés. Mr Ambler is a novelist who analyses the sense of apprehension, the conduct of men in situations of veiled danger as carefully and seriously as others may analyse the sense of guilt or love. The cinema has taught him speed and clarity, the revealing gesture.' Greene replaces death in the library with death in the sewer, which is artistically a gain. But whether it is the 'spiritual' aspect of Greene's thrillers that deserves praise is not easy to decide. The mixture of innocence and worldly knowledge on the part of Else, D.'s maid at the hotel, jars horribly. A spiritual thriller is no new thing, as some critics seem to imagine. It is possible that the Catholic religion, with its dramatic apprehension of the war between good and evil, fosters such a form. *The Confidential Agent* certainly bears a strong family resemblance to Chesterton's *The Ball and the Cross*. In each book there are a chase, hints of anarchy, the contrast of a warm and clumsy tradition with a cold and efficient science. In the beginning we see that D.'s worst enemy is a stranger, but their enmity cannot be avoided because he belongs to a completely antipathetic way of life: Captain Currie, who appears again at the end to frustrate D. 'God, he thought, could only really be pictured as a joker—it was absurd to have come all this way to encounter Captain Currie at the end of it.' I am always

sceptical when an author leads his characters into a particular
situation and then blames God for it. Even the detectives turn out to
be agents in disguise. (Again, G.K.C. had done it all before.) The
Lido is something like the model prison in *The Ball and the Cross*.
The vision of the 'modern, northern, barbarian' coldness is sure
enough—but where is the warmth of our traditional ways? It does
not appear in this novel.

The novel is carefully planned, and the planned structure is
adequate for its needs, but it fails in other respects. Else in particular
worries me. What is she, who is she? Another example of Greene's
corrupted childhoods? A symbol of suffering, abused, innocent-cum-
worldly humanity? Such symbols constantly recur in Greene's
work. He affects a deep horror for the condition of the child who is
psychologically raped by our merciless society. He shows no signs of
being what we term a 'child-lover' but he seems to implore us to
give the young a chance. He, who is tempted so keenly by the adult
vices, begs that the children should be left alone. We have taken the
wrong turning, he has already said; let us at least not *direct* those who
follow us into the same ways. In the Prologue to *The Lawless Roads*
he recalls the vicious youth of his home town when he returned in
later life. The Irish servant girls could not be kept in at night, 'they
would return with the milk in a stranger's car. The youths with
smarmed and scented hair and bitten cigarettes greeted them by the
traffic lights with careless roughness. There were so many fish in the
sea . . . sexual experience had come to them too early and too easily'.
A boy of twenty and a girl of fifteen had been found headless on the
railway line. She was expecting her second child. Her first had been
born when she was thirteen and it had been impossible to fix responsibility among fourteen youths. (There is an echo of this horrible
affair in *Brighton Rock*.) Greene saw others of the same age and with
the same deadly knowingness in Mexico. But Else, as a prospective
victim, does not fit into the framework of *The Confidential Agent*.
One objects less to the romantic melodrama of finding Rose on the
ship with D. at the end—perhaps it is an affirmation of love when it
had been least expected, and even if it is ingenuous it is a familiar part
of the genre. But Else belongs to a different kind of novel. She cannot coexist with Captain Currie. She gives the impression of having

strayed out of *Brighton Rock*. The world of *The Confidential Agent* is merely crazy; that of *Brighton Rock* is evil.

D. is directed to his hotel and Else addresses him with passionate yet innocent warmth. 'It's good working for a gentleman', she says. 'Here they are all "short time"—you know what I mean—or else they're Indians.' Here we have the jarring note that taints all Greene's earlier work, the naivety that rushes to assert its intimacy with the world. We find it hard to accept that a child of fourteen, knowing what she does yet unable to keep her mouth shut, should be left in charge of the hotel. (Madam is out.) Once again Greene is succumbing to his major technical weakness, the desire to bully reality into unnaturally stark forms. Whenever he deals with the world of tarts and 'short times' his obsession blots out his sense of proportion, and by relating the obsession to the naivety we come to a possible conclusion that is a little startling: that this is the work of a man who is immensely curious about the intimacies of loose women (remember *Stamboul Train*) but is not really familiar with them at first hand. Or if he is, he fails to recreate them (because excitement destroys his balance), just as he fails to recreate a plausible dream.[1] It is parallel to our suspicion, felt while reading *Brighton Rock*, that he really knows very little about gangsters.

D. is a familiar Greene character; he is tainted. Coming from a land at war with itself, he carries the war 'in his heart: give me time, he thought, and I shall infect anything.' Like Raven and Pinkie, he trusted no-one. When he handed his revolver to Rose 'it was his first action of trust'. He felt immense gratitude that he could trust someone beside himself. What is more, he is not betrayed; D. does not die, he escapes from his pursuers with a woman who loves him. It is a strange departure for Greene, a happy ending. The happiness is, of course, not complete—there is hardship and uncertainty ahead and the love affair is of the most uncertain kind, that of a young woman and an ageing man, but a grudging admission by Greene that doom does not stare us in the face is worth all the wedding bells in the world from authors like Hugh Walpole or even J. B. Priestley.

D. declares that the modern world presents us with a desperate choice. We must choose between one side or the other, there is no

[1] See chapter XI.

middle way and there is no escaping the choice. Later, in *The Quiet American*, Greene was to say the same thing again, emphasizing the unreality of any possible Third Force. In *The Confidential Agent* the leading character is engaged. It doesn't really matter what he is engaged to—it happens to be in this case the side that Greene would probably reject. But D. knew that the choice had to be made. He chose his side, not for its leaders (they were all corrupt) but for the people they led. They had had the lean portion for centuries. There was only one job left, that of sticking to a job. Billings, in the unfinished novel, 'The Other Side of the Border', even came to the conclusion that to work was to pray. Morality did not count, except the morality of fidelity. Truth is ignored, although it presumably has its importance at the moment of choice; D. revives once more the arguments of the Assistant Commissioner in *It's A Battlefield*. It is worth noting that the Assistant Commissioner is also anonymous. He and D. are projections of Everyman, and are linked by their anonymity with the whiskey priest in *The Power and the Glory*. The only philosophy that was left to D. was a sense of duty. There is a very close parallel between D. and the whiskey priest. Each carries on, even when the situation appears to be hopeless, out of a kind of detached loyalty; in the end their success will be accounted to the faith or organization they represent, but the power that sustains them is derived largely from a momentum whose initial impetus has been checked and half forgotten; D. is a model for the later, more successful characterization.

D. is oppressed by the massed forces of corruption and their facile victories. When men corrupt each other (and this really means, when men corrupt the young, for if adults cannot protect themselves there is no-one else to do it) they reveal their own inhumanity—that is, their nature has been twisted out of its natural shape or texture. At the beginning of *The Lawless Roads* Greene quotes the following couplet from *Wit's Recreations*, 1640:

> Man's like the earth, his hair like grasse is grown,
> His veins the rivers are, his heart the stone.

The corruption, the dead heart, is already there, in place. It is the corruption that is quickened into life; it is not introduced from outside.

The youths by the traffic lights are merely fulfilling the promise of original sin. 'You learned too much in these days before you came of age. His (D.'s) own people knew death before they could walk: they got used to desire early—but this savage knowledge, that ought to come slowly, the gradual fruit of experience. . . . In a happy life the final disillusionment with human nature coincided with death. Nowadays they seemed to have a whole lifetime to get through somehow after it. . . .' D. had hoped to find decency in England but, probe beneath the surface, and there lay the familiar suspicion and malice. The only difference between his own country and England was that in the former these qualities had come to the surface. People everywhere were united by their vices. Conversely, there was honour among adulterers and thieves. (In *A Gun For Sale* the only admirable emotional relationship existed between the perverted Acky and his deplorable wife.) *The Confidential Agent* is not normally regarded as one of Greene's 'Catholic' novels, but the stimuli that lay behind *Brighton Rock*, *The Lawless Roads* and, in a more refined manner, *The Power and the Glory* are to be found here too. The difference is that they are not labelled. And the fragments of Catholic psychology bring the familiar scenes of Greeneland into a new and more significant focus. 'The soap-box orators talked in the bitter cold at Marble Arch with their mackintoshes turned up around their Adam's apples, and all down the road the cad cars waited for the right easy girls, and the cheap prostitutes sat hopelessly in the shadows, and the blackmailers kept an eye open on the grass where the deeds of darkness were quietly and unsatisfactorily accomplished. This was technically known as a city at peace. A poster said: "Bloomsbury Tragedy Sensation".' We have come across these scenes before and I have drawn attention to them. In this world no-one goes shopping or tells stories to children. And now we are told why. All are doomed in Greeneland. It is not our world, after all, it is a phantasmagoria out of the early Fathers and expressionist film directors like Robert Wiene.

There is still pity for the underdog. This is finally eroded away by the action of Greene's Catholic pessimism, but D. is professionally aware of social injustice. His vision of a world made safe for the rich and comfortable, as desired by his enemy L., the aristocrat, is an analogue of the human being whose heart is a stone. 'A world full of preserved objects labelled "Not to be touched": no religious faith, but a lot of Gregorian chants and picturesque ceremonies. . . . There would be excellent libraries, but no new books.' D. preferred distrust, barbarity, betrayal, even chaos. And towards the end of the book we are given glimpses of that advancing chaos, spreading relentlessly into the previously organized areas like the new dust areas of abused continents. D. did not trust his leaders. He knew that the trade union leader he met in the colliery village had already forgotten the men's ultimate interests. This man had worked his way up by night-school and he was already half-ashamed of his origins. Immediate advantage was all he cared for. The unceasing awareness of the end of social and industrial action that some Communists and Anarchists never lose, whatever else they may lose in the process, had gone from him. He gives himself away when D. breaks a window in his exasperation. 'Here', he said in a shocked voice, 'that's hotel property.' Like the aristocrats they were supposed to be fighting against, these orthodox Labour men still ranked property above the human spirit. In a story entitled 'Brother', which had appeared three years earlier, Greene had already expressed his admiration for the solidarity and integrity of the Communist rank-and-file. Their values might be falsely materialist but they had not allowed them to destroy their human loyalties. The young men who helped D. escape and who blew up the mine did not do it for the 'right' reasons but because they had scores to settle and it was fun. These young men are as unacceptable as Greene's gangsters but at least they are an attempt to project a truth that he had perceived: the springs of action are psychological, not economic; men are always looking for psychological satisfactions, even when night-schools and hunger have urged them to concentrate on their bodily appetites.

Greene shows a stronger contempt of the drinking, sporting middle classes in this novel than in any previous one. (The contempt had lain like a seed in his mind ever since he wrote *The Bear Fell Free*.) He records fatuous bar-room conversations with a flat disgust ('What about another Scotch all round?'—'This one's on me.'— 'No, you did the last. This is my turn.'—'As a matter of fact, it's my turn.'—'No, you did the one before the last.') His irritation with royalty that had gained expression in *It's A Battlefield*, where the queen's visit to the cinema causes a traffic jam and Milly wonders why she wears such hats, is again evident. D is mystified by the ceremonial that attended a visit by the two princesses to Harrods. He was surprised to see no-one kneeling. But Currie's sharp admonition to him to take off his hat strikes a false note.

We return to the world of Ida Arnold with the appearance of Hogpit. He plays no essential role in the novel but he is brought in as the representative of that aspect of modern life that Greene was coming to detest more and more. Hogpit is Civil Rights, he is arrogant Protestantism, he is the abstract right-or-wrong busybody. He has a set of Shaw at home, the Life Force courses through his tidily kept veins, and royal totemism is just the other side of a rather tedious penny. He asserts himself against a policeman because in his opinion it is the duty of every citizen to assume that a police-man is an enemy of freedom. (Admiration for the police is a fairly constant factor in the writings of English Catholics.) It does not matter to Hogpit that Mr K., who is in danger, actively wants to be arrested. Right and wrong have an importance denied to mere human wishes. And this Ida Arnold strain is developed in *The Law-less Roads*. In its constant insistence on those abstract values it actually loses all sense of human value. Steadily and inevitably the northern barbarians have lost their power of discrimination and have tried to replace them with various forms of snobbery. Greene quotes, for instance, a journalist who visited Mexico and wrote that 'Mexican cookery appeals to the eye as well as to the palate'. His comment is, 'It is all a hideous red and yellow, green and brown, like art needlework and the sort of cushions popular among decayed gentlewomen in Cotswold teashops.' And rather like the minds of Ida Arnold, Mr Hogpit and Miss Frances Toor, a characterless mush streaked with powerful prejudices. In 'The Lottery Ticket' Mr Thriplow tries to explain the benefits of democracy to the hotel-keeper. But all he does is to anger the man and to goad himself into shouting 'Pistoleros. Asesinos.' Later a woman also shouts at him until Thriplow is made to realize how little he understands of the situation. But there is the implication that this lack of understanding is not merely factual; it is metaphysical and spiritual. In Monterey an old American gentleman in Greene's hotel, immensely self-satisfied and aware of his position at the end of a long and distinguished evolutionary line, gave bulletins on the state of his bowels. All the time goodness, a childlike goodness, flowed out of him. Artistically Greene finds goodness boring; morally, childlike goodness in an adult is a perversion.

The Lawless Roads is frankly propagandist—on the whole not aggressively but sometimes unfairly. Greene loathed Mexico. His religion had been banned in some parts and so discouraged in others that it was accompanied by despair. Yet Mexico was not so depraved as the rich and confident republic to the north. In Mexico were 'idolatry and oppression, starvation and casual violence, but you lived under the shadow of religion—of God or the Devil'. In the United States there were journalists who could quote the bible without knowing the source of the quotation, who associated such lines with talent tests called 'Rating for Dating': it wasn't evil; it wasn't anything at all, it was just the drugstore and Coca-Cola, the hamburger, the graceless sinless empty chromium world. It was the boundless vacancy sensed in *It's A Battlefield*, the film Americans revering Longfellow and keeping Mother's Day. It is the vacancy rather than the cruelty that impresses Greene with the inescapable meaning of Original Sin. This book is prefaced with a quotation from Newman on the appalling hopelessness of man. If there is a God, Newman had written, man is discarded from his presence: 'the human race is implicated in some terrible aboriginal calamity.' Greene is beginning to realize that the living symbols of this exclusion from God's presence and the instruments of God's anger are the very people he has been portraying; the Anthony Farrants and Ravens and even the D.'s of this world, despite the good intentions of some of them. And so in his next novel he introduced a traditional enemy of God, the Mexican lieutenant, to mark his awareness that such people have a closer relationship to God than those who ignore Him.

By now Greene's theology has fallen into place. He can write nothing without our knowing where it fits into his scheme of things. His next tasks were to be the development of his artistic powers and the intensification of his human relationships. For instance, he came across much ugliness in Mexico—but why not? Has not man a need for ugliness? If horrors are not to hand men create them. This is an exceptionally important insight into man's nature. Much criticism of fiction is vitiated by its absence. 'Moral' criticism is usually faulty because it derives not from an understanding of man's moral nature but from adherence to a moral code. As moral codes decry ugliness they cannot deal creatively with ugly human actions, they can only deplore them. Here and there, Greene says, you come across 'little storehouses of human cruelty'. He was appalled by the beggars on Huichapan station, fighting each other tooth and nail in their scramble for alms. He was reminded of a zoo beside a pleasure park on the outskirts of London, 'tucked away like petrol from air-raids', another place in a street off the Tottenham Court Road, 'and in a place I know of in the Midlands'. They can always be drawn on in case of need.

For the wretched Mexican peasants the only happiness lay through the experience of further pain. After a day in the fields they struggle along the stone floor on their knees to the altar, they hold out their weary arms for five minutes at a time. 'You would say that life itself for these was mortification enough: but like saints they seek the only happiness in their lives and squeeze out from it a further pain.'[1] God knows the opposite of pain, he writes, not we. (There were the first suggestions of this particular preoccupation in *England Made Me*, with Kate gaining her only true and deep satisfaction out of her brother's company, which could only bring suffering on the superficial view.) The day he began to hate the Mexicans, he said, was when they covered up death and pain and suffering with big hats and tight trousers, a procession of horsemen and a band of fiddlers. It was for a cock-fight. This seemed to be perversion, at war with the acceptance of pain in their own lives. It was all mummery, fake emphasis on a natural function. 'We die as we evacuate.'

All the time he was obsessed with the contrast between this degenerate civilization and the depraved one he had come from. At

[1] In the short story entitled 'The Lottery Ticket' the Mexican bank manager takes the English visitor to the dentist's. 'Pain', he said with satisfaction, 'pain'. Artistically, it sounds forced, but it underlines one of Greene's preoccupations.

home they played Monopoly, fifteen-year-old girls lay down on railway lines, the land was sold for building estates and the little villas went up with 'garages like tombs'. In Mexico City and the other towns the politicians stood about on balconies, always waiting for something to turn up. They were an intrusion, they belonged to the outer world. The shops were full of junk and the taxis tooted all the time. (He had forgotten this in Chiapas, where he had sometimes longed for his return to the world he came from.) The schoolmaster had replaced the priest; 'he sat there like a poster advertising something of no value to anyone at all.' In the Prologue Greene had written of the sordidness and ephemerality of contemporary life and institutions back home (the area included Mexico City) and had called it 'The Anarchists'. In the first chapter, 'The Border', he referred to the old, old war between faith and anarchy in England. He had shone a light on it in *The Confidential Agent* where indifference had produced boredom and boredom primed the inevitable explosion. Mexico had ostensibly rejected the Catholic faith and replaced it by a socialist society. In effect it had created a vacuum and something would have to fill it. There is no future in vacancy.

The most explicit of all Greene's Catholic propaganda is to be found in *The Lawless Roads*. The recently built bishop's palace near Monterey was evidence of the Church's vitality. He compared it with the hideous little Baptist chapels that were being built in England at the same time. 'I have no sympathy with those who complain of the wealth and beauty of a church in a poor land. For the sake of another peso a week, it is hardly worth depriving the poor of such rest and quiet as they can find in the cathedral here. I have never heard people complain of the super-cinemas. . . .' I cannot object to such an argument, but I do object to this: 'Within two months of Pro's landing, President Calles had begun the fiercest persecution of religion anywhere since the reign of Elizabeth.' What does he mean by this? The fiercest persecution *during* the reign of Elizabeth occurred in the Netherlands, and Catholics were not the chief victims. Greene must know that the Elizabethan persecution of English Catholics was comparatively mild. He must have heard of the Armenian Massacres and the Bulgarian Atrocities. One cannot help suspecting, however, that this careless statement is meant to mislead the unwary.[1] In San Miguelito he was shown some decaying examples of Mexican engineering, which were compared with sturdy Spanish masonry that still stood. The implication was that Catholic engineering was essentially superior to Protestant, Atheist or Buddhist engineering. Four legs good, two legs bad. He writes of the horror experienced by many Mexican Catholics when there are children born without baptism. Such parents are robbed of that great blessing, 'the holiness of the child. You are not allowed to shelter innocence in your house.' The world takes its 'tarnishing account', even if the child is baptised later; it has 'no bank of sanctity to draw on'. In these harsh, despairing phrases Greene's religion can fill the reader with a cold horror. It represents an aspect that was preying more and more relentlessly on his mind at this time: the fierce mercilessness of God, His refusal to give a second chance. Bewildered, we wonder where is the intellectual content that attracted Greene in the first place. We wonder if we may believe, with intellectual propriety, in a Lucky Dip God.

Anyone who indulges in popular Catholic apologetics must risk a comparison with Chesterton. Orwell wrote that Catholic writers suffer from a compulsion to be as unlike Chesterton as possible. There is much truth in this, for Chesterton's exuberance and unfailing cheerfulness eventually infect the reader with the opposite emotions—but it is a sad truth. Greene, for instance, comes off badly in such a comparison. There is a nastiness, a kind of malicious impatience about him which contrasts unfavourably with Chesterton's impressive good nature. Greene might win a despairing misanthrope to the Catholic faith, but his effect on a more normal person is likely to be antagonistic. When he is presenting the irrational Greene seems to take the line, 'If you don't agree with this you must be a fool and I can't do anything for you.' Chesterton, on the other hand, with his load of paradox, always managed to make the

[1] I am willing to admit, on the other hand, that English Protestant history and its reflection in popular belief are immensely irritating to a Catholic. Greene had let himself go before this, as in a review of the film *Fire Over England*: '. . . the distinction is between papists who burn their prisoners in the name of religion and the honest Protestants who sail round the world and singe Philip's beard, sportsmen all. No stench from Campion's quarter offends the nostrils here'. (*The Spectator*, 5th March, 1937).

irrational appear logical (which is not the same as rational, I hope I may be forgiven for pointing out). He never considered the possibility of your not agreeing. It was only necessary to explain the situation and there could be no further objection. After reading this book one is left wondering whether Greene is more concerned with the Catholic faith or with the way of life in those countries which have adopted and clung to Catholicism. Sometimes one feels that he is attracted by a culture and then decides that if it isn't Catholic it ought to be. Thus adultery is a Catholic sin and the Cardinals might well consider adopting it as a Catholic virtue. The corruption of children can be left to the Protestants. Religio-geographical frontiers could be drawn on the maps, and Brighton and Nottwich could be brought under different dispensations. I have already suggested that Greene bullies facts to make them tell in his stories. I suggest that he would also like to bully his religion.

On the other hand, Greene is prepared at times to criticize Catholic policies, especially social policies. He points out that capitalism has been condemned quite as vigorously by Papal Encyclicals as by the Communist Manifesto, but that this fact is generally overlooked because most Catholics have chosen to ignore it. His awareness of the great Left Wing Farce, implied in *The Confidential Agent*, is here referred to more explicitly. Briefly, the socialist leaders are in politics for what they can get out of it. But in this book Greene has extended his target and his criticism suffers from a lack of discrimination. He so far forgets the rank and file that he lumps all socialists together, leaders and led, and subjects them to the whole force of his bitterness. Much of what went wrong in Mexico and in other states which underwent a similar revolution was the result of well-meaning ignorance and emotion wrongly directed. The politicians who waited on their balconies thought only of themselves, it is true, but they acted with the support of men whose good will was not matched by sufficient intelligence. Greene's answer would be that the Church could provide this intelligence, but history denies this. The Catholic faith was not being eradicated merely because a few intellectuals desired a social vacancy to match their own spiritual emptiness. It was being eradicated because too many men and women had become convinced of its omissions. In fact, the

Church had been guilty of that great northern barbarian crime, indifference, over too wide an area of human activity. Politicians are symbols of madness to Greene. Boats in Liberia are overloaded with them (*Journey Without Maps*) and in Mexico they cram the balconies; there is no room for ordinary people. In fact, the politicians stare emotionlessly at other people, who possess a reality they have lost, they hang streamers on trains and indulge in wild orgies that bear no relation to ordinary life but instead seem to be mysterious acts in some arcane ritual. Even if a politician is not a socialist he is probably evil.[1] The Church could manage affairs so much more justly—or perhaps it would leave them unmanaged. (But the justice would probably be beyond human understanding and at times divinely cruel.)

Entering Mexico, Greene experienced the same rather vague sensations of passing from one human state of being to another as when he went to Liberia. He recalled the green baize door that divided his childhood home from school. It lay in a passage by his father's study and when you went through it you passed from one country to another. On the one side were the croquet lawn, the raspberry canes, the greenhouse, the tennis court, his mother's bedroom; on the other, the school orchestra, matron's room, the changing rooms, the classrooms. There were different smells on each side of the green baize door. He inhabited both countries, he lived on a border. Both were childhood worlds, but qualitatively they varied enormously. Passing from one to the other was like sailing from Liverpool to Freetown, crossing the bridge from the U.S.A. into Mexico. The impressions clung to him with an excessive weight of significance which he could never grasp and later could only hint at tantalisingly. But of one thing there was no doubt: there were enormous ranges in human sensibility and experience, even if the crude human apparatus could not apprehend them clearly.[2]

---

[1] There is a group in the Catholic Church that regards all political activity as the work of Satan.

[2] A greene baize door had divided the upstairs, parental world from the mysterious basement world of the Baineses in 'The Basement Room'. In *The Ministry of Fear* Rowe decides to get into the sick bay at his sanatorium. 'Ahead of him was the green baize door he had never seen opened, and beyond that door lay the sick bay. He was back in his own childhood, breaking out of dormitory, daring more than he really wanted to dare, proving himself.'

On the Mexican border two little frontier towns faced each other like twins who at first glance appeared identical, but on examination were seen to be subtly distinguished. Over the border everything will be different, the traveller tells himself, but when he goes to look what does he find? 'The money-changers' booths in Laredo formed a whole street, running downhill to the international bridge; then they ran uphill on the other side into Mexico, just the same but a little shabbier.' When he got to Nuevo Laredo he found dirt and darkness, not so many lights. The same point is made in a short story called 'Across the Bridge'. A detective is looking for an embezzler and crosses the frontier into Mexico. He thought life would be different, he expected more colour and sun, and all he found were wide mud streets where the rain lay in pools, mangy dogs, and cockroaches in his bedroom. Superficially there is not much change and what there is seems to be for the worse. Later one decides that one's values were wrong, that what appeared worse may perhaps be better. It is very difficult to formalize Greene's feelings about the bridge and the green baize door, although they are obviously important to him. At times they appear to conflict, we are not always sure which side of the door corresponds to which side of the frontier. All we can say for sure is that a powerful but hidden symbol proliferates in the mind. It is, in fact, as near to an actual dream as we can come in our experience of literature. In the dream we are often mystified and frustrated; it is only later, in waking analysis, that we sometimes understand. But Greene's peculiarity, and his strength as a poet, is that his waking consciousness is as free and uninhibited, and yet at the same time anarchic, as most people's dream consciousness. He uses symbols which possess a kind of protean power but which are not tied to any external significance. (This is, of course, the true nature of a symbol. No symbol should ever be directly translatable.) An example is the 'land of the skyscrapers' of which D. in *The Confidential Agent* kept dreaming. What was this land? We cannot say with any precision. It was a land of oppressive moods, fears and condemnations. In *The Lawless Roads* we are told, 'In the land of the skyscrapers, of stone stairs and cracked bells ringing early, one was aware of fear and hate, a kind of lawlessness— appalling cruelties could be practised without a second thought;

one met for the first time characters, adult and adolescent, who bore about them the genuine quality of evil.' Thus on one level it might be New York, the United States of America, northern barbarism; on another it might be school and a sadistic schoolmaster; on a third it might be the vacancy of indifference; but in addition it was something more, something that would not surrender to words.

There are one or two matters of technical interest in these works. One of Greene's distinctions had so far been that he had developed a tough way of writing that was recognisably English. It owed nothing, or only the permissible minimum, to Americans such as Hemingway and O'Hara. In *The Lawless Roads* there is an occasional American accent. Consider this paragraph, a typical hybrid:

> 'I went to a cinema and saw William Powell and Annabelle in *The Baroness and the Butler*—it wasn't any good; then I went to Pete's Bar and had a brandy and Coca-Cola highball. Pete was a Greek and had been in America for thirty-seven years, but he couldn't speak enough English for you to notice it. Germany was a fine country, he said; America was no good at all; Greece wasn't so bad—his opinions puzzled me until I realized that he judged every country by its drink laws—I suppose, if you are in the business, that's as good a way as any other. We writers are apt to judge a country by freedom of the Press, and politicians by freedom of speech—it's the same, really.'

This starts off like a little collaboration between Hemingway and Saroyan, who had just established his reputation. The second half is English—reflective and mildly intellectual—then it drops back into the fluffy inaccuracy of 'it's the same, really'. I draw attention to this development because after the publication of *The Quiet American* one transatlantic critic hailed Greene as an American author!

But the more original tricks of style, such as the close observation of small but derogatory details, remain. We are told, for instance, that Father Pro, the Catholic martyr, had entered the country in 1926 in a badly cut suit, striped tie and brown shoes! Heaven alone knows if this is a historic fact, but it is more likely to be part of Greene's method: that is how Father Pro should have been dressed if he were doing his job properly. In both the books of this year we are told that shady hotels have their doors always open. (D.'s did, for instance, and the alert reader knows immediately what D. will find there.) Again, I don't know whether this is true but such meticulousness is all part and parcel of the Greene style. As was noted in the discussion of *England Made Me*, it is useless to hope that any detail can escape the all-seeing eye. If you possess any smallest mark of seediness, it is better to declare it. As Greene tells us in his unfinished novel, 'The Other Side of the Border', you can disguise frayed cuffs, holey socks and a dirty shirt but you cannot hide your shoes. 'That's why strange women always look at your shoes.' Greene's Harpies do, anyway.

In addition to these items, however, Greene did begin to use a new type of image in this year which I do not remember any other writer using so consistently. It is the normal metaphor reversed, turned inside out; instead of comparing two concretes with each other one contrasts the abstract with the concrete. Here is an example from *The Lawless Roads*: 'a little blonde girl of two lay wearily asleep . . . like *goodness* dying out in the hot *seaport*.'[1] It is very effective—this one especially so when we consider Greene's personal attitude towards goodness. Back in 1935, reviewing *Fierce and Gentle*, a volume of stories by H. A. Manhood, Greene had written rather petulantly: 'Mr Manhood has a trying habit of comparing something concrete with something abstract ("a bat entered in chase of a moth, disturbing as a seed of nightmare").' Whether Mr Manhood was chastened or not by this rebuke I don't know; the image Greene quotes is not a good one. It is certain, however, that the possibilities of the method remained alive to Greene. In 1936 we come across 'he wore hospitality like a flower in the buttonhole'. That is striking, but three or four years later it would have been changed to 'he wore a flower like hospitality in the buttonhole'—for a different occasion, it is true. In *The Confidential Agent* one moment of extreme dullness (for the novelist, particularly) is relieved by our learning that 'Dr Bellows moved here and there erratically like love'. *The Lawless Roads* sparkles with these quaint similes: 'the water lapped like doubt and the turkeys moved'; 'the world was all steel and gold, like war'. It is a valuable acquisition to English usage and I hope it finds its way into school text books with a formidable academic label.

[1] My italics.

X

THE RIGHT TO SUFFER

Nineteen Forty
'The Power and the Glory'

Each book gathers together the same set of symbols, the same irremovable memories, and binds them into an increasingly meaningful whole. In a very short time Mr Tench, the dentist, is remembering Nottingham and a 'Metroland birthplace'. His lost childhood throws images at him across the chasm of years. 'There is always one moment when the door opens and lets the future in.' Tench glimpsed his manhood in his father's waste-paper basket. Greene enters the novel for a moment and says, 'We should be thankful we cannot see the horrors and degradations lying around our childhood, in cupboards and bookshelves, everywhere.' Then he retires. The value of congratulating ourselves on the events that do not happen remains a nice moral point. Another memory rears up like a mastodon: the boy's temptation by Meccano. Mrs Baines had tried it on Philip in 'The Basement Room'. Tench remembers it, and its failure. In a later story, 'The Hint of an Explanation', the agnostic baker will tempt the boy with an electric train. On a small scale it is the challenge of the modern revolution to the old religion. TV *v.* the Eucharist.

If the childhood fails the whole life may follow it into hell. That is a terrible truth. Why was the lieutenant such a lost soul? Because his childhood had been a combination of suffering and deprivation. He wished to eradicate as ruthlessly as he could anything that reminded him of his sufferings. 'He wanted to destroy everything: to be alone without any memories at all. Life began five years ago.' He desired this so passionately the surfeit of emotion carried him beyond the rationalism he so much prized into a mystical state, but his experience was of vacancy. It infuriated him that people should believe in a merciful and loving God. He knew there was

nothing, and everyone ought to know this nothing. That was his
mission. He was so very close to the priest in many ways, as the
priest knew and as the reader knows. But he himself would have
een horrified to hear it. He knew that the priest was more dangerous than the American gangster because he was possessed by an idea.
It never occurred to him that he himself was equally possessed by an
idea.

The lieutenant is an old friend by now. An intelligent Ida Arnold,
a Hogpit with room to work in, Shaw's metaphysic sprung to life
where least expected. He loved his people—they were his people for
he alone could defend and help them. He would drive out everything
that brought misery, poverty, superstition and corruption. 'They
deserved nothing less than the truth—a vacant universe and a cooling
world, the right to be happy in any way they chose.' There was a
curious bond of modernism between him and Coral, the daughter of
an English planter, a little girl whom he had met but had probably
forgotten. Her mother was giving her the right kind of education.
She shelters the priest and feeds him and he, in his gratitude, offers to
pray for her. 'You can', she said patronisingly, 'if you like. If you
come again I shall teach you the Morse code. It would be useful to
you.' That would have appealed to the lieutenant. That every child
should know the Morse code—it was an ideal as noble and visionary
as Shaw's extended alphabet.

Coral is not the only little girl. (There is a mystery about her.
She was innocent but she appears to have died a violent death. I also
believe she was pregnant.) The other girl is the priest's daughter.
Born in sin, of course. According to Greene's philosophy, she hadn't
a chance. In her we see the child who has been deprived of the
Church's wisdom and God's grace. We are reminded of the rather
portentous phrase I quoted from the previous book: the child has
'no bank of sanctity to draw on'. She is horrifyingly mature. Her
childish mind has been rushed through a saturnalia of adult passions
and attitudes; we feel there is nothing she does not know, little she
understands. She leers enticingly, she has the brash confidence of the
adolescent who has come on too quickly. 'The world was in her
heart already, like the small spot of decay in the fruit.' She was her
father's sin made living and whole. We can believe in this girl. She

is a second Else but much more convincing. In her alone we can measure Greene's advance. It was particularly rapid at this time.

There is plenty of irony in the book. In one delicious scene, where the Governor's cousin, the Chief of Police and a beggar get drunk (in a 'dry' province) on the priest's brandy, their modernist notions fall away as the spirit releases their natural feelings. They praise the priest when he announces, through his tears, that the hope of the world is draining away. (Brandy formed a large part of the priest's store of hope, not only as a personal stimulant but also as a substitute for the wine of the Eucharist.) The beggar, made a heretic by drink, said, 'A poet is the soul of his country.' The jefe dismisses Yankees as materialists. A storm rages outside and the crashes of thunder punctuate the talk of 'mystery' and 'soul' and 'source of life'. The conversation goes on interminably and the priest slips out, leaving the others to discuss wistfully all those things that they have combined to drive out of their lives. On the following day they will return to duty, offering more hostages to vacancy. The priest, too, suffers from the same kind of disloyalty. He who should urge love upon his fellows has become cynical. He was tempted once by love and he sinned. When he talks with the lieutenant after his capture he mentions bitterly the practical results of loving: 'a girl puts her head under water or a child's strangled'. Greene was still unable to drive out of his mind the memory of that girl with her head on the railway line. It was another event that had pierced his very being and taken on a new life as a symbol.

If we are to establish the point where the priest and the lieutenant meet and immediately part, it must be in their attitude to pain. In the village the priest talks to the peasants before celebrating the Mass. 'One of our Fathers has told us', he says, 'that joy always depends on pain. Pain is part of joy. We are hungry and then think how we enjoy our food. . . .'[1] He bids them pray that they may suffer more. 'That is why I tell you that heaven is here: this is a part of heaven just as pain is a part of pleasure.' The idea sends up a flock of associations: the oft-quoted line from Marlowe, 'Why, this is hell, nor am I out of it'—but the priest has seen through that one; the worn-out

---

[1] Remember how in *Journey Without Maps* he had said that tears are evidence of happiness.

peasants dragging their way to the altar after a day in the fields; that almost loving Mexican contemplation of pain in connection with toothache. Through the interaction of idea and image Greene reaches his conclusion, not through any rational process. The Church possesses wisdom (which, it is true, its human representatives often abuse and warp), a wisdom which the modernists have forgotten. Greene's chief fault lies in his lack of charity. He is angry with those who have turned away from the Church's wisdom—in this case, awareness of the necessity of suffering. Such people should be regarded as lost sheep, no matter how vicious their frustration may become. Many must learn through personal experience. This could also be part of God's plan. Greene has no authority to condemn those who lack wisdom and will not trust those who possess it but abuse it, or perhaps no longer understand it, but cling only to wisdom's empty shell. Greene does come close, at times, to rebuking men for not being saints and I am sure he accepts his share of the rebuke. The priest tries to reason with the lieutenant, but it is useless. After all, reason is the lieutenant's speciality. His aim is to abolish suffering. But suppose men want to suffer? asks the priest, feeling sure this is a point the lieutenant has not considered. But to the lieutenant suffering is something more than undesirable; it is wrong. A man may want to rape a woman. It is the very point discussed by the World Controller in *Brave New World*. For suffering is not an isolated emotion. From it spring religion, love, tragedy and pity.

Now and again we are reminded of that distant first novel, *The Man Within*. Once more Greene grapples with the problem of cowardice, another product of suffering, or at least, of the potentiality of suffering. The priest knows he is a coward, he refers to it nearly as frequently as Andrews had done. Each of them had managed to screw moments of courage out of their cowardice, the priest using brandy as an ally, Andrews love. But in this novel there is a contrast in cowardice, for in addition to the whiskey priest there is Padre José who has lost more than courage. There is not a shred of self-respect remaining to him. People still go to him occasionally and beg him to pronounce the burial service over a grave, or even say a brief prayer, but he hasn't the courage even to do that. He is one of the defeated, he has forsaken God. He knows he is fat and ugly and old and humiliated and God's mercy alone can save him. As he miserably tells an old man that he is too much of a coward to do what he asks, the shrill voice of the wife he has consented to take reaches him with its mocking message: 'Come to bed, José, come to bed.' He is guilty of the unforgivable sin, despair. The whiskey priest never sank to such a fearful level. He had sinned grievously in other ways, broken his vows, known woman, but he had kept on taking the sacrament to those who needed it. Something that was not himself drove him on. It could not be said that he retained any positive hope, yet he had not despaired. His virtue was that he had never rejected the divine spark, as José had done. When he was thrown into prison some of his fellow-prisoners mocked his cowardice and attributed it to his religion. That is true, he commented, if one has a faith and breaks it one gets frightened. If you believe in nothing then there is nothing to be frightened of. 'Believing in God makes cowards', they said to him. Andrews had been contemptuous of God and yet he was a coward. There is undoubtedly a topsy-turveydom apparent here, which one comes across frequently in the course of Catholic apologetics. (I am not referring to a possible change of opinion on Greene's part, for that is understandable.) The normal claim of religion is that faith brings strength, which is moral strength, or courage. Here the opposite is stated. Another mystery occurred to the priest when he was taken before the lieutenant: 'it sometimes seemed to him that venial sins—impatience, an unimportant lie, pride, a neglected opportunity—cut you off from grace more completely than the worst sins of all.' This is not a random peculiarity of the priest's, it is something one comes across fairly frequently in intercourse with others of the same faith, who have been drawn into the same corners by over-refinement and excessive subtlety. The effect in action, of course, is obvious; it is safer, for instance, to tell a big lie than a little one.[1]

The Power and the Glory attracted the attention it did because it dealt with a theme unusual in a Protestant country—and at a time,

[1] It was one of the charges made against Catholics at the time of the Reformation, for instance. 'When he lies sick on his deathbed, no sin troubles him so much, as that he did once eat flesh on a Friday: no repentance can expiate that; the rest need none'. Joseph Hall, *Character o Virtues and Vices*, 1608.

moreover, when the political descendant of Protestantism, Socialism, was dominant in English literature. But once we have perceived that the theme is unusual and have made allowances for it, the novel seems less impressive. One tends to forget that the virtual triumph of the priest is due less to the sustaining power of his faith than to the nihilism of the opposition. When we ask ourselves why the priest was able to carry on it becomes clear that he was sustained by habit. If a Catholic apologist objects that the habit was formed by God's intercession we can only reply that such an interpretation does not emerge from the novel. If it is asked why this priest alone was sustained by habit we can point to the prevalent dullness of his personality—only a third-rate person such as he could have become such a creature of habit. In its treatment of a religious dilemma the novel is very successful, but in human terms it lacks the interest that belongs to some of Greene's later works. It may seem invidious to claim that a novel that concentrates on religious relations should of its nature be inferior to one that concentrates on human relations, yet in the assessment of fiction this must be so. In *The Power and the Glory* the Catholic faith is a thing-in-itself, something that has been practically withdrawn, that lives or does not live, irrespective of human beings. In *The Heart of the Matter* there is an absolute integration of religious doctrine and human feeling, and the same is attempted from a much more difficult angle of approach in *The End of the Affair*. In *The Power and the Glory*, therefore, there is an element of something that is not quite artificiality and not quite non-human detachment, but which participates in these qualities.

We still notice the occasional odd moment of insensibility. It dogs Greene throughout his fiction and still evades even his most careful vetting of the text. When Coral tells her father that a priest is hiding in the barn he nervously tells her that they mustn't meddle in politics. 'This isn't politics', she answers. 'I know about politics. Mother and I are doing the Reform Bill.' This falsity is always caused by the same thing, Greene's over-urgent desire to score off the dead tone of modern culture. It is nearly always expressed by his women (not his Harpies, who only jeer or put their tongues out), and usually by young girls. Anne Crowder, Else and now Coral are

involved—Greene's inner feelings are touched by them and his sense
of reality crumbles.

Apart from these points, the one general and the other particular,
there is little fault to be found with this novel. Comparison with
The Lawless Roads impresses us with the extent to which Greene
draws on his personal experience. This, and the constant repetition
of certain stock symbols, suggest that all his fiction is constructed in
the same way. Where it seems false he is not drawing on experienced
models. In both these books we have the dentist, the German couple
at the *finca*, the 'law-abiding' schoolmaster, the man who knew the
route by hearsay. Sometimes there is a change of nationality but
never of gesture. Black crosses on a hillside, bullet holes in a verandah
post, are transferred from travel book to novel. Odd phrases straddle
the two books. One can say with certainty that Greene's talent is
imaginative, not inventive. I fancy he resembles most of the great
novelists in this.

Greene does not spare the Catholic equivalent of the unco guid.
One feels that the climax of the novel comes when the priest is
thrown into prison and among his fellow-prisoners finds a pious
woman. His enemies have got him in their hands but do not
recognize him. We wait for someone to betray him and feel instinctively it will be this woman. She is horrified by the activities of
two lovers and urges the priest to reprimand them. He refuses and
she says, 'I can see you're a bad priest. . . . You sympathize with these
animals.' The whole of this episode is handled with great skill and we
see Greene and his faith in their most attractive light. He has never
been slow to criticize the Catholic who is also a Pharisee. In *The
Heart of the Matter* the priest condemns Mrs Scobie's pietistic over-
literalism. On this occasion there is no comment on the woman who
rebukes the priest, but in an essay entitled '*Paradoxes du Christianisme*'
in *Essais Catholiques* he refers to her and writes '. . . *cette même sorte
de pieté figure dans une scène de mon livre, celle où la dame pudibonde qui
partage avec le prêtre mexicain la cellule de prison, est si scandalisée par ses
compagnons. Elle, et le Rev Dr Hyde, ont tendance à simplifier . . .*' Dr
Hyde was the missionary who attacked Father Damien for being
dirty and lecherous, and who was attacked by R. L. Stevenson in
turn. It is worth recalling that this woman does not betray the priest

after all. That is a very good thing, as one gets sick of novelists who always do what their readers tell them. The episode is an example of cleverly manipulated climax and anticlimax, thus making way for a second climax. The building up of a succession of climaxes is one of Greene's ways of creating the suspense for which he is so famous.

The spell works insidiously. Like all good art, we cannot explain it. When the sergeant orders the prisoners out to wash but takes the priest away with the news that they had other plans for him, we feel a sense of relief. We want him to be taken away and executed immediately, not because we hate him but because his agony is becoming intolerable. In the same way we always wanted Christ to die quickly on the cross, to escape further suffering. In fiction we normally wish to protect the innocent and oppressed but here we want the death to come quickly because, like the priest, we cannot regard it as a catastrophe. We do not need to share his religious beliefs to extend this sympathy. We may be persuaded to hate the lieutenant's philosophy (if we didn't hate it already) but we cannot hate the lieutenant. One easily recognizable moment of psychological perception occurs when the lieutenant gives the priest a five-peso piece. The lieutenant is no cardboard villian; he really does hate poverty and misery and it is in keeping with his character that he should be capable of charity. The priest says, 'You're a good man', and he means much more by this than the lieutenant realizes. Once again we are brought round to that basic conviction of Greene's, that opposites have an attraction for each other because they have the passion to care about something. His admiration for the Communists, although normally hidden beneath a façade of doctrine, constantly shows itself; in *It's a Battlefield*, 'Brother', *The Confidential Agent*, in French Indo-China and *The Quiet American*, his news reports from Poland.

In the end the priest is executed, another takes his place, God wins a victory and the lieutenant has lost his old unshakeable conviction. He tells himself it will come back. The boy Luis is won to the Church by the priest's martyrdom. (It is assumed he died bravely; actually, his legs failed him.) Symbolically this is essential but it is not as well handled as some of the other psychological developments. He had been listening unwillingly to his mother's reading from a book about a Catholic martyr. He himself had been far more impressed by the bloodthirsty heroes of modern Mexico, Villa and Madero, and he admired the local lieutenant of police. There had been something insipid about the early life of the martyr. But when the latter faced the firing squad, calling out 'Viva el Cristo Rey', and when this coincided with the whiskey priest's own execution, the boy was swept into Catholic allegiance. It is the sort of conversion that many people sneer at; they call it superficial, say it cannot last. Greene is saying, as he always says, 'You cannot dismiss blood and pain merely by romanticizing them. They are as real as dirt and hunger. There may be a meretricious element in martyrdom but you need to be a critic to feel that. Most people are not critics'. Luis, boylike, sways easily from one extreme to the other. He hasn't yet learnt to admire a faith, only the men who die for a faith. The novel ends with his act of affirmation, which thereby gains a special importance. Whether the conversion will be permanent or not does not matter. We attribute too much significance to permanence, and in any case it is an entirely academic matter. What is important is that the faith should carry on. Here on earth it depends on human beings who have only a limited period of activity. When we speak of permanence we do it from a supposed vantage point we cannot attain. Continuity should be the main preoccupation of mortal man. Luis is gained for the Church. Will it last? It is not of first importance. At the moment in time when the novel ends the Church is one up on its enemies. There is a strong quantitative element in the Catholic reckoning. Unlike the Buddhists, they lay especial emphasis on individuality. This characteristic comes out in the confessional. 'Father, I have committed adultery'. 'How many times?' asks the priest—at least, we have the evidence of Greene's fiction for it. It is another Catholic paradox. It is the spirit of man that matters, we are told. But once we have accepted that we are brought to heel with the insistence that number is important. One must never take anything for granted.

XI

THE RATIONAL DREAM

Nineteen Forty-Three
'The Ministry of Fear'

Eᴀᴄʜ chapter is headed by a suitably haunting quotation from Charlotte M. Yonge's *The Little Duke*. The war slowed down Greene's output considerably—from April to October 1940 he served as a specialist in the Literary Section of the Ministry of Information, and from then until 1945 he worked for the Foreign Office. During this period he produced only one novel and it reflected keenly the fantastic atmosphere of wartime London. But the reflection is dream, not reality, and it is in keeping with the story's character that it should be associated with the innocent work of a Victorian lady novelist.

Much of the material he used is by now familiar. Arthur Rowe, the central character, longs for his childhood and adolescence. He reads *The Old Curiosity Shop* and *David Copperfield* over and over again, not because he likes them particularly but because he first read them as a child and they carry no adult memories. He wants to forget the last twenty years because they have been stained by his wife's suffering and his own in consequence, and finally his killing of her on what he believed at the time were grounds of mercy. Now he knows that he killed her to protect himself. His desire to wipe out those years is actually granted him, for he loses his memory as the result of a bombing incident. But his childhood was only enhanced by his unfortunate experiences in later life. His childhood was in fact a symbol of certainty and simplicity. In the person of Arthur Rowe, Greene presents his own view of man's development. There is nothing in the following passage that he has not expressed before, but it is a very useful piece of stocktaking. 'He learned before he was seven what pain was like—he wouldn't willingly allow even a rat to suffer it. In childhood we live under the brightness of immortality—

heaven is as near and actual as the seaside. Behind the complicated details of the world stand the simplicities: God is good, the grownup man or woman knows the answer to every question, there is such a thing as truth, and justice is as measured and faultless as a clock.[1] Our heroes are simple: they are brave, they tell the truth, they are good swordsmen and they are never in the long run really defeated. That is why no later books satisfy us like those which were read to us in childhood—for those promised a world of great simplcity of which we know the rules, but the later books are complicated and contradictory with experience; they are formed out of our own disappointing memories—of the V.C. in the police court dock, of the faked income tax return, the sins in corners, and the hollow voice of the man we despise talking to us of courage and purity. The little duke is dead and betrayed and forgotten; we cannot recognize the villain and we suspect the hero and the world is a small place. The two great popular statements of faith are "What a small place the world is" and "I'm a stranger here myself".' The last phrase in particular haunts Greene. His commentary is vital because it arises out of things that are actually said and done by people, not out of a critic's systematized notions of their behaviour.

The point is made in this novel that in the modern world murder pays, and when a thing pays it becomes respectable. The old-fashioned murderer killed from fear, the new type does it for position. It is an interesting theory, though rather of the kind that is developed enthusiastically on the spur of the moment, with any possible objections (such as the history of the Renaissance) conveniently forgotten. Secondly, the murderer, though he is regarded by the conventional world as a monster, is a perfectly ordinary man to himself, with perfectly ordinary tastes and habits. This had always been implicit in Greene; with the exception of Pinkie, his murderers had always wanted to be regarded as ordinary people. (It was Raven's tragedy that he could not, for an obvious physical reason.) What is really

[1] This is very close to Mr Polly's view of experience, enunciated when the pattern of his life had become clear. 'One seems to start in life expecting something. And it doesn't happen. And it doesn't matter. One starts with ideas that things are good and things are bad—and it hasn't much relation to what *is* good and what *is* bad'. Greene and H. G. Wells were afflicted by the same kind of disillusion at about the same time in life—but there the resemblance ends.

agitating Greene is the injunction to kill that was being laid upon every Christian in the British Isles at that time. Killing is murder and the faith forbade it. But the leaders of the faith condoned it—and so Greene was caught up in that weary roundabout of doubt and justification that always assaults the sensitive Christian who attempts to reconcile the irreconcilable. But Rowe is a very special case—he once killed out of pity, which he equated with love, and although he has forgotten this he is disturbed by the idea, rumbling like a ground-bass, that one does not always kill out of hate, that it might be because one loves . . . but he cannot go so far as to excuse it on that ground. Then he thinks of Tolstoy refusing to participate and he endeavours to dismiss that attitude as selfishness—as though a few unselfish killings would redress the fault. And finally Rowe becomes so tied up he has to admit that as he is granting himself the right to kill he cannot withhold it from his enemy. 'And why not? he thought. It excused anyone who loved enough to kill or be killed. Why shouldn't you excuse your enemy? That didn't mean you must stand in lonely superiority, refuse to kill, and turn the intolerable cheek. "If a man offend *thee* . . ." there was the point—not to kill for one's own sake. But for the sake of people you loved, and in the company of people you loved, it was right to risk damnation.' Rowe, it will be seen, was as awkward in his intellectual movements as was his creator. Certain conflicts that we have noted previously in Greene seem to come to a head here: feeling warring with intellect, trying to force itself into logical shape, and the Catholic ingenuity in proving that the worse is really superior to the better. The danger is that twisted reasoning will impress some people just because they cannot understand it and therefore think it immensely clever.

Much of Greene's discontent with the familiar modern attitudes, their gentility, niceness, politeness, rationality, false democracy, is thoroughly justified. His view of love has helped to rescue the English from their antiseptic notions. In this novel he relates cruelty and pity—it was time someone did it. In fact, it was time someone pointed out that very rarely does any emotion exist without the active partnership of its opposite or what may appear to be its opposite. That cruelty and pity may work simultaneously is obvious; that they may work together and to the same end is not nearly so obvious and is rarely portrayed in our fiction. Greene repeats this, or a variant of it, so frequently that one might be justified in calling it the message of the book. If another creature is in pain you will do well to kill it. Why? Conventionally, out of pity. But that is rarely true. It is more likely to be out of selfishness (its pain worries you) or out of cruelty even, for the one can shelter behind the other. Rowe dreamt he killed a rat, he actually did kill his wife, he wanted to kill Major Stone. But it is when he transfers his intuitions from individual cases, where individual understanding is possible, to the mass-slaughter of war that Greene's perception fails. And it fails here for the very reason that it succeeds elsewhere. You cannot transfer emotions and reasons. Knowing the lives of individuals in modern cities does not necessarily fit one for an understanding of the psychology or 'natural history' of war. Vaguely Greene sensed this, when he bestowed on this novel the weird intensity of a dream. Once again, his instinct was right. War is a dream and we cannot understand it in the waking days of peace. Hemingway could do it because he spoke out of war.

We are back with the old pessimism. Looking through a Roman missal in a junk-shop Rowe came across the words, 'Let not man prevail . . .' How right, he thought. It is not merely evil men we must not let prevail, as the modernists believed, but any and all men. Left to themselves men resorted to bloodshed and violence. Although this is not a 'Catholic' novel we are nevertheless brought to the truth through the Roman Church. I compared the Lido in *The Confidential Agent* with Chesterton's cold and heartless prison in *The Ball and the Cross*. The sanatorium in this novel makes an even closer parallel. It is an image of inefficiency without love. The significance is all the more poignant when we consider that the chief claim made for it is efficiency. This type of vision is the characteristic Catholic contribution to the thought of our time. It resembles Eric Gill's horror of work performed without love, existing in a waste of shame. The apparent object is health, but merely clinical health, which lacks charity or purpose. Psychology ceases to be the understanding of the mind and has become the regimentation of the mind. Psychiatry has been used to reconcile man and his society, however corrupt. Norms are established and the slightest failure to adhere to them is (and quite logically) treated as abnormality. But a semantic trick causes abnormality to be equated with insanity. In Greene's vision of wartime society (its perfection would be a legitimate war-aim for some) there was never any benefit of the doubt. A single mistake would condemn. There are occasional references to They, the people who in some mysterious way control society. They are never specified, sometimes They appear to be a gang whose path Rowe has unwittingly crossed, at other times They are all oppressors all over the world. We are told that whereas Justice (a big name, which had no reality apart from the massed wills of millions of unimportant people)[1] was against the infliction of pain, that whereas the Rowes of this world cannot bear their own pain and will kill to escape it, They, the heartless, cruel masters, can always bear pain. But the pain they can bear is other people's. They simply don't care. Some area of feeling which the rest of us possess has been anaesthetized in them. They set up a Ministry of Fear and blackmail all those who are susceptible to pain. The atmosphere soon spreads.

Hence the dream. If we view the book realistically it is absurd. Rowe's visit to the hotel and his meeting there with Miss Hilfe is quite unacceptable in normal terms. There is a brooding sense of anxiety (it is as though the reader is the dreamer), probability and likelihood are forsaken. At the same time it is recognizably Greene-land, and it has been given just that little extra push which tilts it within the orbit of the dream. The air-raid heard from the public urinal is vintage Greene; the sudden malevolence of Hilfe as the bombs explode and the water flushes is dream. Greene's fascination with the 'bombing pilot's eight-hour day' is another sign of his pre-occupation with the normal and the fantastic merging together. The murderer is a 'man-in-the-street', but so is the bombing pilot. In 1941 he had published a story called 'Men at Work' in *Penguin New Writing*. It was a scalding account of waste and frustration in one of the vast wartime ministries. Greene probably ate his heart out doing nothing of importance, while the Minister announced that 'we are one of the fighting services'. He expressed his sense of frustration in a slogan which appeared on the hoardings after the meat ration

---

[1] A less thoughtful conception than the one expressed in *It's A Battlefield*.

had gone down to a shilling: DON'T GROUSE ABOUT MUTTON. WHAT'S WRONG WITH YOUR GREENS? And looking out of the window he could see 'far up in a pale enormous sky little white lines, like the phosphorescent spore of snails', which showed 'where men were going home after work'. The dream atmosphere was being constantly reinforced.

But dreams vary in quality, and some are more convincing than others. Greene's personal level of creation is naturally so close to the dream level that his conscious attempts to simulate the latter have a disturbing falseness. In the first place there is his private dichotomy between thought and emotion, most commonly expressed by his failure to decide permanently on the correct attitude to adopt towards, say, an aesthetic theory. He notes the same weakness in Herbert Read and repeats it in himself. He dislikes oddity and crankishness but refuses to be anti-intellectual on principle. The dividing line is often thin and requires a keen intuition to perceive it. He attacks Evelyn Waugh in *Horizon* for mocking the art of Alfred Wallis, but at roughly the same time he pokes fun at Miss Pantil in *The Ministry of Fear* for her 'quite extraordinary powers of painting the inner world'. Alfred Wallis and Miss Pantil are not of the same school, it is true, but Greene's approach to art is never convincing. He seems tentative when he should be certain; certain when he should be tentative. He wants to be advanced but he doesn't want to make a fool of himself. There is an area of his mind which has been deprived of nourishment. When it is brought into play it lacks the grasp that is so distinctive of the rest and produces little verbal monsters of slickness and insensitivity. At the murder of Cost, for instance, the mind spins like a roulette wheel and one of the murder dons takes charge; the scene is efficient and smug and quite incredible. The absurdity is attractive at first, we can even get a little malicious pleasure out of murmuring, 'How like Professor Crispin', or 'Now Dr Innes takes over', but there is a limit to what we can absorb. All the time he is taking on too much, trying to carry too heavy a load, and as though this book does not provide sufficient victims he adds idealism. We are told that 'it ended up with a bullet in the stomach at the foot of the stairs', and we shudder. Idealism benefits from well-directed assaults, but small arms of this description do not touch it. 'One can't love humanity. One can only love people'. But this is no place for bathos.

Towards the end, when Hilfe emerges as some kind of a devil, who spends 'a long day with Lady Dunwoody about woollies', when his sister longs for his death but daren't say so openly, the absurdity reaches the pitch of insanity. Greene completely loses his normal control, his mind appears to become dissociated. There is a type of insanity to which the artist is peculiarly susceptible; it is temporary and does not unfit him for the normal acts of living. It does, however, distort and warp his art. This happens to Greene in *The Ministry of Fear* and the evidence of it becomes increasingly apparent as the book proceeds. The old skill is thrown off balance, what had previously produced a sense of psychological intensity now results in a monumental woodenness of feeling. It has nothing to do with the characters, they are too insignificant to possess it—and in any case, they do not live. The brother-sister relationship, so subtle and true in *England Made Me*, is here false in every respect. One can only treat it as a nightmare. There is a type of killing that we can almost regard as healthy in so far as it is the product of blind hatred, fed by shame. These at least are human emotions. But in this novel the event is brooded on, it is washed by an ebb and flow of sentiment. It is really very hard to know what it is all about. Two people are going to find a lifetime of evasion together very difficult. Is this meant to be a picture of all married couples? This is an extreme case—but suppose they all have pasts to hide, what has been said that is worth saying? 'One could exaggerate the value of happiness'. But it doesn't follow from the story. That there is a Ministry of Fear to which all who loved belong? 'If one loved one feared'. The real weakness lies in the machinery used to reach this conclusion. It would be more impressive if it were reached by a more familiar road. Why could he not leave this as a thriller instead of trying to pass a judgment? To take *The Ministry of Fear* seriously for its 'moral' would be as unreal as to accept the Marquis as one's sexual guide or *Frankenstein* as a sermon on destiny.

The Ministry of Fear is interesting for two reasons. First of all, it affirms the notion accepted by all true artists, that the conditions of modern war suffocate art. This novel is a parody of Greene's best work, and it has the fascination of all perversions—the obverse view, the distorting mirror, the slightly unhinged mind. Secondly, it deals directly with an aspect of Greene's outlook (or inlook, in this case) that until now has only been expressed implicitly. 'War', he writes, 'is very like a bad dream in which familiar people appear in terrible and unlikely disguises'. The implication, certainly supported by the evidence, is that normal peace-time life resembles a less horrifying dream, when the disguises are less terrible and unlikely.

I know of no other writer who makes as much use of dream material as Graham Greene. In the whole of his published output I have counted sixty-three dreams. They are distributed as follows:

Novels	29
Entertainments	11
Stories	2
Travel	14
Children's books ..	5
Plays	2

(I have counted *Brighton Rock* as a novel. The American and Penguin editions were classified as Entertainments but the list of 'works by the same author' given in *The Quiet American* restores it to the status of Novel.)

Here are one or two points worth rescuing from these statistics and, as I am in a formal mood, I will tabulate them.

(a) Dreams referred to in 'Travel' are, of course, personal ones. This in itself is evidence of his interest in the subject for there are only two travel books. (Four are recorded in *Journey Without Maps*, five in *The Lawless Roads*. The other five are to be found in his West African journal, published in *The Mint*, and in his Indo-China journal, published in *The London Magazine*.)

(b) One dream is recounted in *The Third Man*. This was written specifically for filming and was not touched up later. In other words, Greene finds the dream atmosphere essential for his method of working.

(c) Two 'dreaming states' are referred to in his play, *The Living Room*.

(d) The most dreams in any one book are to be found in the best, *The Heart of the Matter*, where there are eight. This is followed by *The Power and the Glory* (six) and *The End of the Affair* (five), which are probably the next best in that order. *England Made Me*, on the other hand, has only one. There are two in *Brighton Rock*, both belonging to Pinkie, although we are told at one stage that he did not dream. This is significant. Pinkie stood against the world, and when the world began to close in on him he began to dream.

The odd and obvious thing about Greene's literary dreams is that at first they do not ring true. They have an unreal note—unreal as dreams, too much like what we feel in our waking moments a dream should be. In *Stamboul Train*, for instance, they were too sharp, too clear, too much what the conscious mind would expect. This might have meant, of course, that Greene was not particularly adept at describing them. The dreams in the travel books, which were experienced, not imagined, had the same quality.

Apparently no work has been done on the dreaming of artists. This might well be a fruitful field of research, for the artist is in close and continual contact with his subconscious, also the source of his dreams. Is it possible that Greene is in more direct touch, in closer contact with his subconscious than other people, even other creative writers? There has always been an obsessive quality about his work, at times toppling over into nightmare. We must always be careful how we use spatial metaphors in discussing the mind. With that caveat, however, I would like to suggest that Greene is consistently and naturally aware of the subconscious elements that normally make themselves felt only at odd times. A great part of his normal, waking experience is in fact dominated by subconscious influences. He is closer to dream than most people, but this in turn affects his own species of dreaming. It may be that the more one draws upon what we might call dream-stuff for creative and artistic purposes, the less one will call on it for actual dreaming. The dreams recorded by Greene were not at first dreamlike at all, i.e., they did not have that dream logic that is so hard to analyse but is so easily recognizable. In fact, they seemed to be rational products, dreams that the conscious mind would have if it could invent its own dreams. The question really comes to this: does he, when he tries to record a dream, fail because he feels compelled to move outside the dream area, which is his native ground? We are all guilty of secondary elaboration, of course, when in recounting our dreams we unthinkingly make them more logical and rational than they actually are. But this is surely too obvious a pitfall for an author of Greene's subtlety to fall into. There is another possibility that if a man's writing is exceptionally emotional or irrational (and Greene's is, despite his occasional intellectual tidying operations) his dreams may appear in more rational form to restore the balance.

The dreams become more convincing as time passes. Those recounted in *The Heart of the Matter* are fully acceptable. This was Greene's optimum moment as an artist: the war was over, he had recovered the spiritual freedom he required (he made it clear at about the same time that he considered disloyalty to any cramping philosophy of conduct as a duty), and the mysterious relationship between conscious mind and subconscious drives, so important to an artist, was functioning smoothly and richly. The marriage between that ill-assorted pair, his intellect and his emotional apparatus, was temporarily at peace. But before he reached this moment of perfect balance he had examined in two of his books the relationship which, perhaps unknown to him, decided whether his work was to be artistically successful or not. The first was *Journey Without Maps*.

In that book Greene had devoted a lot of space to the digging, cultivating and turning up of his subconscious mind. His wisdom does not come from the outer layers of his being and it is therefore not easily understood. In fact, it is often mistrusted or ridiculed by those whose lives are spent on the rind of existence. Because of this, when he tried (i.e., his outer, acting mind) to grapple with, express and present the internal layers in the language of rational experience, he failed. When awake he tried to set forth the inner life, sensed through dreams; to do this he was compelled to use the language of logic, and the result was invariably unreal and invented. His dilemma was similar to that of the Javanese politician who could only get angry in Dutch. His dreams were actually the most prosaic portions of his writings. Now men of this type, poets in psychic construction if not in the language of expression (Greene actually had more in common with Dylan Thomas than any other among his contemporaries), are rarely taken seriously by the prose-men, the logicians and intellectuals. Hemingway is another; his far-seeing, exact apprehension of reality is often mocked by those who analyse experience into pieces and away from living relevance. When critics like Kingsmill and Pearson (both of whom worked by formula) gently deride Greene, they do so because they cannot recognize the reality hidden by the surface gaucheness or grasp his angle of orientation. Greene's prose is often praised for its effectiveness, but it is effective in the way that Hemingway's is effective; it doesn't smooth out experience, it reproduces its roughness and corrugations. But the dreams are the very worst kind of surrealism. They do not haunt like Chirico but console like Magritte. They are usually meant to transplant the reader over the border, take him through the green baize door, and at the most they take him for a walk on the front at Brighton.

In *The Ministry of Fear* he makes a great effort to understand this subtly hidden relationship. The examination itself produces a bad novel and the results of it lay the foundation for an excellent one, *The Heart of the Matter*. I have noticed that all really talented creative writers have to pass through a moment of crisis, during which they balance on a knife-edge (of course, the moment may be months or even years long), before taking the plunge into heaven or hell. It is more than a moment of crisis, it is a moment of madness. Chapter V of *The Ministry of Fear* is called 'Between Sleeping and Waking' and it serves as the no-man's-land through which Greene had to pass—or turn back. 'There are dreams', the chapter begins, 'which belong only partly to the unconscious; these are the dreams we remember on waking so vividly that we deliberately continue them, and so fall asleep again and wake and sleep and the dream goes on without interruption, with a thread of logic the pure dream doesn't possess.' In that paragraph he seems to grasp momentarily the truth about himself that had been hidden in the past. There was only the slightest distinction between wake and dream. (One notices exactly the same quality in the work of de le Mare, who will be considered as one of the major literary talents of this period. Greene has recognized this, and has paid his homage.) Just as the war seemed to realize the visions of the surrealists, so it brought situations which were strikingly familiar to Greene. It occurred to Rowe that his new life of the war was a bad dream of the old life. First he dreams that he is a little boy again, telling his mother that he has killed his wife. She laughs at him, for her little boy wouldn't kill anyone. He wakes up, and yet the dream continues, only now he has mastered it. He tells his mother what is happening, how London is being pulverized, and now she becomes upset because she doesn't like people to recount such unpleasant dreams. Yet is it all true, he *has* killed his wife and London *is* being bombed. The old security and calm have disappeared and the contents of a thousand cheap volumes have become true: *Death in Piccadilly*, *The Ambassador's Diamonds*, *The Theft of the Naval Papers*, *Diplomacy*, *Seven Days' Leave*, *The Four Just Men.* . . . After this the dream takes control again, it becomes a jumble of memory and fantasy, the same pregnant images press upon him, even the ground whines when he treads upon it.

In his dream he had killed the suffering rat. In reality he had killed his suffering wife. Many of the things you do you do because you first dream them. This could be a theory of prophecy. The subconscious mind may not make excursions through time via another dimension; it may, instead, make its own decisions and then see that they are carried out. After the death of his wife Rowe never daydreamed; during his trial he had not dreamed at all. 'It was as if that side of the brain had been dried up: he was no longer capable of sacrifice, courage, virtue, because he no longer dreamed of them.' But Rowe could not dream because he had ceased to distinguish between wake and dream. You cannot dream when your life is a dream. Or, if you make the attempt, the resultant dream will be as clear-cut and logical as a waking epexrience. The two categories have been reversed. Rowe was Greene's guinea-pig and from his suffering emerges the figure of Scobie—or not so much Scobie, who is not a great character, but the author responsible for Scobie, a man who had finally argued and puzzled his psychology into its most fruitful pattern.

XII

ENTER HENRY WILCOX

THE exceptional and naked activity of Greene's subconscious mind is marked in another way: the prevalence of certain names and of certain types of name. We could learn a great deal about any author merely by relating the choice of names in his fiction to the people he has known, but this is a research normally denied to us.[1] Nor can we do this in the case of Greene but thanks to the energy of his unconscious processes we can deduce far more than he ever knew he was giving away.

First of all, a mild example of how the censor was caught napping. (That is the secret, of course: Greene's censor is usually napping.) In *Stamboul Train* he introduced a Central European character. He named him Richard Czinner. As a film critic Greene must have come across the film director Paul Czinner, if only by name. One would therefore expect that this would be one of the names he would avoid. It was scarcely less remarkable than calling him Korda.

He is fascinated by his own name, which I believe to signify a profound concern with the problem of identity. This has been expressed on at least three occasions. First of all, Robert Greene was one of the very few Elizabethan playwrights singled out for praise in *British Dramatists*. Graham Greene had been led to a closer consideration of Robert's work, which does not normally come in for a great deal of commendation, by the fact of nominal identity.[2] There is a

---

[1] Now and again the veil is raised, as when Stevenson named Mr Hyde after the missionary who slandered Father Damien. Dickens's Fagin is another case in point, and the choice of the name is not necessarily a sign of malice, as some critics have suggested.

[2] Graham was almost certainly attracted by Robert's accounts of low life and cockney lewdness. These probably emphasised his sense of clanship with the suggestion of once a Greene, always a Greene. Robert Greene was the seediest of the Elizabethan authors.

much more striking example in *The Lawless Roads*. The chief of police in Villahermosa said to him. 'You've come home. Why, everybody in Villahermosa is called Greene—or Graham'. It is important to note that he said 'Greene', not 'Green', though how he managed the distinction orally we are not told. But Graham took the final 'e' for granted. And then, thirdly, his expressed reason for wishing to visit the Naga Hills in 1956 was to investigate the activities of his namesake, who was in gaol. It may seem a slight reason to undertake a long and difficult journey. The point is that, slight though it may seem on the surface, it was immensely powerful for him.[1]

In Greene's earlier fiction certain names keep recurring (sometimes with slight variations).[2] It is probable that they are associated in his mind with certain ineradicable childhood memories which it would be fruitless for us to attempt to trace: the green baize door, the witch on the landing, the croquet lawn. These memories may not associate with actual people bearing the repeated name, but with other incidents for which a particular name serves as a symbol. It is noticeable that this type of repetition does not occur in his later work. Perhaps a friend pointed it out. It is very strange that the mayor in *A Gun For Sale* should be named Piker, and that the name should be used again for Pinkie's old schoolmate turned barman in the next book, *Brighton Rock*. Piker is not a familiar name. There may have been a Piker in Greene's past, perhaps only a chance acquaintance but one who caught his fancy on account of some pronounced characteristic or memorable incident. Or it may be a direct borrowing from American slang where a 'piker' is a timid gambler. In *A Gun For Sale* Piker, the mediocre provincial councillor, is contrasted with Sir Marcus, the industrial magnate who plays for high stakes. Pinkie is openly contemptuous of the other Piker for his ready acceptance of a servile position.

There is one name which occurs so frequently in the novels that one feels it must have a special significance. What that significance is we cannot say, and even Greene himself might find it hard to explain it without some very deep probing into the past. The name is Davis,

---

[1] This may have been one of Greene's hoaxes, of course.

[2] He also gives a symbolic value to anonymity, as in *It's A Battlefield*, *The Confidential Agent* and *The Power and the Glory*.

always spelt without the 'e'. It first appears in *The Bear Fell Free* and it is interesting to note that every mention of the character is charged with emotion. Davis does not appear except in the chaotic mental impressions of Carter, the war hero. He was someone who had been killed in the war, perhaps a batman, and all thought of him was tangled up with Carter's sense of guilt. Perhaps Carter had betrayed him, as he was already betraying Farrell. Davis returns in *A Gun For Sale* as the man of many aliases (he is sometimes Davis, sometimes Davenant, sometimes Cholmondeley), the panto backer and the shady contact man. The room booked for D., at the Lido in *The Confidential Agent*, was taken in the name of Davis. He actually has two small parts in *The Ministry of Fear*, one as a hotel clerk and another as a patient at the sanatorium, as though there were a shortage of names to choose from. When Scobie pretends to read a story to the sick boy in *The Heart of the Matter* he invents a character named 'Batty Davis, so called because of his insane rages'. The importance of being Davis, like the importance of being Greene, is confirmed in *British Dramatists*, where one of the few actors or actresses mentioned by name is Moll Davis, the sexy Restoration performer. Perhaps it is unfair to mention Bette Davis, although she sounds like a close relation of Batty. 'It is unfortunate so many of us said once that Miss Bette Davis was potentially a great actress, for now she plugs the emotions with dreadful abandonment'. It is very difficult to get a picture of Davis from all this. I have tried to trace him but have failed. [1]

Here are some other names which are repeated, sometimes with a slight change in the spelling.

Crowle, the murdered woman in *It's A Battlefield.* The murdered girl in *The Confidential Agent* is named *Crole*.

Pinkie's girl in *Brighton Rock* and D.'s in *The Confidential Agent* are both named *Rose*. The chorus girl in *Stamboul Train* (a born failure) and the young daughter of the English planter in

---

[1] In the first edition I inexplicably overlooked Colonel Elwood Davis, the Dictator of Grand Bassa, who figured prominently in *Journey Without Maps*. 'There was something attractive about him', Greene wrote. 'He had personality.' He also had a reputation for atrocity.

The Power and the Glory, who dies in unusual and possibly shameful circumstances, both bear the unusual name of *Coral*. (I think it is significant that this is not a 'Christian' name in the true sense, but is flashy and modern.)

In 'The Basement Room' *Baines* is the butler; in the unfinished 'The Other Side of the Border' he is a dead minister on the West Coast. (Baines had been a Coaster.)

There is a character named *Savage* in the story 'Men At Work'. In *The Ministry of Fear* there is a Sunday School teacher named Savage. The private detective agency in *The End of the Affair* was run by a man named Savage.

Bellows in *The Confidential Agent* becomes *Fellows* in *The Power and the Glory*, and shows off as *Bellairs* in *The Ministry of Fear*. In *The Heart of the Matter* he reverts to *Fellowes*.

Tench in *The Power and the Glory* becomes *Trench* in *The Ministry of Fear*.

In *The End of the Affair* Bendrix calls on Smythe and says first that he is looking for someone named *Wilson* (*The Heart of the Matter*) and then for someone named *Wilcox* (*The Ministry of Fear*).

It may be stretching a coincidence to make anything of Andersen (*England Made Me*) and *Anderson's* Store ('The Other Side of the Border'), but the other parallels I have quoted sharpen one's powers of observation.

Round about 1940 Greene began to plunder the fish world for his names. There was Tench in *The Power and the Glory* and Skate in 'Men at Work'. In the previous year there had been Salmon in a story called 'The Case for the Defence'. Rowe in *The Ministry of Fear* is close enough to Roe to qualify. (Roe: eggs or spawn of fish. Soft roe: milt of male fish.) Also in *The Ministry of Fear* was a Fishguard. Earlier, in 'The Other Side of the Border' (1936), one character had had the suggestive name of Billings, and in the same work Greene invents Codling's Cough Cure. It is always difficult to know how much significance to attach to these discoveries. It is possible, for instance, that Greene was quite conscious of his borrowings from fish in the sometimes troublesome business of choosing names. (At other times it was birds: Raven, Henne-Falcon, Chick.)

On the other hand, the Freudians attribute a strong symbolic value
to fish. Language often enshrines the concealed or forgotten wisdom
of a race; in Hebrew the word for fish (*dag*) also means 'to be fruitful'. Fish was connected with the worship of Aphrodite and appeared
on her monuments. I need hardly stress the additional significance of
fish to a Roman Catholic. Friday, the fish day, was once called *Dies
Veneris*. T. Inman, author of *Ancient Faiths Embodied in Ancient
Names*, says: 'Fish symbolizes the male principle in an active state'. It
has been pointed out that the bishop's mitre is shaped like a fish.
Statues of Isis often showed her with a fish on her head. If the fish is
to be regarded as a sexual symbol, whose significance is unconsciously
grasped by any human being, its application to Greene is obvious.
The sexual drive is consistently sublimated in his writing. Most of
these fish-names belong to the early war-period, when Greene was
acutely aware of the frustration of his creative instincts. In the light
of this we can regard them as protests.

But in the case of one name we can, I think, find a little more
scope for our detective instincts. In *The Ministry of Fear* there is a
character named Henry Wilcox. Although he has no integral place in
the story, he stands in the limelight for a few pages. Inevitably one
wonders why this importance was given him, and supposes that he
has a personal significance for his creator. Now Henry Wilcox is the
name of one of the chief characters in E. M. Forster's *Howards End*.
Both Henry and Wilcox are familiar names, but the two in con-
junction are bound to remind the reader familiar with modern
fiction of the earlier and more famous bearer of them. The fact is,
Henry Wilcox is an important name in modern English fiction, as
important as Leopold Bloom, Catherine Barkley or Basil Seal. But
is there any reason why Greene should wish to refer to E. M. Forster
in this indirect manner? I doubt if his choice of the name was
deliberate. In fact, I doubt if Greene consciously remembered the
character of Henry Wilcox in *Howards End* at all when he introduced
the name into *The Ministry of Fear*. But here and there he gives hints
that, although he has a certain amount of admiration for Forster's
technical ability, he abhors his outlook. (It will be remembered that
Forster had ceased to believe in belief.) There are one or two references to him in the essays that make up *The Lost Childhood*. In his

tribute to François Mauriac he states that 'the characters of such distinguished writers as Mrs Virginia Woolf and Mr E. M. Forster wandered like cardboard symbols through a world that was paper thin'. In his Preface to *The Third Man* there is some gentle irony at Forster's expense. In the story itself we are told that Benjamin Dexter (who was modelled on Forster) was 'old-maidish', took a passionate interest in embroidery and calmed 'a not very tumultuous mind with tatting'. Later Martins thinks of him as a 'complacent, tiring, pompous ass'. In *Why Do I Write?* Forster is referred to condescendingly as the kind of person who signed appeals to *The Times* in the 'thirties. There is a cutting reference in *The End of the Affair*.

It is the calm of Forster's mind and the absence from his work of any sense of sin that irritated Greene. I believe that the wholly unnecessary intrusion of Henry Wilcox into *The Ministry of Fear* was an expression of this irritation. The Henry Wilcox of *Howards End* was Forster's representative man, the outwardly strong man of the modern, protestant, barbarian North, with his fatal moments of unexpected weakness, resulting from his divorce from spiritual reality. Forster was not an apologist for Wilcox but he had no-one to set against him. His Schlegels and Rickies and Fieldings are not strong; they only conquer through the brittleness of their opponents. The Henry Wilcox of *The Ministry of Fear* was one of Rowe's few friends, who stood by him after his wife's death, believing in his innocence. When Rowe admitted his guilt Wilcox also dropped away. His wife had been a hockey player who had disliked Rowe's wife, and in any case would not have approved of him. Wilcox was now an Air Raid Warden. His wife had been killed by a collapsing wall. He feels responsible but tries to allay his conscience by saying he had warned her. He knows, however, that he could have saved her by holding her or knocking her down. Having escaped his wife, however, he is immediately dominated by his mother, who has already beatified the dead woman. At the last moment, as the funeral moves off, he feels the pull so strongly that he runs after the cortège, although he had decided not to accompany it. He reappears once more after Rowe has lost his memory. He has to remind Rowe who he is, and when they last met. From the little we know of him we recognize his pathetic futility. It is a criticism, from a subconscious mind that is barely covered, of a ubiquitous type in modern society and literature.

Forster's Wilcox drove a motor-car (in the early nineteen-hundreds), appeared to be rather boisterous and extrovert, hadn't much faith in the continent, and was very kind. His wife had been vague, rather frail and (although Forster may not have known it) silly in the precious way that people protected by money often are. Wilcox was greatly upset by his wife's death—he could not eat and his eyes easily filled with tears. His sentimental affection for her *goodness* and her innocence (adult innocence!) must have irritated Greene. But as soon as Wilcox received bad news (that Howards End had been left to Miss Schlegel) he recovered his *sang-froid* and became cold and businesslike. Margaret Schlegel (representing culture) admired the kind of life led by the Wilcoxes. 'It fostered such virtues as neatness, decision and obedience, virtues of the second rank, no doubt, but they have formed our civilization. They form character, too . . . they keep the soul from becoming sloppy'. Now Greene detests 'virtues of the second rank'—they are the product of the Protestant heresy. (Needless to say, the Wilcoxes were almost arrogantly C. of E.) The deeply Protestant nineteenth century worshipped character. Greene admires holiness, or the failure to achieve holiness, but never a secular good character. These words of Margaret Schlegel to her sister Helen stress the difference between the two attitudes: 'Don't brood too much on the superiority of the unseen to the seen. It's true, but to brood on it is medieval. Our business is not to contrast the two but to reconcile them'.

In Helen's words, Henry Wilcox becomes a 'prosperous vulgarian'. He has far more force of character than Greene's Henry Wilcox, but perhaps he is what the other would like to be. Forster's H.W. had set up a row of defences against the world, he could not bear emotional talk or shows of sympathy. Greene's H.W. had no need of defences, not because he was strong enough to deal with attackers but because no-one would ever trouble to attack him. If there is any relationship between the two it is certainly not a direct one. But Greene's mind is far too subtle to enjoy direct relationships. It may be true that by 1910, as Margaret Schlegel said, the Wilcoxes had made a settled and cultured life possible. But by 1940 the same people might have lost caste and influence and self-confidence (social decline of this type is always in process) and have become frightened little men in overalls and tin hats. *Howards End* stinks of money. It is an attempt to be cultured and grateful for money at the same time. Greene, with his Catholic insistence on the unseen, presumably hates such blatant philistinism, or neo-philistinism. Because you cannot regard both money and culture as the most important thing in life, you must choose one or the other. Forster is really saying, although apologetically, that it is money. The character of H.W. becomes gradually clearer and gradually less admirable. 'He must be one of those men who have reconciled science with religion', says Helen. 'I don't like those men. They are scientific themselves, and talk of the survival of the fittest, and cut down the salaries of their clerks, and stunt the independence of all who may menace their comfort, but yet they believe that somehow good—it is always that sloppy "somehow"—will be the outcome...'

Margaret said that so long as the Wilcoxes governed England and the world it wouldn't be a bad place. But look what the Wilcoxes have brought us to and what they have come to themselves, might well be Greene's retort. There are hints enough in *Howards End*. Charles Wilcox, Henry's son, for instance, hadn't enough money to go on living in his accustomed style, and he certainly hadn't the ability to make more. Greene's Henry might well be the grandson, in logic if not in heredity. The first H.W. had been, in Margaret's words, 'a man who insults his wife when she's alive and cants with her memory when she's dead'. Such men are 'muddled, criminally muddled'. The second H.W. was dominated by his wife while she was living. When she is dead he sees his chance to escape and even plays with the possibility, but he cannot do it, it is too much for his exhausted nature. It was Forster himself who wrote, in an aside, that the Wilcox imperialists will bequeath and inherit a grey world. Nothing was more important to them than property, and their main energies were concentrated on its defence. And now, a generation later, the Wilcoxes were destroying property wholesale and their decadent sons and grandsons were making futile efforts to protect it. (The second Henry, it should be remembered, was an Air Raid

Warden.) We live in the world produced by 'the inner darkness in high places that comes with a commercial age', as Margaret said.

I have devoted so much space to this extremely hypothetical relation between the two H.W.s that some explanation is probably necessary. I have tried to show that, if only we had the background information, Greene's choice of names for his characters might be seen to be extremely significant. In one case, and one only, it may be possible to follow a line of enquiry: I have followed it not only because Henry Wilcox is an important name in English fiction but because I believe Greene expresses his attitudes unconsciously through this type of symbolism. I have already given my opinion, in the previous chapter, that Greene's subconscious mind is less subject to censorship than is normal. It is extremely active, insistent and dominating. It is quite capable of collecting some odds and ends, attitudes attached to names, approvals and disapprovals, from a novel read in, say, 1922, brooding on them, making new patterns with them and, finally, disgorging them twenty years later. This is, after all, the normal behaviour of the subconscious mind. My only claim is that the workings of Greene's are more visible, the walls of his psychological compartments less opaque, than is usual. With Forster, for instance, we never get a glimpse of what goes on beneath the smooth and tidy exterior. With Greene, we see vague blurs moving as through frosted glass.

I will end this chapter with a prophecy. In 1971 Greene will publish his last novel. In it Scobie will be hunted by Bendrix and a cloud of Davises. A Rose will love a condemned man and a Coral will commit suicide. Various Savages and piscine creatures named Dab, Crab and Flounder will assist in the chase. Wilcox will shake in his shoes and Mellows will disapprove.

XIII

THE BLITZ AND LITERATURE

T HE war was a bleak period for Greene. Between 1940 and 1948 he only published one novel, *The Ministry of Fear*, and that was a nightmare that itself tried to define the links between wake and dream. During this period, however, he also published minor works and some rather fugitive pieces, which must be considered in a survey of his total work. It also gives me an opportunity to halt and take a look at Greene himself.

His photographs nearly always show him wearing a puzzled expression, a slight frown as though he is trying to work something out. Sometimes the brow is wrinkled. One naturally wonders to what extent this may be significant: is he naturally worried or suspicious? (He appeared to be suspicious of my desire to write this book, and was strongly opposed to our meeting.) Does he feel people are getting at him? As a Catholic publicist, he probably does. (Ask me any questions you like, he finally wrote, except about my religion.) Has he a sense of insecurity, emotional or intellectual? Again, as I have already stated, I believe he has and that it is largely intellectual. When he wrote an Introduction to Herbert Read's *The Green Child* (dated March 1946) he wondered at the gap between *The Innocent Eye* and *Art Now*, between the supporter of surrealism and the child from the Yorkshire farm. He sensed a division in sensibility. I believe this to be partly his own predicament. Although Read had creative talent which at times overwhelmed his critical prejudices, the latter were dominant most of the time and he was thought of by his contemporaries primarily as a critic, and an intellectual rather in the continental sense. Greene on the other hand is nine-tenths creative energy, but he has a respect for critical, intellectual ability which is often found in men of his type. Read is the kind of man he would sometimes like to be, and he has therefore become something of a literary deity for him. He is not able to treat him as a model because the gap between them is too great. The admiration is probably of long standing. *The Green Child* first appeared in 1935 and in 'The Basement Room' (1936) there is a passing reference to Sir Hubert Reed. Something about Read clung to Greene's fancy and he could not quite forget him.

With Read the head wags the emotional tail; with Greene the emotions wag the head. 'A whole world of the imagination seems to separate the rather dry, sophisticated critic from the vale, the orchard, the foldgarth and the stockyard', he wrote. (Sir Hubert Reed had been called 'withered'.) Read constantly returned to his origins but never to stay. Greene has scarcely ever left his. His visits to Africa are, symbolically, not so much returns to childhood as to the consolidations of childhood. Biologically we must leave childhood behind but spiritually one can stay. Greene envies Read for his mobility. To put it in a vastly different way, he would probably like to be better at chess. In his West African convoy journal and elsewhere he has hinted that he is not very good at chess. Creative talents rarely do shine at it. It is a game for the critical, analytical temperament which Greene occasionally wishes he possessed.

There are two references to Greene in Kingsmill and Pearson's *Talking of Dick Whittington*. In one he is puzzled. In the other they are rather hearty with him, and he is puzzled again. There is a suggestion that they were accustomed to tease him, that they felt he took his religion too seriously. Kingsmill and Pearson sound like prefects who are getting a bit of fun out of ragging one of the juniors. If it isn't condescension it is liable to be scorn. Max Plowman, for instance, writing to Geoffrey West in February 1941, praises Eric Gill's *Autobiography* and then adds, 'I see Graham Greene found Gill "eccentric"—not revolutionary! I wonder if he'd know a revolution if he saw it?' Greene felt uneasy in the face of Gill's enthusiasm. He hates any form of brashness, and gives the impression that his loyalty to an institution increases in proportion to its failings. There was practically no common ground between men such as Greene and Plowman. Greene is a formalist who has decided that the only true revolution is the Counter-Reformation (which was not a revolution at all) and sees every other movement as a mere intensification of Protestant heresy. Plowman disliked the Catholic Church (we know it by its fruits, 'which are horrid', he wrote), but felt that Gill transcended its limitations. Greene rejoices in limitations. The only happy picture I have ever seen of him was taken when he had been expelled from Puerto Rico. His cheeks bulged with amusement. Circumstances had answered the call of his spirit for persecution, things were going very well and very badly.

Apart from *The Ministry of Fear* Greene did publish two other books during this period. One was his *British Dramatists*, which was no more than an essay for the Britain in Pictures series. In 1947 he collected his stories under the title *Nineteen Stories*. In a note he wrote: ' I am only too conscious of the defects of these stories, written at long intervals between 1929 and 1941. The short story is an exacting form which I have never properly practised: I present these tales merely as the by-products of a novelist's career'. There is no false modesty about this statement. Few of the stories are good, often because the treatment is much more trivial than any that Greene would use in a novel. I have already referred to some of them. On the whole, they are Metroland stories with the familiar Greeneland atmosphere, but there are also one or two attempts at humour. Typical of the first type is 'The Case for the Defence' (1939). A man is accused of murder and the case against him appears to be absolutely water-tight until it is discovered that he has an identical twin brother. One witness, a Mrs Salmon, says she would have known that face anywhere. After the man's acquittal the crowd rush at the brothers and one of them is knocked under a bus and killed. The surviving brother looks accusingly at Mrs Salmon. 'If you were Mrs Salmon,' we are asked, 'could you sleep at night?' The literary level is that of the *Evening News*. Such a trite question may stimulate the tired brain of the straphanger but would never be asked in one of the author's novels, not even the Entertainments. It obviously illustrates his concern with identity, which he has exhibited elsewhere far more subtly. It also reiterates, in a commonplace way, his dissatisfaction with the efficiency of human justice.

But arguments from twin brothers were never impressive, even in Shakespeare.

The chief character in 'A Little Place Off the Edgware Road', belonging to the same year, is named Craven. We are immediately reminded of Raven in *A Gun For Sale*, and the name also suggests Greene's preoccupation with cowardice. The atmosphere is characteristically squalid, being compounded of wealth and love, poverty and lust. Craven, who is worried by a recurrent dream that dead bodies do not decay, goes to a cinema where he is annoyed by a little man whom he believes to be mad. Later he discovers that the little man had already been murdered. It might be a dream, logically it could only be a dream, with another dream within it. This kind of horror is very much to Greene's taste. Here and there he shows himself to be fascinated by the possibilities derived from a literal acceptance of religious belief. For instance, Craven would hate to live again in his inadequate body—Raven had already hated his first life because of his body. The story poses the question: does a man who has died violently live again with his mutilation? Once more, it doesn't come off. The question is not serious enough to make a story of it. It is sufficient for a passing remark, and no more.

'Alas, Poor Maling' (1940) is a humorous story and should be regarded, I think, as an example of the kind of unsatisfactory outlet Greene's frustrated creative spirit began to find once the Blitz was upon him. Maling's stomach picked up sounds and repeated them like a parrot. Sounding the air raid warning, it sent a Board meeting to the shelters where they stayed for twelve hours, and so were unable to carry out the business for which they met. The story is slightly revolting because it turns on a disordered stomach. This is a representative Greene trick but it is easier to derive seediness from it than humour. 'When Greek Meets Greek' (1941) is, on the other hand, a rare and charming story, with humour grafted on to crookedness, rather in the O. Henry manner. The humour is in the situation, not in someone's physical failing. Two old crooks cheat each other and their young ones see through it all and turn the situation to their joint advantage. There are only two moments of serious criticism, and each of these points out that there are bigger, if more respectable, frauds in the world than these two.[1]

The short story is not one of Greene's successful forms, although the four new ones which appeared in *Twenty-One Stories* (1954) show an improvement. He is happier with the journal and the critical review. During the war period he kept journals on two separate occasions, and selections from them were both published later. The first covered the period of the Blitz, 1940–1, and appeared in *The Month* of November 1952 under the title of 'The Londoners'. In it we can see the novelist flexing his literary muscles, while the Catholic propagandist occasionally peeps out. It opens with a description that could easily set the tone for a new novel of failure: 'They got into the bus at Golders Green after the pantomime: a dyed blonde woman in the late forties and her old husband, with the relics of histrionic good looks. The old wrinkled tortoise-skin and the heavy-lidded eyes might have belonged to a Forbes-Robertson —somebody who had played *Hamlet* too often. Now he was tired, very tired, and the vulgar woman he had married nagged and bullied and insulted him all the time in the public bus, and he made no reply but "Yes, dear", "No dear". He hadn't noticed or understood anything in the pantomime, and this was her excuse to bait him. Slowly a whole wartime life emerged. They lived in a hotel and had nowhere to sit without having to buy drinks. So after the pantomime they were going to the "flicks" for an hour, and after the flicks, dinner, and after dinner, bed in the big steel-built reinforced hotel. And the next day, just the same again'. Two whole lives are set before us here, exactly and mercilessly, but the lack of mercy is

---

[1] Another story, published in the *Strand Magazine* (June 1940) but not included in his collected stories, is of considerable interest to the Greene fan. It is called 'The News in English' and is about a Lord Haw-Haw. His voice is recognized by his wife, who later realizes that he is passing messages to her in code. She informs the War Office, and has to adopt a kind of double consciousness: her husband is a hero but everyone else thinks he is a coward and a traitor. It is extremely characteristic of Greene's distaste for heroic attitudes. If the priest in *The Power and the Glory* is a hero, it is entirely fortuitous; David Bishop in this story really is a hero (I believe the only orthodox one in the whole of Greene's output) yet fate will not allow him to assume the title publicly. A decidedly subtle manifestation of failure, with an ecclesiastical name.

not the author's. They belong to the defeated. But at the same time men can triumph. This was the case of the fire-watcher who, being told that the Alert had sounded, stayed on the roof in the biting east wind for an hour, until somebody reminded him it was April Fool's Day. One of the men remarked, 'Now you might say we lost one man's work for an hour—but it was worth it for the merriment it caused. Made everything go smoother'. Greene's appreciation of this point of view can be related to his Catholic psychology—although I certainly do not mean that only a Catholic could appreciate the situation. But it is the view of the inefficient, irrational, non-planning section of humanity. Ida Arnold might have been shocked. On the whole, however, the real flavour of Greene comes out most strongly in two short passages at the end of the journal. One is a footnote which reads, 'For days afterwards there was the sweet smell of corruption in Store Street'. And the other is the final paragraph. 'Looking back, it was the squalor of the night, the purgatorial throng of men and women in dirty torn pyjamas with little blood splashes standing in doorways, which remained. These were disquieting because they supplied images for what one day would happen to oneself'. It will be remembered that he said the same thing of dreams in *The Ministry of Fear*. The blitz was not a real event. It was a nightmare, and it preluded something worse to come. There is no doubt that Greene was deeply affected by the bombing of London. I believe that the mood of apocalyptic piety which he exhibited during 1952 and 1953 was a delayed reaction from this wartime fear.

The other journal was kept while travelling in convoy to West Africa during December and January, 1941-2, and it was published in *The Mint* in 1946. He actually calls this 'an indication of the kind of raw material a novelist stores', yet it is curiously flat. There is quite a lot about the books he takes and reads. There is more poetry than any other single category: Rilke, Wordsworth, Browning, Shakespeare. Several Trollopes—and we remember he was reading Trollope in Mexico. (Trollope is the perfect antidote to the dreamwriter.) He read and was unimpressed by Hanley's *The Ocean*. It seemed unreal and there was no mention of 'the Cold'. But later we find him reading *Grey Eminence* with 'unexpected pleasure'. There is less human observation in this journal, more description of inanimate objects, as though he were deliberately trying to improve his weaker points. 'We leave Belfast. Again the showers of sparks from the oxy-acetylene welders and the blue and green lights of the electric welders. The open hull of an aircraft carrier lights up like a toy stage as a welder gets to work and a tiny figure can be seen against the confused background of steel—then darkness again and then again the green light and the tiny figure'. Human observation, when it takes place, tends to concentrate on the non-Sunday school aspect—a steward demonstrates how to test a French letter, later blows some up to the size of balloons for Christmas decorations. Another pre-occupation, a lesser one, gets an airing: on Christmas Day they listen to the 'King's rather lugubrious speech at lunch'. He records two nightmares. One is of 'the traditional kind—being trapped in darkness'. Does this mean he *will* be trapped in darkness at a later date? Like Scobie?

He was writing *British Dramatists* on board. We learn nothing about Greene from this performance—except, perhaps, that he is interested in the theatre. He is always associated with the cinema and a few years later he was to tell Walter Allen, in a broadcast interview, that he prefers the films to the stage. The most interesting parts of this essay are his comments on contemporary drama. The Morality Plays, he said, were bones without flesh. Today we more frequently have flesh without bones: 'characters who act a plot before us and have no significance at all outside the theatre, who are born when the curtain rises and die when it falls'. It is lit up by spasmodic shafts of Greenesque wisdom: 'a man dies in the way he lives'; 'nobody who lives escapes a private agony'; 'one admires the quality one lacks'. He obviously feels happier when he reaches his own world. Up till then his prose has seemed slightly restricted, but at this point it resumes its normal tough masculinity: 'The three-act play was here: the drawing room set, the library set, and after a few more years the bedroom set. Cigarette cases were being offered, and very soon now butlers and parlour-maids would be crossing the stage, as the curtain rose, to answer the telephone. The panelling in the library looks quite Tudor, the club is lifted straight from St James's (and now that acting has become a respectable profession the actors can be lifted from there, too)'. This is the familiar voice of the film critic.[1]

There was one other activity during this 'bitty' period which should be mentioned. It was a brief spell of reviewing done for the *Evening Standard*, for a few weeks in the summer of 1945. These reviews attracted a great deal of attention at the time and their level was well above the normal literary level of a popular daily newspaper. Greene treated his readers as adults and did not deliberately cheapen his values as some other authors of reputation have done in similar circumstances. One gets the impression that he took this opportunity to affirm some articles of literary faith at a time when standards were debased and he himself had been through a period of unproductive frustration. It is strange that one of his most important and forthright declarations appeared in this form, masquerading as a review of John Farleigh's *Fifteen Craftsmen on their Arts*. A novelist on his craft is always of interest and because Greene has written very little about his I intend to quote at length. He says far more here than Walter Allen was able to elicit from him in a rather sticky broadcast interview, although the express purpose of the latter was to get him to talk on his view of the novel and his method.

> 'Craftsmen, one is inclined to think', he writes, 'should live in the hurly-burly of cities: some of these contributors are conditioned disastrously by the ghastly good taste of the Cotswold village, the false simplicity of the cottage, the admiration of undiscriminating female pilgrims, by the beauty spot. Wedgwood and Chippendale did not find it necessary to live in reverent and self-conscious isolation.
>
> Among the fifteen craftsmen you will find no novelist, and yet his is a craft, or should be as well as an art.
>
> I would distinguish the craft of the novel as the means the novelist takes towards his end. A novel, like an epic, has its dull passages: the writer must find a method to make his links shine, but not shine too much. He must describe the passage of time (perhaps a novelist's most difficult problem): only craft will enable him to do this—or to avoid the problem altogether.

[1] Greene did in fact write some stage notices for the *Spectator*, though they were mostly of revues and musical comedies.

How is he to convey simultaneously the way a man talks, the tone of voice he uses, and the place in which he is standing? How is he to avoid *telling* the reader too much, instead of allowing the reader to find out for himself?

These are all problems of craft which a great novelist may fail to solve (at his peril), but which a popular commercial novelist may solve triumphantly and yet produce nothing of value.'

It is true that Greene only states the problems here, but we really do not expect more. It is the problem that fascinates the layman, the means of solving it is not his business and is too remote to be of much interest. A fortnight before, Greene had already discussed the relationship between the book and the reader, or at least a particular aspect of it, in a joint review of a novel by D. L. Murray and a book on Virginia Woolf. Are the popular novelists read, he wonders, or are they merely background noises like the B.B.C.? He makes a typical comparison between popular fiction and agriculture—they both go on all the time! 'The point is not the author's sincerity or lack of it, but the harm done by his popularity', he says, and it is worth saying for this type of writer is too often excused on the ground that he is sincere. So were Hitler and most murderers. A course in D. L. Murray damages your mind. You cannot expect to read him day in and day out and then switch over to Virginia Woolf. Finally one feels an insidious charm in Rebecca and only irritation with Mrs Dalloway. One has lost the capacity to share the latter's thoughts and feelings. He ended with a characteristic jab at the Americans. 'Publishers decide on their best-sellers beforehand, confident that publicity will beat down the public resistance weakened already by a long course of best-sellers. Authoresses are groomed like actresses for stardom.'

Animal Farm cheered him up. It renewed his faith in writers as a fraternity. 'Whatever you may say about writers—their private lives, their feeding habits or their taste in shirts—you have to admit, I think, that there has never been such a thing as a literature of appeasement. Writers may pass, like everyone else, through the opium dream of Munich and Yalta, but no literature comes out of the dream.' The review was dated 10th August, 1945. The war in Europe was over and it would be possible to live again. The writer, he said very pointedly, keeps quiet in wartime. Officials take charge, like the type of official at the Ministry of Information who asked if it might not be possible for the dictator and his friends in Orwell's book to be portrayed as something other than pigs. *Animal Farm*, he said, was a welcome sign of peace. One would be able to write the truth again. One would be able to leave the Foreign Office and settle down to another book. It turned out to be his best.

XIV

PITY DESTROYS

Nineteen Forty-Eight
'The Heart of the Matter', 'Why Do I Write?'

'Round the corner, in front of the old cotton tree, where the earliest settlers had gathered their first day on the unfriendly shore, stood the law courts and police station, a great stone building like the grandiloquent boast of weak men.' This was where Scobie worked, and the tragedy of Scobie is inherent in this simile. For Scobie was not a boaster, he was a weak man who could not hide his weakness. When the novel opens we hear he has been passed over for promotion. He might as well have been told publicly that he wasn't good enough. The criticism glances off him and wounds his wife Louise. The climate was just right for it. Long before Scobie met Helen he told himself that hate or love would madden a man, but meanness, malice and snobbery would come as naturally as sweat or thirst. Scobie is not an emotional man. He bears a strong resemblance to the Assistant Commissioner of *It's A Battlefield*. Like him he cannot altogether hide his disgust with the uselessness of his work or his impatience with an unjust society. It becomes clear early on that Scobie is riddled with pity and a desire to help the victims of injustice. His pity is his weakness, for there is no place for it in the official routine. Now and again he wishes it were all over, he fears retirement like an inevitable hell, and he is incapable of dissembling. In this he is a distorted reflection of his creator, a man who cannot disguise or hide his feelings. He can always be seen through.

And yet he loved the Coast. Wondering why, he supposed it was because human nature hadn't time to hide itself. Nobody there could possibly talk about a heaven on earth. 'Here you could love human beings nearly as God loved them, knowing the worst.' But this seemed to conflict with the insincerity that flourished everywhere. Scobie noticed, for instance, that when Wilson first arrived he sounded sincere. A few months would change that, and Wilson would be talking like the rest of them, saying one thing and meaning its opposite. How then was it possible to say that human nature could not disguise itself? The answer was that you were expected to try. Everyone was expected to set up the correct façade, to put on the socially accepted mask. Scobie's fault was that his efforts were too amateurish, or perhaps he didn't even try. In the latter case, it was an example of snobbery, he was setting himself above the others, judging them. But he wasn't a snob. He didn't really believe the truth had any human value. His honesty was a habit. 'In human relations kindness and lies are worth a thousand truths.' Pity demanded white lies. The truth too often hurt.

He was much concerned with happiness, of course. Experience had taught him that no human being can really understand another and that no-one can arrange another's happiness. Under the stress of circumstances, trying to puzzle things out, he often forgot this. As his depression thickens (Louise had been getting hysterical with disappointment and had been sent to South Africa, while his own dreaded retirement approached inexorably) he comes to the conclusion that only three kinds of people can possibly know happiness: the egoists, the evil or the absolutely ignorant. It was absurd for an ordinary person to expect happiness in a world so full of misery. There was one moment when Scobie believed that he had reached the borders of happiness, that he could expect nothing more. He was alone in the dark and rain, without love or pity. He was empty and featureless, and in that state one could approach happiness. For remember, he had told himself that a truly positive emotion was out of the question.

Then came Helen and a moment of happiness which he was too bewildered to notice at the time and which he looked back upon afterwards, almost disbelievingly. He told himself pedantically that it was a mistake to mix up the ideas of happiness and love. He had once told himself that an evil man could be happy. That was the prospect now dangled before him—commit a sin and be happy. He was a Roman and didn't believe it. It wasn't entirely a matter of religious belief. He wasn't the forthright type of character who is prepared to snatch at happiness, to sin and be damned. He knew he had sinned and he couldn't guarantee that he wouldn't repeat his sin. That was his despair, for even if he did repeat the sin he would not recapture the happiness he had once tasted. It would be a slow and painful process of selling oneself to the Devil for nothing at all, just nothing at all. In desperation he goes to confession and the priest fails to produce the magic formula. 'When he came out of the box it seemed to Scobie that for the first time his footsteps had taken him out of sight of hope. There was no hope anywhere he turned his eyes: the dead figure of the God upon the Cross, the plaster Virgin, the hideous Stations representing a series of events that had happened a long time ago. It seemed to him that he had only left for his exploration the territory of despair.'

Scobie is like so many of his forerunners in that he loves failure. The difference between him and, say, Anthony Farrant, is that he exists in a metier where failure is unforgivable. It didn't matter to Anthony, no-one expected him to succeed. When Scobie was passed over for promotion it was not he who suffered but his wife, Louise. When the decision was reversed it was she who exulted in it and immediately recovered her desire to live, while he found himself hating her. She was so cheerful, so smug, one of the saved, and he was nauseated by her adult innocence. He told himself that even God was a failure—a useful rationalization, and it enabled him to love God. Just before he committed suicide he found himself loving Louise again (at least, it was a feeling that resembled love) but only because his heightened perceptions saw beyond her complacent delight in the forthcoming social triumph, and knew that she too was a failure. She was no longer beautiful. You can't love beauty for long. 'It wasn't beauty that we love, it's failure—the failure to stay young for ever, the failure of nerves, the failure of the body.' He slid into a desire to protect her, he settled back into pity. And pity is a retreat from love, not a part of love. It is in its insistence on love rather than pity, or its more generalized conception, compassion, that Christianity rises above all other religions.

How truthful was Scobie? He is, like all English Catholics, torn in his loyalties. The Portuguese ship captain would never have dreamed of trying to bribe an English official, but as soon as he discovers Scobie is a Catholic he offers money. Greene has always drawn a distinction so sharply between wrong on the human level and evil on the spiritual level that at times he is tempted to praise wrong-doing merely because it is not a divine transgression. *Brighton Rock* exemplifies this tendency most clearly. Here we have the implication that British official incorruptibility signifies nothing more than a kind of stodgy, unfeeling rigidity. It is useful but masks an inner void. This is an additional suggestion that Scobie did not admire the truth for its own sake—he had already decided that truth is frequently harmful in human relations. Yet all his close acquaintances reprove him at one time or another for his habit of sticking to the truth: Louise, Wilson, Helen. They cannot bear the truth, its naked power. But there is something petulant about their rejection of it, something exaggerated and false. Helen also resents his pity, which is a reflection of the truth he knows. There is one very revealing scene. Automatically he pities her and she bursts out furiously, 'I don't want your pity'. There follows this significant passage. 'But it was not a question of whether she wanted it—she had it. Pity smouldered like decay at the heart.' Sometimes one feels that Greene is succumbing to the pressure that afflicts every serious writer, the compulsion to elucidate a previously unknown truth. But no truths are unknown, though some may be obscured. A novelist, under the scourge of originality, is tempted to seek one out.

But even if the touch is not always quite sure, even if there are occasional inconsistencies in the delineation of character (and we should be wary of demanding too much consistency in literature), this is the first occasion on which Greene writes wholly out of human sympathy and understanding. *England Made Me* had been a work of clever observation. *The Power and the Glory* had been an affirmation made out of faith. But this comes out of love and knowledge, in the sense of understanding. Although the leading character is a Catholic it is not what is understood by a 'Catholic' novel. No attempt is made to pour scorn on Protestants and heretics. The only concern is the soul of Scobie, attention is not diffused by a blurring of focus. And the achievement is performed with the simplest words in the language. This book is proof, if it is needed, that the highest accomplishment in literature is not necessarily reached through verbal pyrotechnics or tricks of style; if it were, then none would stand higher than Thomas Nashe or Walter Pater. Greene's effect is cumulative, and is derived from a simple tautness and directness that is never relaxed. I find, for instance, that I have marked the following passage on page 219 of the Uniform Edition: 'Could I shift my burden there, I wondered: could I tell him that I love two women: that I don't know what to do? What would be the use? I know the answer as well as he does.' Now standing in isolation these sentences are probably much less impressive than many that could be quoted from Galsworthy or even Nevil Shute, yet in their context they produce an effect of which those authors are incapable.

The moral heart of the matter was this: Scobie, a Catholic, had ceased to love his wife and had fallen in love with another woman, Helen. He was faced with the following alternatives: he could reject Helen and stay with his wife; he could leave his wife to live with Helen; he could stay with his wife but keep Helen as a mistress; he could commit suicide; there was also the possibility of the problem being solved by a miracle, and Scobie actually prayed for this. This would presumably have been the sudden death of Louise. (It is worth noting that Greene considered the possibility of miraculous intervention, but reserved it, though with a less decisive application, for his next novel.) It is fashionable in modern criticism to treat a work of art as the simultaneous posing and solution of a problem. I have no sympathy with this attitude at all because I believe it encourages art to usurp a function for which it was never intended and is not really fitted. In the present case such a critical attitude would reject one of the five alternatives in particular, as offering no solution. This, that of suicide, is the one that Greene bravely selects. This novel is therefore a valuable reply to a false critical outlook, its value lying in its literary excellence, for no reputable critic dared to attack it for its 'lack of solution'. Incidentally, so chaotic (or, to be kind, varied) is the literary scene today that each of the possible solutions would be heartily attacked by one school or another. Thus, the first would be dull and bourgeois, the second would be falsely romantic, the third would be immoral (or dishonest, for people are selective in their morality), and the last would be impossible.

When literature has passed through its present phase of self-consciousness, it may be recognized again that there can and should be no limitation on characterization, event or 'solution'. There is no formation of character that life does not provide examples of (we are incapable of imagining beyond reality), and the solution of a human situation is the moralist's task, not the artist's. Glib terms such as 'consistency' and 'convincing' should be avoided. The evasion of critical responsibility, which is a task demanding accuracy and exactness, conveyed in the term 'inner consistency' does not bring us nearer the truth. Naturally, a writer's work must be convincing but we should beware of relating such a quality to the narrow terms of a critic's possibly inferior imagination. One too often is compelled to say of life, 'If I read that in a novel I wouldn't believe it.' While the best critics are worth more attention than the worst novelists it should never be forgotten that many critics stand in their relation to the best novelists as, say, Dean Church stood to Wordsworth. And so, putting 'solutions' on one side, we can say that *The Heart of the Matter* is a fine novel though not a great one, because a great artistic achievement can only be performed by a great man. Greene is not one of the great. His work can be superb in its own terms. Parallels are always helpful. This novel puts him on a level with, say, Browning.

When a particular matter (a problem, as the *Zeitgeist* prefers it) exercises Greene's mind he often resorts to a short story for its elaboration, as well as the novel he is currently working on. Here he wants to know how some things that palpably exist can be reconciled with God. Why do children die? Why do they suffer at all? How could you reconcile with the love of God the fact that a child had survived forty days and nights in an open boat, and then died? A French officer said to Scobie, 'Of course, they looked after her on the boat. They gave up their own share of the water often. It was foolish, of course, but one cannot always be logical. And it gave them something to think about.' And then comes the author's comment: 'It was like the hint of an explanation—too faint to be grasped.' The Hint of an Explanation! The phrase catches his fancy and he makes it the title of a story, published in the same year. The corruption of children had become an obsession with him: *The Confidential Agent, The Lawless Roads, The Power and the Glory*. And now the suffering and pointless death—they were marked by the same horror beyond reason. In the story the agnostic traveller on the train says to the Catholic, 'When you think what God—if there is a God—allows. It's not merely the physical agonies, but think of the corruption, even of children . . .' And the Catholic replies that now and again we catch hints. They are not scientific evidence, they only have meaning for those who experience them, but the believer will act upon them.

Scobie's slow corruption came into existence through his pity. Pity led to a shunning of the truth and a retreat into cowardice. It blasted a breach through his integrity. In concrete terms, it put him in Yusef's clutches. It finally destroyed him, for there was a chain leading back directly from the final act, his suicide, to his first surrender to pity, expended on his wife. (On the whole, the more familiar fault of self-pity was not Scobie's.) Every critic of *The Heart of the Matter* has commented on the role played by Scobie's pity. In 'A Note on Graham Greene' in *The Wind and the Rain* (Summer 1949) W. H. Auden calls pity 'that corrupt parody of love and compassion which is so insidious and deadly for sensitive natures'. He then goes on to treat the subject with his characteristic violence and says much more than Greene ever intended. 'To feel compassion for someone is to make oneself their equal; to pity them is to regard oneself as their superior and from that eminence the step to the torture chamber and the corrective labour camp is shorter than one thinks.' It may be shorter, but it's still immensely long. The point which Auden missed was that Scobie's pity was the instrument that killed *him*, not the victims of a brutal rationalization. This was by no means the first occasion on which pity had played a leading part: Conrad Drover felt it for Milly in *It's A Battlefield*, Mr Lever felt it for his wife in 'A Chance for Mr Lever', Fellows for *his* wife in *The Power and the Glory*, Rose Cullen for D. in *The Confidential Agent*, Rollo for Anna in *The Third Man*. In each case pity is a poor substitute for love, and it is its possessor who is injured. It appeared with especial virulence ('the horrible and horrifying emotion of pity') in *The Ministry of Fear*. It is true that it caused Rowe to kill his wife, but its significance really began there, not ended. For Rowe entered his nightmare at that point and at one time began to pity his own suffering to such an extent that he considered killing himself

as he had killed his wife. Scobie actually does. The question arises
whether pity is to be regarded as a distortion (or perhaps a simplification) of love, or as 'the worst passion of all'. Greene says both at
different times. I think it would be unwise to systematize the outlook
of this novel. What is far more important to Greene is the refusal to
regard pity as a substitute for love. When separated from love, pity
actually becomes destructive, a negative sharing of failure, whereas
love is creative. Love is 'an eternal affirmation' of human personality,
as Berdyaev says. When Greene can follow his own feelings and
experience without interference he recognizes love as this eternal
affirmation. And then the Catholic viewpoint interposes, and hi
intuitions are warped and explained away.

Scobie was assailed by a temporary slackening of faith such as
comes to everyone who possesses a faith of some kind. He tells the
confessor this and the confessor replies that there is nothing unusual
about it. It seems fairly certain that Greene himself had suffered in
that way. Scobie said he felt empty, the Absolution sounded like
hocus pocus. There is something very touching about this passage, it
bears that ring of authenticity that is so difficult to define. Like the
passage concerning Scobie's hopeless effort to shift the burden,
quoted earlier, it communicates perfectly. Again, it is not the actual
language used, although that is apt and impressive and not in the
least portentous. The passage owes much of its success to its position,
and this is probably as close as we can go to an awareness of two
excellences, of structure and of timing, without resorting to the
soul-destroying practice of chopping the novel into pieces to see
how it works. Another moment of the profoundest conviction
occurs when Scobie writes that terrifying letter to Helen, asserting
that he loved her more than he loved himself, than he loved Louise,
than he loved God. In previous books Greene had often resorted to
sensationalism, deliberate attempts to excite or horrify the reader.
Here he does both, and there is not the slightest suggestion of
strain. Obviously all treatment of faith in this book comes from
experience and sincerity, but how it is imparted is a mystery. It is,
after all, what distinguishes art from science.

My praise of this novel may seem extravagant, especially as
there were others who found fault. Elizabeth Hardwick reviewed

it in *Partisan Review* under the title 'Loveless Love'. She criticized the 'exhausted dialogue' but this is surely unavoidable for the realist novelist of today. It is *our* language that is exhausted, or rather the common use of it, not the author's. One might write in a poetic style and record 'live' dialogue (like O'Casey) but the result would not be realist. Greene has chosen to be realist (he probably could be nothing else, but in that lies his representative quality). She also criticized what she called the 'snobbishness' of serious Catholic writers, what I have seen described elsewhere as their 'smoothness and smugness'. The odd thing is that Miss Hardwick's criticism has no relationship to *The Heart of the Matter* but would have been a valid comment on *Brighton Rock*. In fact, there is in this novel an element of impatience with Catholic dogma and Scobie more than once questions the Church's teaching. When he found Pemberton's note after the latter's suicide, his pity took control. He told the priest that God would forgive him, and when Father Clay began to pronounce the attitude of the Church, Scobie put in impatiently, 'Even the Church can't teach me that God doesn't pity the young . . .'

The best art comes out of resolved conflict. There had always been conflict in Greene's mind but it had not found its point of rest until now. He had always, so far as we can judge, been a faithful Catholic. He had not criticized his Church although he had occasionally found fault with its priests. But now stirrings of revolt were occasionally noticeable, and their effect on his work seemed beneficial. In a review written in 1945 he had said there is always a Jones Minor who sees through even the most successful schoolmaster, and that there is a Jones Minor in every human heart. Non-Catholics (and, of course, non-Communists) often claim that a rigid intellectual discipline is fatal to the artist. Greene had apparently come round to this way of thinking himself, for about this time he began to talk and write about the necessity of disloyalty. The idea seemed to act as a talisman, and it allowed him to produce his best work.

In a broadcast discussion with Elizabeth Bowen and V. S. Pritchett called 'The Artist in Society' (July 1948) he said: 'Disloyalty is our privilege. But it is a privilege you will never get society to recognize. All the more necessary that we who can be disloyal with impunity should keep that ideal alive. If I may be personal, I belong to a group—the Catholic church—which would present me with grave problems as a writer if I were not saved by my disloyalty. You remember the black and white squares of Bishop Blougram's chessboard? As a novelist, I must be allowed to write from the point of view of a black square as well as of a white. Doubt and even denial must be given their chance of self-expression, or how am I freer than the Leningrad group?' In the same year the same three authors published an exchange of letters under the title *Why Do I Write?* Greene again mentioned this newly discovered privilege. The greatest pressure on the writer comes, he wrote, from the society within society. If his conscience were as acute as M. Mauriac's he would be unable to write a line.

Undoubtedly this new attitude freed Greene's spirit. He had found a formula which excused those critical attitudes which the creative writer must indulge, and at the same time his fundamental loyalty to his religion was unimpaired. His letters, however, are marred by a kind of pretentious flippancy; Bowen and Pritchett seem to write out of greater sincerity and try to answer the perennial question without being clever. Greene started by saying that, like Charlotte Brontë, he could not write on the topics of the day. From this he passed to a position of almost complete detachment, stating that he considered even the supporting of press appeals as mistaken. Certain human duties he owed in common with others: supporting his family, not robbing the poor or disabled, dying if the authorities required it. He added two other duties which he considered peculiar to the artist: to tell the truth as he sees it, and to accept no special privileges from the State. Catholic novelists in particular had to defend themselves from attacks of piety, 'that morbid growth of religion'. In a later letter he reverted to the importance of disloyalty, which he now called a virtue. It was so much more important for the writer than purity. 'Honours, State patronage, success, the praise of their fellows all tend to sap their disloyalty. If they don't become loyal to a Church or a country, they are too apt to become loyal to some invented ideology of their own, until they are praised for consistency, for a unified view. Even despair can become a form of loyalty. How few die treacherous or blaspheming in old age, and have any at all been lucky enough to die by the rope or a firing squad? I can think of none, for the world knows only too well that given time the writer will be corrupted into loyalty. Ezra Pound therefore goes to an asylum . . . (the honourable haven of the uncorruptible—Smart, Cowper, Clare and Lee). Loyalty confines us to accepted opinions: loyalty forbids us to comprehend sympathetically our dissident fellows; but disloyalty encourages us to roam experimentally through any human mind: it gives to the novelist the extra dimension of sympathy.'

The writer has a duty to be grit in the State machinery, he goes on to say—but it is not the State he is thinking of primarily. His conscience was finding a new level and whatever he said about the demands of the State could be applied equally to the Church. Here the temptations were in fact greater because the Church did not possess the means of persuasion open to the State. Sooner or later the question might arise as to how far disloyalty could be allowed to go. He could say that he disliked State patronage, distrusted a tax on classics to help contemporary writers, that literature should be left alone and no attempt should be made to plan it. It all sounds a bit self-satisfied. Pritchett wrote that after twenty years of writing he still couldn't live on the proceeds of his creative work. Greene can, and appears to have little constructive sympathy for those (the great majority) who can't. And all the time he writes about the State he is really thinking about the Church. He doesn't want to be patronized by his Church, he doesn't want to be regarded as a 'Catholic' writer, he doesn't want Catholic doctrine to be applied to his work or specifically Catholic judgments to be made about it.

It is a strange and difficult position to uphold. After all, Greene's Church publishes an Index of Forbidden Books and even teaches that some thoughts are forbidden. Greene is surely claiming the right to say what he likes, to be the keeper of his own artistic conscience. But this is Protestantism, a damnable heresy. He is claiming a privileged position for himself—after declaring that writers must not accept privileges from authority. Hector Hawton, an ex-Catholic who is now editor of *The Humanist*, made some shrewd comments on this attitude in an article contributed to *The Plain View*

(Winter 1953): 'Graham Greene', he wrote, 'seems to think that as a Catholic writer he is more free than he would be as a Communist writer. Certainly he is not being interferred with; he is too useful. He is the kind of attraction the Church in this country likes to display in the shop window. Communists are taunted with practising "double talk".[1] But satirical shafts are seldom directed nowadays against Catholics. Yet all Catholic talk about freedom is "double talk". They, no less than the Communists, demand freedom in order to suppress it. You must tolerate them because they are right; they must suppress you because you are wrong.'

The Catholic dilemma is admirably expressed by Claudel in the account of his conversion. Entering the church of Notre Dame on Christmas Day as an atheist, he suddenly believed. All doubts were swept away and since then nothing had been able to shake his faith. Yet his philosophical opinions remained intact: 'God had contemptuously left them where they were. . . . The Catholic religion still seemed to be the same treasure house of absurd fairy stories.' In the end he found that everything that had been most repugnant to his opinions and tastes had turned out to be true, and he had to adapt himself to it whether he liked it or not. And here, says Hawton, we have the true heart of the matter. The Catholic intellectual must at some time or other become aware of the incompatibility of his religious beliefs and the world as it is revealed to him. Greene had noticed this early on and had (rather contemptuously, as I think) asserted his *intellectual* belief. But you cannot cheat yourself for ever. The psychic split, particularly evident between intellect and feeling, widened and led to an unsure and even phantasmagorical view of his environment. Unification had to be found, at any price, and for a brief period he managed to persuade his unconscious will that a satisfactory formula had been discovered. *Fundamentally* he could remain faithful but it was allowable to make certain breaches in the faith that could be treated as *superficial*. It could not satisfy for long, of course. Already, by the time he came to write his next serious novel, *The End of the Affair*, the tension was beginning to show again. And in consequence he entered upon a period in which the

[1] Greene gives instances of Communist 'double talk' in his article on Poland, contributed to the *Sunday Times* in January 1956.

defence of his religion appeared to be of the first importance. He felt that the Catholic Church was under fire, although he did not realize that the aggression was to some extent his own. As he quietly sapped at the foundations of its discipline he organized sorties against the obvious and official enemies, Communism and Materialism. He even trembled at times on the edge of piety, the 'morbid growth of religion', but managed to withdraw without injury.

XV

RACKETEERS AND TODDLERS

Nineteen Fifty
'The Third Man', 'The Little Fire Engine'

GREENE produced no major work during the two years that followed *The Heart of the Matter*, but 'The Basement Room' was re-issued (under the meaningless title of *The Fallen Idol*, an example of the falsity immediately imposed by film work) with the story of the successful film, *The Third Man*. This was an Entertainment, of course, but it lacked the nightmare quality of *A Gun For Sale* and *The Ministry of Fear*. Greene had now recovered that grasp of reality that he seemed to lose after writing *England Made Me*.

The Third Man has no intrinsic importance but is interesting for its setting and once again many of those preoccupations and obsessions with which we have become familiar. Perhaps it establishes for the first time one that until now has only been guessed at. Greene is fascinated by the police rather than by the criminal. One of his Catholic critics, Neville Braybrooke, has in fact said that Greene's books are about the hunters rather than the hunted. There is a case for regarding the Assistant Commissioner as the chief character of *It's A Battlefield*. In *A Gun For Sale* Mather's importance nearly equals Raven's. We have already noted the close and at times sympathetic relationship between the priest and the lieutenant in *The Power and the Glory*; they could easily exchange roles. In this new book the 'I' character is the hunter, a policeman. The main character, Martins, works on the same side. In a story not originally intended for publication Greene felt he was able to indulge one of his favourite dream-wishes more openly. There had been evidence for some time, however. Despite his talk of disloyalty he had declared himself against extending any helping hand to the underdogs of his own profession. He was almost openly contemptuous of Civil Liberties (which he portrays unattractively as Busybodiness) and seemed strangely reluctant to assist the victims whom he pitied.

Martins writes Westerns but has feelings like the author of *The Heart of the Matter*. At Lime's funeral he could not keep back his tears —'the few meagre drops that any of us can squeeze out at our age'. (Martins was thirty-five, Greene forty-six—but I don't think the supply of tears varies much during the intervening period.) Although Martins was a third-rate writer his views on literature were in some ways similar to Greene's. (Greene has never been donnish about his profession.) Crabbin[1], the secretary of the Literary Society which Martins was mistakenly called upon to address, angered him by saying that Zane Grey was 'just a popular entertainer'. Martin's comment was, 'Why the hell not?' No-one deprecated Shakespeare for being a popular entertainer. When someone asked him where he would put James Joyce he replied, 'What do you mean put? I don't want to put anybody anywhere.' This passage refers back to Greene's statement made twelve years ago, that the film must be popular. There had undoubtedly been an implication that the novel should also be popular. A similar impression of impatience with academic formalism occurs in *The End of the Affair* when Bendrix is interviewed by a little review editor.

We also get the repetition of image and phrase that is so characteristic of his work: the witch on the landing, the land of the skyscrapers. Here it is a child that whimpers, 'I saw the blood on the coke'. There is also a reappearance of anti-Americanism, which had been quiescent since the film-reviewing days (perhaps that was why) but was soon to find its maximum expression in *The Quiet American*. Cooler's ideal was good citizenship. He is in some ways a reincarnation (not an exact copy, of course) of Ida Arnold and Hogpit and even Kapper from *The Name of Action*. He resembles the old man, also American, whose insipid goodness irritated Greene so much in Mexico. Martins could not bear Cooler; 'he wanted no more of that kindly tired humanitarian face'.

One last comment on this story. It is a film story and bears all those cinematic marks of style that distinguish the genre from the

[1] As the crossword puzzler would say: In front a *fish*, behind a receptacle for rubbish, the whole is a withered specimen of *homo sapiens* (7).

normal novel. (I drew attention to this in *A Gun For Sale* where the characters often did not behave like human beings but like film beings.) It is very rarely that a film character behaves like a human character. One considerable difference is that the film character reacts far more positively and alertly to hints and suggestions than a human character. Naturally, as life models itself on art we now have human characters who also react in this way, and the consequences are often laughable, for the conditions of ordinary life are not arranged as are the conditions of film life. I will give one example of this mode of existence. Martins suspects that Lime's death has been faked long before he has cause to. No human being would have been suspicious so soon as he was. In ordinary existence we cannot take it for granted that a mystery exists. In film existence (as in the religious sphere, which may be significant) a mystery *always* exists. Also, this does not imply that film beings are more instinctive than human beings. In fact, they rarely are. They resemble automata much more closely than they resemble human beings. There is really little need for instinct—they know that there is a puzzle to be cracked. There is in fact little in common between the rules of development in the two worlds, although their furniture is identical.

Another recurrence (it is quite a *mélange*) is the Catholic outlook: only a whiff of it this time. It occurs during that typically Greenesque meeting between Martins and Lime in the Great Wheel. It is the first landmark of its kind since those flushing lavatories in *The Ministry of Fear* and we are beginning to get just a little bit weary of it. Another one, and we'll start complaining. Lime is telling Martins how much money he makes (tax free) and how easy it is. 'In these days, old man, nobody thinks in terms of human beings. Governments don't—so why should we?' Then Martins makes that very significant remark, 'You used to be a Catholic'—significant in view of the author responsible. 'Oh, I still *believe*, old man,' Lime answers. 'In God and mercy and all that.' Now how are we to take this? As an admission by Greene that there are bad Catholics? Or as a statement, whether conscious or not, that this is where the Catholic faith may so easily lead? For such an attitude can relentlessly follow from the brave protestations of *Brighton Rock*, with its contempt for notions of right and wrong. The particular racket that Lime profited from resulted in death or idiocy among children. Lime started by selling penicillin stolen by military orderlies. Later he decided his profits weren't big enough so he diluted it with coloured water or mixed sand in with the penicillin dust. After all, he could argue, he was only breaking the law and what was the law? A formalization of Ida Arnold's despised right and wrong.

I think the connection must have crossed Greene's mind. If it did, he must have felt as troubled as Martins did when he discovered the human results of his friend's actions. For the corruption of children has always been for Greene the major evil. Corruption can be mental or physical, and Lime was managing to perform both. There was no need to make him a Catholic, his religion did not pose any special problems in the treatment of the story, as did Scobie's. It has a kind of ghost-like role, rising up accusingly like an unpleasant memory. Greene's personal religion did its best to excuse adultery (yet, having swallowed that camel he nearly chokes on the gnat divorce!) because adults must be left to answer for their own actions. But children cannot. I shall refer once again to this tenderness Greene shows for the condition of children and the tight corners it can get him into. For the time being, however, I shall concern myself with another aspect of his interest in children.

This was the publication of a book for children, called *The Little Fire Engine*, in 1950. There had in fact been a previous one, *The Little Train*, in 1948 but his name had not appeared on it. (One never knows when one might be going too far in criticism; is there a possibility that he wished to be known as a children's author in the year when the miserable fate of some children in Vienna caused him to reconsider his moral attitudes?) Altogether he was to write four children's books, all Transport Novels, one might say, and in each case they were illustrated by Dorothy Craigie. In a letter he told me that the books were written for fun and relaxation during the flying bomb raids. This means that they were actually designed and executed during the last stages of the war, but were only released at intervals later.

I must confess that the world of children's books baffles me. It appears that it is very difficult to write a bad children's book. My authority for saying this is a collection of reviews I read recently in

The New Statesman and Nation, normally a very critical journal except on certain reserved subjects. Eighty-two children's titles were reviewed and apparently they were all good. (Didn't someone once say—

> There are two-and-eighty ways
> Of writing children's lays,
> And every blessed one of them is right?)

Children's stories seem to resemble humour—judging by the books that do appear almost anyone can write a funny book. What is very rare, both among funny books and children's books, is excellence. Usually the author finds a formula or a trick, and the rest falls into place. One joke serves for a book, in its many avatars. Similarly one situation satisfies the children. They love the good joke to be repeated, and once they've discovered it they'll read it out to you *ad nauseam* and *ad* utmost irritation, for that matter. Charity forbids me to mention by name professional humorists who are not funny —in any case, *Punch* is easily available. The point is, 'humour' and 'child-appeal' have lost definition. They have become mechanical constructs and any reasonably proficient artisan can manage them. Genius being so rare, we forget what it's like and laud mere talent.

Now Greene found his trick without any difficulty. A vehicle, always a despised one (a failure), performs some meritorious and even fantastic feat. Later there is to be an emphasis on crime. The vehicle, of course, is on the side of law and order—an expression which would probably appal the author, but is more acceptable if we say that the vehicle becomes a hunter. The Little Train dreamt of a visit to 'the world outside where the great expresses go'. His bid for freedom failed. The outer world was ugly, noisy, frightening, and a Scotch express pushed him home. This is perhaps a warning to the kiddies not to get mixed up in the rottenness of grown-ups. The dedication 'to the guard of the twelve o'clock to Brighton' hints at a world that is never far from Greene's thoughts. In the other book Sam Trolley, the fireman, lost his job because fires were to be put out in future by a superior fire engine from Much Snoreing. He set up as a higgler, with the old engine and Toby, the horse. All three of them manage to have dreams in a very short space. In the end they redeem themselves by putting out a fire while the new team is drunk. This is a triumph for the more realistic and less moralistic Catholic view of misdemeanour, for little Protestant boys and girls are not supposed to know that their mummies and daddies get drunk! I will leave the other books until we come to them later.

XVI

FAILURE AS A CAREER

Nineteen Fifty-One
'The Lost Childhood and Other Essays'

THE publication of this volume of critical and reminiscent essays, collected from a variety of magazines and periodicals, gives me the opportunity to continue my exercise of building the onion. Many layers are here on view, most of them old skins that are beginning to thicken. An essay on Beatrix Potter also raises the vexed question of criticising and discussing the work of authors who are still living. Greene decided that Miss Potter must have been undergoing an emotional disturbance when she wrote *Mr Tod*. In a 'somewhat acid letter' she denied this. I can only hope that I will not receive an acid letter from *him* on account of a bad guess or even a bull's eye, and that he will remember that he himself has been tempted to probe into another's private life. Miss Potter's displeasure brings up the whole question of biocriticism, the weaving of work and life, in the manner of Lytton Strachey, Hugh Kingsmill and Peter Quennell— what Miss Potter objected to, not very accurately, as 'the Freudian school' of criticism. It can be very revealing and it is probably essential for a full understanding. But should it be applied to living writers? It is a tasteless practice, to say the least. To hint at emotional disturbances may be justifiable, but it may also reopen wounds. The question is, where will it stop? Some critics would not refrain from spying on their victims or rigging up concealed mikes, from reading syphilis or dementia praecox into their work.[1] All in the course of a 'sacred duty', for it is easy for the most flippant scribbler to persuade himself that he *is*, for the time being, Literature. But if we do not resort to these tactics there is no decision to make, or perhaps it is

[1] I may confess now that I tried to persuade someone to break into Greene's flat to get hold of one of his personal publications. I can only admit this because my persuasion failed.

made for us. We can never know enough about the living to write the last word on their works. We have not access to their letters, and the mere fact that we have to suspect 'emotional disturbance' (itself a very vague condition) underlines our ignorance. We are compelled to guess and make hypotheses, and then wait for confirmation or denial—if we live long enough.

One thing is made clear by this collection, and that is the veneration Greene feels for Henry James, whom he calls The Master. No fewer than five essays are devoted to his work. Henry James is enlisted to clarify an attitude towards evil which had been latent in Greene's work since the beginning but which began to be given especial emphasis about this time. One of the functions of this book, indeed, is the focusing of attention upon certain matters that fill Greene's mind—the reality of evil, for example, and failure. He decides that James's later novels are mainly concerned with corruption, but that 'to render the highest justice to corruption you must retain your innocence'. It recalls that old and familiar oscillation between adultery and the corruption of children, the ambivalence of standards according to experience. 'Evil was overwhelmingly part of his visible universe', he wrote in the same essay ('Henry James: the Private Universe'). He is always on the lookout for this recognition of evil and finds it in the least likely places. We usually associate Dickens with a wishy-washy goodness that does not impress. Greene fastens on to this very point and asks, *Why* does it not impress? *Why* is it that the punishment of the wicked in *Oliver Twist* is so unconvincing? *Why* is it that the truly creative aspect of that novel is to be found in Oliver's 'temporary escapes' and his 'inevitable recapture'? It is because even Dickens could not deny the omnipresent evil and his attempts to meet the tastes of his time were sadly banal. *Oliver Twist* is a nightmare with agreeable fripperies tacked on. Is it too fantastic to imagine, Greene asks, that there creeps into many of Dickens's novels 'the eternal and alluring taint of the Manichee, with its simple and terrible explanation of our plight, how the world was made by Satan and not by God, lulling us with the music of despair?' And in another essay he quotes T. S. Eliot with approval: 'Most people are only a very little alive; and to awaken them to the spiritual is a very great responsibility: it is only when

they are so awakened that they are capable of real Good, but that at
the same time they become first capable of Evil.'

This obsession with evil could be attributed to his religion but in
fact is only confirmed by it. The Church of England, in its doctrine,
asserts the existence of evil but very few of its members really believe
in it. More Catholics do because their spiritual education is more
intense and imaginative than that of Protestants. All the same, the
belief of most English Catholics in evil is an intellectual matter and
does not touch their conduct. Most of us are Pelagians today. Greene
is an oddity in that he seems to have been born with a belief in
Original Sin. He was not brought up to believe in it—at least, he
makes no mention of such teaching, and if there had been any I am
sure he would have referred to it at some point or other. But as a boy
he was immensely impressed by Marjorie Bowen's *The Viper of
Milan*, a tale of unrelieved treachery. He was fourteen, he says, and
from that time he began to write. This book seemed to release a
creative flood in him, and the key to it was the character of della
Scala, whose corruption was so accessible. It was useless for Greene
to hope that he could one day become the Sir Henry Curtis of *King
Solomon's Mines*, but della Scala was a different matter. He 'turned
from an honesty that never paid and betrayed his friends and died
dishonoured and a failure even at treachery'—even young G. Greene
could manage that. In later years he learnt to recognize the whiff of
corruption in others; his well-trained nose sniffed round the library
shelves and found it here and there, in the few authors who had
sufficient understanding to write truthfully. He recognized the
quality in James—I feel inclined to believe that it was his initial
admiration of James that convinced him that James had stumbled on
the secret, despite his apparent disinterest in religious interpretations,
rather than the other way round. Then it became easy to find evidence of James's awareness of independent evil: 'there was no
victory for human beings, that was his conclusion; you were
punished in your own way, whether you were of God's or the
Devil's party.[1] James believed in the supernatural, but he saw evil as
an equal force with good'. So did Dickens, according to Greene,
and so, I suspect, does Greene. For Greene's sympathy with another

[1] The same view is expressed in *It's A Battlefield*.

person is a kind of pell-mell action, revealing a number of practically identical souls wearing different masks. Greene was obsessed with failure, and was constantly nagged by a past failure of his own. So, then, must be James. It is hinted that James may have evaded military service during the American Civil War, and the guilt of that memory, that failure, haunted him forever after. Greene becomes a Catholic. It is rather galling to think that James was so unimpressed by religious interpretations, but this does not prevent Greene from doing his damnedest to show that Catholic doctrine and Catholic ritual impinged rather forcefully on James's consciousness. But even he cannot go so far as to capture James for the Roman Church. Nevertheless, he is able to state that his novels 'are only saved from the deepest cynicism by the religious sense'.

We are told that this religiosity of James was always a mirror of his experience, i.e., it was not doctrinal. Experience taught him to believe in supernatural evil but not in supernatural good.[1] I have no doubt at all that Greene is using James as a mouthpiece in all this religious discussion. There is plenty of evidence that he finds the discipline of his Church irksome. It is all very well to write about the duty of disloyalty but not many fellow-religionists are likely to support such a heretical claim. In essays like this he can express his doubts and misgivings and give them more positive utterance than he would dare in his own person. Then he can write *The End of the Affair* under his own name, a novel which simply throbs with Manichæan tensions, and he can even attempt to portray a good woman. No-one is really impressed, of course, although I doubt if anyone would call her a fake. Many people, however, have called her creator a fake, and on her account. As for Greene, he is pretty well convinced that a good woman is a contradiction in terms, although at times a rebellious voice cries out, That's all very well, but Evil cannot exist without Good, and you cannot express Evil without also being capable of expressing Good! James is again shanghaied into Greene's service when the latter writes, 'There is no

[1] There are contradictions in these essays. 'James believed in the supernatural, but he saw evil as an equal force with good' ('The Private Universe'). 'Experience taught him to believe in supernatural evil, but not in supernatural good' ('The Religious Aspect').

possibility of a happy ending: this is surely what James always tells us.' It is certainly what Greene always tells us. And so it goes on, an interesting ventriloquist act. 'You must betray or, more fortunately perhaps, you must be betrayed.' Greene, on a score of occasions; attributed to James; and in direct descent from *The Viper of Milan*.

It is well known that James's dramatic efforts were flops, and tears have been shed on this account. Greene knows better. 'Fate was kind to him: other artists have had the same intention and have been caught by success. James found neither cash nor credit on the stage and returned enriched by his failure.' The failures that mean so much to Greene first beckoned from *The Viper*. In the moment of success the seeds of failure are sown. Even at school, he tells us, he had an intuitive conviction of this condition of life. The champion runner would one day sag over the tape, the head of the school would 'atone' during forty dreary undistinguished years (the strange use of that word hints at an unbearable tyranny) . . . 'and when success began to touch oneself too, however mildly, one could only pray that failure would not be held off for too long'. Is it insincere? Probably not. It could have started as an exciting pose but we can grow into our poses, as Koestler says. The title essay traces all the salient acts and beliefs of manhood back to childhood—in AE's words:

> In the lost boyhood of Judas
> Christ was betrayed.

Greene says he often wished he had not passed beyond *King Solomon's Mines*, and had become a consular official in Sierra Leone. I can believe this. It's pretty dull being a successful novelist. It's only exciting when you're not. But he also says the attraction of failure began at a much earlier date, before success had been won. At seventeen he believed that love and despair were inextricable, that a successful love is a contradiction in terms.

Every creative writer worth our consideration, he says, is the victim of an obsession. With Henry James it was fear of treachery, with Hardy pity for human beings, with de la Mare it was death. There is no need to search for Greene's. Without failure and waste his emotions cannot be roused. Think back to that story, 'Men At

Work', where Greene laid bare the falsity of the immense wartime propaganda machine. We can be quite sure that if the Ministry of Information had been efficient and well organized he would have remained silent, perhaps frustrated. He would not have praised because praise only appeals to the mediocre side of his talent. He is quickened by failure, and he can only praise when there is something magnificent about the failure or when , in an obscure way, the failure is indicative of a greater success (as in *The Power and the Glory*). But if we follow this predilection to its logical end we have to discover a failure in every object of his admiration. This is, in fact, not difficult, and Greene has faced up to it. (Did he not once find God lovable because He was a failure? Or was that Scobie?) James's failure was in the theatre, but it was a much more serious failure than we may have imagined. 'Unwillingly we have to condemn the Master for a fault we had previously never suspected the possibility of his possessing', runs the last sentence of the essay—and the fault is incompetence. There could not be a worse one in Greene's eyes. Like many men who have wrestled with the intractable problems of right and wrong, good and evil, he reverts with relief to the manageable problems of craft. Incompetence is failure, but it is a particularly shocking form of failure, for it can be overcome. The kind of failure that Greene most admires and even desires is that imposed by God.

Greene is deeply conscious of his craft. He is careful not to overwrite—in two or three places he has stated that five hundred words a day are his quota. Much of his craft is obviously instinctive and in addition he is extremely chary of pontificating about it. (There is a strong temptation for writers to become as portentous as politicians about their work.) When Walter Allen tried to persuade Greene to talk about his craft in a broadcast programme ('We Write Novels', May 1955) he met with very limited success. One got the impression that Greene didn't like being interviewed and even that he didn't like Allen. Perhaps it *is* embarrassing for the professional chronicler of failure to describe publicly how he ensures success. He began by saying that at first he wanted to separate his thrillers from the ordinary novels and write them under another name, but his publishers objected. 'In one's entertainments one is primarily interested in having an exciting story as in a physical action, with just enough character to give interest in the action, because you can't be interested in the action of a mere dummy. In the novels I hope one is primarily interested in the character and the action takes a minor part.' In his insistence on action he was conscious of revolting against the best writers of his youth, such as Virginia Woolf. When Allen tried to nudge him into talking about the novelist's job in terms of 'significance', Greene wouldn't bite and even called the practice a 'little pompous'. He then said, 'It comes incidentally, I should say, but it's more of an obsession, one has got to walk down that particular street, certain emotions may come into one's mind as he walks down the street, but one's first motive was simply to walk down that street'. I think Greene's theory of obsession is a valuable one. Self-conscious critics such as Allen and Pritchett fall too easily into the trap of isolating 'significance'. Significance there will be, but the significance of significance dissolves when the latter is abstracted from the generating obsession. Being creative writers themselves, Allen and Pritchett know this at a deep level but are not always conscious of it.

Allen's next trap, again avoided rather contemptuously by Greene, was the one called 'influence'. Conrad, James and F. M. Ford, of course, but: 'Who can speak about influences, I mean there's so much that's in the subconscious, and I've even been influenced by non-fiction'.[1] Did he travel for material? No. (Greene must be one of the most restless novelists since Laurence Oliphant, who was not primarily a novelist.) But his travel was essential for writing fiction? 'No, I think it's to escape claustrophobia, to escape boredom, and incidentally a subject may come.' Allen's last fling, a little despairing,

[1] Apart from the writers mentioned, Greene certainly comes in the line initiated by Turgeniev and carried on by, among others, Gissing and George Moore in England. Although they could recognize good and evil they refused to burden their works with what Henry James called 'the dull dispute' of what is and is not 'moral'. The Victorian novel had almost foundered under its insistence on abstracting man's moral nature. The French had become artificial and mechanical. This new strain managed to present man in all his variety, and did not judge him (or, ultimately, the novelist) by his 'depth' or metaphysical understanding. Every now and again the novel is assaulted by efforts to categorize its purpose, and it must be repeatedly saved by writers who are concerned with the mere fact of being. An occasional philosopher-novelist is a useful stimulus. A tribe of them is a literary tragedy.

one feels, was to try to persuade Greene that his love of practical jokes lay behind his Entertainments.[1] (The connection is not very clear.) Greene didn't think much of that either, and said: 'I don't see any resemblance to one's practical jokes and one's ordinary work, except that one has this wild and crazy ambition one day to write a comic novel'.[2] I noted in a previous chapter how much more likely Greene is to say something of interest about his craft in an unexpected, even fugitive piece of writing. In the same year as *The Lost Childhood* was published he supplied an Introduction to Philip Caraman's translation of *John Gerard, the Autobiography of an Elizabethan*. The book appealed to him because of its 'danger in the familiar lane, death lying in wait in all the peaceful countryside'. Then he adds the little analogy which expresses much more sharply than answers to leading questions how he views his own work: 'The act of writing is very like the act of sculpture: one is provided with a rude block of facts, out of which one has to cut the only details that matter.'

Although there is only one essay, and a very short one at that, on Ford Madox Ford in this volume, compared with the five (amounting to thirty pages) on The Master, there is no doubt about Greene's admiration. During the 'thirties he made a point of reviewing Ford's books, usually in *The London Mercury*. In February 1937 we are told that Ford is 'so incontestably our finest living novelist'. This is repeated in August, with the addition of this revealing comment: 'Human nature in his books is utterly corrupt—but Mr Ford is a Catholic, and it doesn't surprise or depress him.' So Ford had everything: a clear view of corruption, the Catholic faith, and in addition he was, by worldly standards, a failure. Once again one has the

---

[1] Greene is an accomplished practical joker, the best since H. de Vere Cole, some say. His most successful effort was the Anglo-Texan Society, which never existed yet actually had seventy-eight members, including one worthy M.P., and even organized its own barbecue. He also likes to write to the Press under fictitious names, e.g., to *The Times Literary Supplement*, 19th August, 1939, signed Henry Ash, to *Time & Tide*, 27th April, 1946, signed M. E. Wimbush. The first takes up and elaborates a point taken from one of his own articles. The second asks for assistance on a biography of Ella Carney (Mrs Henry Montgomery), 'the children's writer'.

[2] There are so many grammatical errors in this discussion I presume it was unscripted.

feeling that when Greene is describing someone or passing judgment, the someone concerned is seen in a mirror: 'he had never really believed in human happiness, his middle life had been made miserable by passion, and he had come through'. It was written of Ford but I fancy it would fit Greene, except that he was not sure yet whether he would come through. He wonders at Dickens because the 'dead hand' of fame fell on his shoulder so early, and yet he survived. The only success Ford could have would be posthumous. Whatever happens to the author, whether he is a failure or a success, it isn't easy for him to be a pleasant human being. Both roles are usually crippling.

But accompanying this central theme of failure is that of the lost childhood. It is the unhappy childhood that persists, acting on later life like a malignant germ. Unhappy childhoods left indelible marks on Dickens, Kipling and Saki; childhoods that were intended to be happy but which were distorted by over-indulgence, such as those of Browning and Ruskin, were just as influential. It is not that all later unhappiness is related to those early moments of suffering, but later experience. Greene's first treatment of this theme is to be found in a story entitled 'The Innocent', 1937. A man takes a tart back to his childhood home town for the night. He is overcome by nostalgia, 'the smell of innocence'. He slips out to look at a house where he had had dancing lessons. He had once loved a little girl there, but she had taken no notice of him. (Greene noted the peculiar tragedy of childhood love, that it can never find satisfaction.) He remembered how he had left messages filled with a beautiful passion for her in a hole in the gatepost. One was still there and he took it out to read the beautiful passion—but it was an obscene drawing! This story has much in common with the much later one, 'The Blue Film', which describes the tender, even pure, feelings experienced by a man who takes part in an obscene film. The point of the first story is that when the man found the drawing he knew it had been innocent. 'I had believed I was drawing something with a meaning unique and beautiful; it was only now after thirty years of life that the picture seemed obscene.' Now this story takes us further than the miseries of Dickens's blacking factory or Kipling's boarding house at Southsea. Childhood is capable of more than suffering. It has the blessed gift of innocence, denied to adults, a gift that transmutes even the most sordid experiences and circumstances. So the Lost Childhood is a compound of miseries and innocence, but (and this is the horror of the condition) it is the miseries that persist and breed and damn, while any attempt to prolong the innocence is doomed to failure. Again we come to the fact of failure. Greene's works are a maze where all paths eventually lead to the one destination.

In December 1954 Greene wrote a revealing little article for *Time & Tide* called 'The Revenge'. As a boy he read Q's *Foe-Farrell* three or four times. (It is rather surprising that he does not mention this book at all elsewhere.) It is a story of pursuit and revenge. At one time pursuer and pursued find themselves together and alone in an open boat in the Pacific. Greene felt that he could discern the desire for revenge as a motive in his own career. At school he had been bullied by two boys named Carter and Watson. He met Watson ('a foxy-faced man with a small moustache') in Kuala Lumpur in 1951. Watson spoke nostalgically of him and Carter as old friends, absolutely inseparable. 'I wondered all the way back to my hotel', writes Greene, 'whether I would ever have written a book if it had not been for Watson and the dead Carter, if those years of humiliation had not given me an excessive desire to prove that I was good at something,[1] however long the effort might prove.' We have here a cluster of emotions, typified by revenge. If we apply the rule that Greene's choice of names often bears a judgment value, we find our understanding of certain passages considerably enriched. In *The Bear Fell Free* it was Farrell who tried to fly the Atlantic. He was betrayed by the ex-war hero Carter, who slept with Farrell's wife. But there is another reference to Carter in the essay, 'The Lost Childhood'. He was a reincarnation of the dreaded Visconti in *The Viper of Milan*. 'I had watched him pass by many a time in his black Sunday suit smelling of mothballs. His name was Carter. He exercised terror from a distance like a snowcloud over the young fields.' I wonder if it's going too far to connect Drover with Carter? Conrad Drover betrayed his brother. It was another case of adultery.[2]

---

[1] The similarity with Orwell is a close one.

[2] The man who performed in an obscene film and, when he saw it several years later, realized that his behaviour had not been obscene, whatever an audience might think, was also a Carter ('The Blue Film').

The connection of childhood experience with adult behaviour is nothing new. Where Greene goes further than other writers on this theme is his claim that the creative writer perceives his world once and for all in childhood. A writer's career is an effort to illustrate his private world in terms of the great public world shared with others. The intensity of feeling and of involvement that Greene exhibits in his novels, and which I have referred to several times, is a product of the child mind which still remains exceptionally active. Greene is a living refutation of the idea that the child must die before the adult can emerge. It is also clear that what is understood by emotional maturity is not blocked by the persistence of a child's capacity for feeling. Greene is at once more mature and more raw, in the way that a child is raw, than any of his contemporaries. When there is an abrupt break between childhood and maturity, the person is hindered in his adjustment by having only dead material to draw upon. For instance, Greene stated in a broadcast (March 1947) that it is only in childhood that books have any deep influence on our lives. 'In later life we admire, we are entertained, perhaps we modify some views we already hold, but we are more likely to find in books merely a confirmation of what is in our minds already. As in a love affair, it is our own features that we see reflected flatteringly back.' The childhood books hold their power, the dreams are nearer the surface, the primitive land can be reached through a green baize door.

One of the most important essays from the critic's point of view in *The Lost Childhood* is 'The Revolver in the Corner Cupboard', first published in *The Saturday Book*. In this he describes how, at the age of seventeen, he found a revolver belonging to his brother in a cupboard in the bedroom they shared. His brother was away. The revolver had six chambers and ammunition was at hand. Graham was on holiday and bored. The first day of a holiday, especially from boarding school, is all happiness. Afterwards there is too much freedom—and 'freedom bored me unutterably'. That in itself is a revealing remark. Graham decided, not for the first time, to flirt with death. I would like to recall the death-obsession in his poetry, and my statement that it could not be dismissed as easily as we normally dismiss such moods in the work of young men. For from the age of eleven or twelve he had repeatedly played a game with death. (Perhaps, like the little boy in 'The End of the Party', he had been half convinced, as so many of our ancestors had been wholly convinced, that death really was the gateway to a much more delightful condition of existence.) He says he was overcome by boredom. He drank hypo, believing it was poisonous; he tried hay fever lotion, but the cocaine in it seemed merely to neutralize his mood; he ate a bunch of deadly nightshade with only a slight narcotic effect; he had swallowed twenty aspirins; and now he stole across Berkhamsted Common, slipped a bullet into the chamber of his revolver, and spun the barrel. None of these were attempts at suicide. They were gambles, and in the case of Russian roulette the odds were five to one against. The game served as a drug for a while, and he played it six times. The odds had been reduced to evens and he still lived. After the last occasion he lied to his parents that a friend had invited him to Paris, and he set off to find a new antidote to boredom.

This incident, or series of incidents, provided the subject for the first and last of his poems in *Babbling April*. Without the biographical information supplied in the essay they had merely appeared to be pointless exercises in sensationalism. The first is actually called 'Sensations' and contains these lines:

> How we make our timorous advances to death, by
>   pulling the trigger of a revolver, which we
>   already know to be empty
> Even as I do now.
> And how horrified I should be, I who love Death in
>   my verse, if I had forgotten
> To unload.

When I first read that I could not control my excitement. Greene was a swindler, his essay was a fraud, he was deceiving us for the sake of a romantic reputation. But referring to the essay again I saw that this poem was written to be left on his desk so that if he lost his gamble there would be evidence of an accident, and his parents would at least not suffer from the knowledge of the truth. The other poem is an inferior one, and ends with these lines:

Will it be mist and death
At the bend of this sunset road,
Or life reinforced
By the propinquity of death?
Either is gain.
It is a gamble which I cannot lose.

I believe that the risk of death affects, sometimes enriches, the spirit
in a way that cannot be effected by other means. (Similarly, profound suffering is another beneficial agent.) Greene used his revolver
as Huxley used mescalin, to induce dimensions of spiritual experience which would be otherwise acquired only through the
accidents of one's personal life. Whether this type of machinery does
have the required effect is a matter that requires far more discussion
than I can afford to give here. What must be incontrovertible is that
an emotional experience of some kind results. The quality of it is
doubtful. I would like to quote Edward Sackville West, however,
in his essay on Greene in *The Month* (September 1951), entitled 'The
Electric Hare'. He writes: 'This curious confession is disturbing, as
any sign of desperation always is; but when Mr Greene concludes,
after finally returning the revolver to the cupboard, that he simply
went off to Paris, because "the war against boredom had got to go
on", we do not feel that we have been told the whole truth about the
episode.' Why, for instance, if the poem 'Sensations' was a lie and
was written for the purely mundane purpose of putting other people
off the track, was it not only included in *Babbling April* but even
given pride of place? One doesn't even have to question Greene's
honour. Memory can play funny tricks. George IV died believing
he had been present at Waterloo.

It is time to sum up. When Greene's criticism is gathered together we realize how very good it is. He has an eye as quick and
alert for the significant point as Pritchett, but his expression is far
more incisive. Greene has great creative and critical talent yet he is
not what we understand by the term intellectual. Trilling or Savage,
Empson or Tate could probably tie him in knots in rational and
logical argument. But his standpoint would be lived and felt where
theirs would be more likely to be veiled algebra. Perhaps it accounts

for his admiration of Sir Herbert Read, who is imaginative and intellectual in fits and starts, and rarely manages to fuse the two. Rather wistfully he observes the parade of the intellectuals and wishes he could take part. Comedians are unhappy because they are not allowed to play Hamlet, and Mark Twain died convinced that his *Joan of Arc* was his masterpiece. Greene wishes to write a comic novel. There is a hint of ambivalence, possibly depending on his state of health or digestion: intellectualism is the negation of life, intellectualism is what I lack. But he has something much more valuable than the ability to be consistently rational. He has unerring good judgment in all literary matters. He can always be relied upon to see through falsity and to detect the ring of truth in others. His criticism is much more free of fault than his fiction. He does not adopt a patronizing attitude towards Chesterton (not because he is a Catholic, for he can be very hard on a bad Catholic writer) and he recognizes the quality of de la Mare. These are two test cases: it is fashionable to ignore the one and praise the other for the wrong reasons. A good critic does not waste time on obvious faults. He searches for rare virtues.[1]

He is not taken in by Big Man propaganda, for instance. He cannot for long restrain a sneer at the expense of the rationalist enemy, the man in his suit of scrubby black, the man who cannot tell polite untruths, the professional Honest Man. He does not believe that criticism, even with the help of Freud, can ever become a science. He finds the academic brain inhuman and unreliable. He enjoys few things so much as attacking bores and sentimentalists. Back in 1936 he had written entertainingly of a horse called James Agate, with 'his nervous distrust of what he called highbrows (from the names he mentions I think other horses might consider them steam-rollers), his very natural affection for *Cavalcade*' (*London Mercury*). In the following year he applied the same treatment to Godfrey Winn: 'the set boyishness, fifth-form diffidence and thinning hair . . . the eyes look out at us so innocently, so candidly, so doggily . . .' (*Night and Day*, after his assault on Shirley Temple, when Greene was temporarily leaving the ladies alone.) And now, in the book of essays,

[1] There is a deprecatory reference to Chesterton in a later story, 'A Visit to Morin', however.

his 'Portrait of a Maiden Lady' is reprinted. The lady is Beverley Nichols. It is a superb example of controlled, directed venom, and is in the best interests of literature. 'I would hazard a guess that she housekeeps for her brother, who may be a canon or perhaps a rural dean. In that connection she may have met the distinguished ecclesiastics who have noticed a previous book so kindly'—for the author's name must be a pseudonym. Neville Braybrooke, writing in the *Irish Monthly*, criticizes Greene for his cruelty. 'The method is not suited to objective presentation and when so treated appears cruel without excuse; there is no question of its leading to kindness.' That is true, but a little precious. It is intended to lead to extinction, surely an honourable aim under the circumstances! And I would also defend 'Great Dog of Weimar'. This admirable creature could speak by barks! His communications were as unedifying as those of a psychic guide but that worried nobody—hang the sense so long as it comes in an unorthodox way! 'I have always suspected dogs', writes Greene: 'solid, well-meaning, reliable, they seem to possess all the least attractive human virtues.' All very malicious, of course, but for God's sake don't let morality erode humour. Apparently each species has a group-soul. Perhaps Shaw is now merged with Agate, and both wait for Winn and Nichols. And perhaps the Speaking Dog of Weimar will jump the boundaries by virtue of his expressive barks and help guide the living world to vegetarianism, perpetual kindness, weeded gardens and comfortable stables for soft-eyed horses.

XVII

HATRED REVIVES

Nineteen Fifty-One
'The End of the Affair'

CATHOLICS were worried by *The Heart of the Matter*. Waugh said it was a 'mad blasphemy'. Greene was puzzled: 'I wrote a book about a man who goes to hell—*Brighton Rock*—another about a man who goes to heaven—*The Power and the Glory*. Now I've simply written one about a man who goes to purgatory. I don't know what all the fuss is about,' he told a *Time* reporter. It wasn't the Catholics who were upset by his next novel, but the barbarians of the Protestant North. *Time's* review was headed 'Shocker'. Greene's portrait appeared on the cover against a visceral background of greyish cave narrowing to a white cross on blue. The caption read, 'Adultery can lead to Sainthood'. This was an expected reaction, of course. Sarah Miles had committed adultery, therefore she had done nothing else in her life. It was the case of Father Damien all over again. Greene gave a party and told the reporter he felt like hell— he had been up all night drinking with the priest. Certainly a lot of people would think ill of such information, and he rejoiced at the thought.

He had Waugh's approval this time, and it was unqualified. Summarizing the book he wrote: 'That, very baldly, is the story, a singularly beautiful and moving one. This *précis* gives no indication of the variety and precision of the craftmanship. The relationship of lover to husband with its crazy mutation of pity, hate, comradeship, jealousy and contempt is superbly described. For the first time in Mr Greene's work there is humour. The heroine is consistently lovable. Again and again Mr Greene has entered fully into a scene of high emotion which anyone else would have shirked. Instead of pistol-shots there are tears' (*The Month*, September 1951). The novel had a mixed reception, ranging from adulation to contempt. I quote this opinion because it approximates to my own view, for the same reasons. I am glad Mr Waugh drew attention to the craftsmanship. In most criticisms of fiction today there is no reference at all to this very important matter. The 'mutations' of emotion are admirably handled. And it is very true that there is one passage, Bendrix's first meeting with Parkis, that is superb comedy. In other words, Greene is still learning new tricks, an enviable achievement at his age.

A creative writer must have an obsession, Greene has written. Up to now his has been failure, but in this novel there is a switch to hatred. An American critic, Max Cosman, has drawn attention to the obsessive hatred that has in fact been present in a great part of Greene's work. He claims that the word occurs at least two dozen times in *The Man Within*. That may be so, but in his first novel Greene was still an apprentice and had not learnt how to get the full impact of emotional intensity on to paper. *The End of the Affair* is heavy with hatred, and it appeared again, though less overtly, in *The Living Room*. It is probable that *The End of the Affair* was partly the product of a personal crisis, and the hatred had to be spilled out before Greene could recover his balance. (It is an unbalanced novel, verging on insanity at times, like *The Ministry of Fear*, though more dangerously.) But hatred is also one of the emotional portholes through which Greene's genius escapes (they are *data* for the novelist, Thackeray had his cheerfulness and Wells his irritability) and again we can see how *The Viper of Milan* nudged at something only too ready to move: Giannoti hated Visconti, who hated della Scala (though he was believed dead), who reciprocated. Visconti's sister Valentine hated her brother and Graziosa, in her gentle fashion, hated Valentine.

Greene, through the medium of his character Bendrix (also an author), writes out of bitterness. 'What a dull lifeless quality this bitterness is. If I could write with love, but if I could write with love, I would be another man: I would never have lost love'. From the beginning, then, he admits his mental state, and the stage is set for an interesting psychological examination. Now many people object automatically to anything that comes out of bitterness. They say, and rightly, that bitterness precludes sympathy and without sympathy the creation of character is impossible. The only drawback is a very obvious one—if no-one is to write out of bitterness there will be one aspect of experience denied to literature. It is one more product of our senseless demand for excellence and nothing but excellence, and a failure to recognize that no end of demands for excellence will ever produce it to order. Literary excellence comes occasionally, unplanned and unexpected. For the rest of the time we would be advised to welcome the best we can get out of bitterness, fatuity, ecstasy, meanness, jollity, misery and a host of other qualities. They won't be first-rate but they may be interesting. So *The End of the Affair* is written knowingly out of bitterness, and a refusal to accept that is equivalent to a refusal to acknowledge that water is wet.

Now although he is not a superb literary creation, Bendrix is a rounded character. Some of the hatred he feels for his old lover, Sarah, and her husband, Henry, is merely the reaction from frustrated love. Its intensity is a measure of the love that produced it. But there is also a display of unnecessary spite and cruelty which cannot be attributed to the same source. The petty spite is inborn and is therefore a failing in character. Bendrix behaves towards Parkis, the pathetic old detective, with consistent nastiness. He is a person with a considerable store of natural unpleasantness, which has been aggravated and stimulated by circumstances. I find that while reading the book I marked a passage on page ninety-nine and made this comment: 'At this point the book turns rotten—the nastiness is too much. From now on Bendrix can only be a person worth listening to by accident'. (I am not quite sure what I meant by the latter sentence but it has a fine ring to it.) The passage is the one where Bendrix deliberately hurts Smythe by mentioning Sarah's name to him. But a few pages later I find this note: 'On the other hand we must remember the effects of hate and suspicion and envy'. In other words I had been wrong, too hasty. I had been condemning the novel on the basis of a character. No-one dreams of condemning *Othello* because of Iago, but that is because Shakespeare is by now sacrosanct. We have gradually allowed our judgment to be coarsened by a puritanical attitude towards morality and by a

H

false relationship between human beings and abstractions. Bendrix is a cad. This is no criticism of *The End of the Affair*. If his cad-dishness were unconvincing it would be, but in fact he is so credible a cad only great skill could portray him. And not even morality can condemn Greene. He knows Bendrix is a cad and says so frequently (which is more than Shakespeare says about Iago). 'Hate and suspicion and envy had driven me so far away, etc.', he writes.

Then Bendrix begins to treat Sarah like a prey. He follows her silently through London, exulting over her fear. He felt pity for his victim. But the really powerful impression gained by the reader is of Bendrix's moral deterioration. He is behaving now as he could not have behaved a few months before. Greene has achieved the rare feat of depicting a man in process, rather than in a series of discon-nected states, which is relatively easy. A little later, with Sarah dead, the hatred has lost its object, and so it is transferred to God. God had her now, and he should be hated as bitterly as Henry and Smythe had been—and, of course, Sarah herself. Bendrix is insane. If he were to stay in this state for long he would be certified. There is a quantitative aspect to insanity. We are left with the ruins of a man. At the end of Bendrix's talk with Henry and the priest it becomes clear that the author is perfectly well aware of what had happened. He had not been carried away by his emotions and trapped into revealing himself. Bendrix may well be Greene, but the point I wish to make is that Greene can see Bendrix whole. Here is a man, he says, who has been nearly destroyed by frustrated desire, and a very nasty specimen he is. 'I wanted to defend myself,' he says simply, dropping all bravado. For he knows defence is necessary. He did not consider nastiness was an admirable social virtue, like Peter Cheyney. 'Grief and disappointment are like hate: they make men ugly with self-pity and bitterness. And how selfish they make us too.'

We get a good idea of what is in Greene's mind (if not when he starts writing, at least by the time he has finished) from the quota-tions he uses as epigraphs. Here it is from Léon Bloy: 'Man has places in his heart which do not yet exist, and into them enters suffering in order that they may have existence'. One is reminded of

Proust's statement that without suffering there can be no wisdom.[1] Through his suffering Bendrix felt new areas come to life. Intensity of suffering brought first madness, but at the end there is more than a hint that a new and healing sanity is taking its place. There is nothing new in the idea that one can find wisdom (or God) through excess. Although wisdom itself is not quantitative it can be stimulated by surfeit, which produces world-weariness. Many people today believe that travel or acquaintance automatically foster a deeper under-standing, which is nonsense. The kind of surfeit I am referring to is mental, and can be either intellectual or emotional, for there is no defined line of demarcation. But nothing can take the place of experience within its own particular field—analogy is, at best, a poor substitute. A man cannot write about love without first loving, although many think they can. (Greene obviously did when he wrote *The Man Within*.) Paradoxically, he won't get far in his know-ledge of love until he has also experienced the end of love. Once the rage was over Bendrix was certainly a wiser man than he had been before it started, and much wiser than when it had been at its height. We know nothing about the mind (our own or those of others, which we approach through analogy) until it has been under stress. Hence suffering is a necessary ingredient of wisdom. (Shock can help—the shock of near death, for instance. Once again I would like to compare playing with a loaded revolver with the effect of certain drugs. This type of school is only a kindergarten, however.)

A hasty reading might suggest cynicism on the part of both Bendrix and the author. In fact, the book is an exercise in self-exploration. The cynicism belongs to the affect that is being studied,

[1] The Catholic view is that everything depends on the spirit *in which* the suffering is endured. Simone Weil, who was a Jewess but had close affiliations to the Catholic standpoint in her thought, wrote: 'In hours of disaster our vital instinct survives the severing of our attachments and twines itself blindly round anything that can serve it as support, as a plant grips hold with its tendrils ... From this point of view disaster is always hideous, as life stripped naked always is, as a stump is, as the swarming of insects is Life without form. There, sur-vival is the only attachment left—having no other object than itself—a Hell!' The spirit of Bendrix's suffering was self-destruction, but there are signs to-wards the end that he is acquiring grace. The grace comes from outside (he is certainly reluctant to receive it) and we are allowed to suppose that it is the result of intercession.

not the attitude of the study itself. It is obvious that Bendrix is not a very pleasant character but we should not run to the other extreme and assume he is an exceptionally nasty one. He is only that when the stress becomes too great. He has lost a woman whom he still desires and for the sake of his self-esteem he must pretend that the affair is over even from his own point of view. This leads to a boastful, slightly vicious form of expression which is as natural and inevitable as joy and generosity would be to a man whose love is still whole. He is fully aware of his own egotism and refers to it shamefacedly on several occasions. The novel is a good example of one that is unpleasant in feeling, accurate in expression and justified in essence. Its total effect is of truth and the achievement of understanding through intensity.

In this novel Greene shows a mature grasp of sexual relations rare in English literature. Puritanism and nonconformism have so conditioned our attitude to sex that we are still largely incapable of treating it naturally. Few modern English writers have managed to write convincingly of the sexual relation between adults. When they have had the ability, as Swinburne had it, they have had to conceal it beneath verbal canopies or miss it out altogether. A mature attitude is more commonly found in French fiction. Ignace Legrand's *The Land Within* is a case in point, where the sex is taken in the author's stride and is not viewed with awe or sheepishly treated as of no importance. Yet when he leaves the sexual relationship he can be guilty of the grossest sentimentality that causes the English reader to wince —*vide* his *Embassy Train*. It is interesting to note what happens to the French attitude when it becomes self-conscious and is doctored for export, as in many films but notably in *La Ronde*, an immense success in England yet degraded by its coyness. French coyness is as irritating as English gentility. But Greene avoids them both. He had worked through the excitement of prurience and the snigger to an attitude as hard and uncompromising as one's attitude to a landscape. In those early books, *The Man Within* and *Stamboul Train*, for instance, there were the familiar antinomies of romance and lust presented as exclusive alternatives. In the first novel they are presented romantically, in the later one realistically. The gap between the two grows less in subsequent novels but only in this one does it disappear. In *The End of the Affair* there is an undeviating directness of the lover's instinct, without reservations or attempts at justification. Sarah's love touched a point outside time. The approach is similar to Huxley's in *The Genius and the Goddess*.

For the young and inexperienced, of whatever age and whatever apparent involvement in sex, this book will appear nasty and even dirty, in both theme and treatment. One might as well expect a Stone Age savage to appreciate Henry James. It is inevitable, for the sexual theme and sexual act are, paradoxically, dirtied by innocence. The word 'love' lacks definition. It is a pity that it is used for other kinds of association, such as 'love of God', 'platonic' or 'spiritual love'. It is a dilemma the Greeks avoided. For the love between man and woman, which contains and requires lust, is something far removed from them. Love cannot reside in the marriage of true minds alone. Or, another way of putting it, true minds cannot be married without the prior marriage of the bodies. Nor is the temporal aspect to be ignored. When love is complete it can disappear. All kinds of emotions and psychological states may exist before the bodies unite, but they do not amount to love. There are innumerable passages which state this or something like this or something from which this can be deduced. 'It was as if quite suddenly after all the promiscuous years I had grown up. My passion for Sarah had killed simple lust for ever. Never again would I be able to enjoy a woman without love.' What he does not say, and this is very noticeable, is that never again would he be able to love without lust, for he knows that that is a meaningless abstraction. It is the *simple* lust that has gone. Sarah tries to persuade herself (in her diary) and Bendrix that people can love without seeing each other. It is a desperate cry, and no-one is deceived. It is what we *ought* to believe, what the priests and moralists tell us to believe, but we cannot. It is beyond our condition while we are fully alive. God tends to get the half dead for his recruits. And even Sarah surrenders in the end. She thought of a scar on Bendrix's body, but what was the use of a loved scar if she was to be only the vapour of the spirit? 'Then I began to want my body that I hated,' she wrote, 'but only because it could love that scar. We can love with our minds, but can we love only with our minds? Love extends itself all the time, so that we can even love with our senseless nails: we love even with our clothes, so that a sleeve can feel a sleeve.'

The gasping, 'coarse', 'crude', unaesthetic love of Bendrix and Sarah on a hardwood floor is an adult love. It has managed to discard the notions of romance, pity, morality and, equally important, spiritualized psychology. It requires no justification and does not resort to abstraction. It just is. It infuriates some and touches others profoundly. For me this is the most affecting novel I have read since *Ethan Frome*. It is fatally easy for the inexperienced to think of love as they think of anything else—work, holidays, a particular problem in conduct. They apply rational rules and everything seems so simple. Love is beautiful, they say, it is the world of sweetness and light, and therefore it surrenders to the application of sweetness and light. But it does nothing of the kind. It is something that engages the whole personality, it is concerned with evil as well as good, and its manifestations (like those of art) will be found in ugliness as well as in beauty. In her diary Sarah approaches nearer the dark truths than Bendrix. She is wiser than he and it is an indication of Greene's skill and, in a sense, courage that he makes the woman so much superior to the man, when we consider that much of himself must be in the man. He naturally runs the risk of identification, and he invites criticism on the grounds of Bendrix's petty savagery. In her diary Sarah glimpses the many dimensions of love when she writes, 'All today Maurice has been sweet to me. He tells me often that he has never loved another woman so much. He thinks that by saying it often he will make me believe it. But I believe it simply because I love him in exactly the same way. If I stopped loving him, I would cease to believe in his love.' In the face of such perceptions the serious undergraduate view of love, ineffable and yet defined in simple absolutes, is broken to pieces. It is the same when Bendrix looks through her childhood books, after her death, relics of a past when they had both been happy and did not know of each other's existence. The sentiments are exact. We have passed beyond romantic love, undergraduate wisdom, married decency, the Indian Summer, to the final stage in love's scaffolding. I know of only one other book which comes to grips with the lover's situations so realistically and so disturbingly. It is *Words and Darkness*, by Axel Heyst. It was published in 1946 and went practically unnoticed, probably because its publishers did not have what is known in the trade as a 'good imprint'. The farcical conventions of our publishing allow casualties of this kind to take place.

The terrible intensity of love, especially the pains of love, brought Sarah and Maurice Bendrix to God. Bendrix was determined not to believe but as he raged against God he was forced to admit that his animosity implied belief. At the novel's end he is not brought to love God, but he is defeated and tired out and begs to be left alone. Greene does not demand conversion. Recognition is enough. The priest had said as much. Then there are the supernatural events which roused criticism out of all proportion to the part they play in the story. Nevertheless, Greene is perfectly justified in making use of them. As a Catholic he believes in miracles and it is impertinent to tell him that they are not permissible. (He has expressed scorn in another place of those Catholics whose expressed beliefs are in fact only academic.) As I, a non-Catholic, also believe in miracles, I naturally find it easy to accept them when they occur in fiction, providing there are not too many of them. (It is like the famous dog in *Eyeless in Gaza;* one is permissible but we can't have them falling all over the place.) I have heard it stated that as God has created order it is not valid to believe He will on occasion disrupt the order. I don't see why God should be limited by His own creation. Surely there would be all the more reason to intervene where order existed, for intervention in chaos would be unnoticeable. But these matters are not susceptible of proof, nor can they be profitably reasoned about. The only possible criticism is that in a realist novel the action should also be realist. The view that many inexplicable events may one day be explained by rational means gets us nowhere. The only question is: do they happen now? Millions of people and thousands of books and even a considerable number of scientists declare that they do. One is left with one's own personal experience and digestive tracts. For myself, I once witnessed an event that did not belong to the familiar order, and it will take a lot to persuade me that it was not the action of a power that occasionally transcends space and time within the human field of experience.

But modern literature tends to regard the remarkable and

inexplicable (and, of course, the miraculous) as outside the legitimate bounds of fiction. As fiction cannot be allowed to become too dull there must be some kind of compensation, and this is sought through psychological abnormality, best expressed in fantastic acts of violence. These are practically commonplaces in the contemporary novel. By comparison, Greene is staid and yet manages to avoid dullness. It will appear strange to later generations that we accepted *The Naked and the Dead* almost with relief (except for that elderly editor!), yet jibbed at *The End of the Affair*. The novel was originally conceived as a chronicle of significant events. When the desire for realism became strong and did not temper the mode with abnormality, it produced Dorothy Richardson. 'But the final effect, I fear, is one of weariness,' Greene wrote of Miss Richardson's work in *The Lost Childhood* ('The Saratoga Trunk') and yet managed to quote from it what is probably the only passage in the whole massive structure containing the germ of eccentricity. He revolts against monotony, sameness and greyness, but the revolt is subtle and lacks the stridency of the self-conscious rebels. The attitude is implicit in his view of sin, which I shall refer to in a later chapter.

The End of the Affair is not a great novel, not even his best; it is irritating at times and its temporal scheme is unnecessarily difficult to follow. (Huxley managed that sort of thing better, and yet I believe the confusion was intentional. It belongs to the general dream-character that Greene never gets far away from.) But it is a courageous and adult treatment of one of the most important themes a novelist can handle. One is left with an impression of strong emotion, an emotion that overwhelms the aesthetic control.[1] We probably perceive the same emotion at work in a poem entitled 'Behind the Tight Pupils', published in *The Month*, July 1949:

> And love comes like a memory
> Of a face that is not this face, and a hand
> That is not this hand,
> Though it was not lies he told her
> When he cried, 'I love, I love',

[1] Remember Savory in *Stamboul Train:* 'In so far as the novel is founded on the author's experience, the novelist is making a confession to the public.'

When the touch of a shoulder
For a moment stirred a thought
Of once in the dark the light . . .

The sudden resort to verse, the extraordinarily emotive title and the
faint childhood memory of the last line all suggest Bendrix's cry of
pain. In the same year Greene privately printed a poetry pamphlet in
Italy (I believe this poem appeared in it) and a second one in 1951,
the year of *The End of the Affair*. I have been unable to get hold of
copies and they are of such a personal nature (I imagine) that Greene
will not lend me his own. It sounds like Bendrix again, perhaps with
a touch of Norman Douglas in uninhibited mood.

XVIII

CHRISTIANITY ON THE DEFENSIVE

Nineteen Fifty-Two
'The Glory of Mary'

THIS and the following year probably constituted the peak period of Greene's religious enthusiasm. In the past he had shown far more interest in ridiculing and condemning the Church's enemies, explicit and implicit, than in positive argument on its behalf. At about this time, however, he states that the Church is in danger and he goes to its defence. This activity coincides with personal doubts which become more and more persistent and stick out of his work at awkward angles. It seems likely that the more he doubted the more he desired to defend. The propagandist compensated for the backslider.

A new children's book, *The Little Horse Bus*, had some characteristic Greenesque touches. First of all we come across a new preoccupation, semantics, which is also developed in his journalism during the period. (See later in this chapter.) Writing of a shop he says, 'It was called the Hygienic (which only means clean) Emporium (which only means shop) Company Limited (and that means it was owned by Sir William Popkins, who never came into the shop and never put lollipops in bags. He thought lollipops were cough-drops and you bought them at a chemist's. Sir William Popkins is too ugly to draw).' This type of social comment is typically Catholic, in the tradition of Belloc, and once again Greene speaks out to the children, not addressing them as tender little flowers. There is a tendency in England to give children the impression that all Sirs are excellent fellows, even when they are the most obnoxious rogues. The story has its seedy element (derived from spiders' webs and empty bottles and tins and broken china and a chair with only three legs) and a trunk is labelled Brighton-on-Sea. This is the second children's book across which Pinkie's shadow has fallen, however faintly.

The same year saw the significant little publication from Dublin entitled *The Glory of Mary: Written in Homage*. Greene contributed an essay which had previously appeared in *Life* and which was entitled 'The Conflict Round the Dogma'. Perugino's 'Assumption of the Virgin' was reproduced on the cover. Greene's fellow-contributors were St Cyril of Alexandria, St John of Damascus, St Aelred of Rievaulx, M. L. Guerard des Lauriers, O. P. and Louis Lochet. The object of the publication was to celebrate the Holy Father's proclamation of the Dogma of the Assumption of the Mother of God, and to explain the Dogma to non-Catholics who were mystified by it yet not normally antagonistic to the Church. Greene's religious thinking at this time is best typified by the urgency expressed in this quotation: 'Since the defeat of the Turks at Lepanto the battle for Christianity has never been more critical, and sometimes it seems as though the supernatural were gathering its forces for our support, and whom should we expect in the vanguard but Our Lady? For the attack on the Son has always come through the Mother. She is the keystone of Christian doctrine. If you wish to discredit the divinity of Christ you discredit the Virgin Birth; if you wish to discredit the manhood of Christ you discredit the motherhood of Our Lady.' This was, I believe, the first occasion on which Greene had publicly discussed dogma.

He begins the essay by referring to the Protestant profession of belief in the Resurrection of the dead. To suggest that an actual resurrection has taken place, however, seems to them to be a blasphemy. On several occasions in his fiction Greene had referred to this belief and had dwelt on the implications of it. However improbable it seemed to modern man, this was one of the central beliefs of Christianity and one must not evade the issue by refusing to consider it. Mary had never been touched by original sin and so her body never suffered corruption. She remains soul and glorified body in heaven. He then passes on to various cases of alleged resurrection, mentioning the places where Mary is said to have appeared to men: Lourdes, La Salette, Carmel, Fatima, Guadeloupe, Lima. He deals at some length with the report of the Virgin of Guadeloupe, which he regards as established. There have been other claims which have been investigated and condemned by the Church.

He mentions one at Assisi which he visited in a mood of scepticism. There was a report of a similar investigation in *Lawless Roads*. He stresses that belief in these visions is not an article of the Catholic faith. Only belief in the Assumption of the Virgin is that, and in this time of crisis we should pay special attention to any message that the Virgin is said to have brought on her appearances. The message is always the same, the appeal for prayer and yet more prayer. 'Her message is as simple as that, and it may seem unimportant unless we have some realization of the terrible force of prayer, the mysterious untapped power able to move mountains.'

The millions who worship God need help in their devotions now more urgently than they have done for four centuries. That is why this moment has been chosen for the proclamation of this Dogma. It is only the definition of an old belief, there is nothing new or revolutionary about it. There are no obvious signs of heretical belief within the Church today, he wrote (unless the belief in the necessity of disloyalty be one, but he did not say that), yet Catholics cannot remain untouched by the general heresy of our time, the unimportance of the individual. 'Today the human body is regarded as expendable material, something to be eliminated wholesale by the atom bomb, a kind of anonymous carrion.' The definition of the Assumption is partly a blow struck for the eternal destiny of each human body. The emphasis is on the body. The Catholic faith's appeal to Greene was enhanced by its recognition of the body, its refusal to despise the flesh. Once again I am reminded of that early statement of Greene's, that he became a Catholic on intellectual grounds. This has always been puzzling but now it begins to make sense. The Catholic Church actually meant what it said. It did not exist on a double level, stating one thing and believing another. Intellectually this was refreshing. The doctrines might be unscientific but at least they were cohesive.

Greene now began a series of journalistic commitments, all of which were partly religious in purpose. In 1951 he spent two and a half months in Malaya. At the conclusion of an article in *Life* he said that an idea such as Communism can only be defeated by another idea, and that must be Christianity. The war was in the mind as much as in the jungle. His newly aroused semantic interests were again stimulated: he went out to investigate what the Government called an 'emergency', but 'let me call it by the right name', he wrote. It was war. Looking ahead, to 1956, we find him drawing attention to the same kind of verbal evasion or falsity in Poland. He was particularly interested in the Pax movement which was an attempt to reconcile the Church with Communism and was supported by Moscow. It had only 350 members but many fellow-travellers, including priests. Its ostensible aim was to support social and economic changes in Poland ('many of which were both necessary and admirable') and to prove Catholic 'progressiveness'. But the vast majority of Polish Catholics opposed the movement. 'Peace, Democracy, Patriot—these words when spelt with a capital have been taken over in a special sense in Eastern Europe. Certainly among the fellow-travellers of Pax there are many sincere patriots (without the capital letter) who wish to take part in the social reform of their country and if a debt has to be paid by their Catholicism they try to pay it in the smallest possible coinage.' It is worth noting that, despite Greene's conviction of crisis and the emotional climate of those days, he possessed enough sense of proportion to admit that the Communists had committed no crimes in Poland comparable to those of the Nazis.

The feeling that Greene is struggling to maintain his own faith is a strong one, however. He may have felt dimly that the onslaught of Communism was paralleled by his own private criticisms which received increasingly outspoken expression during these years. *The Heart of the Matter*, *The End of the Affair* and later *The Living Room* were not the work of a man who was completely satisfied in his faith. The first had upset many co-religionists and in all of them the opposition to Catholic doctrines expressed by some of the characters was too forthright for comfort. It seemed very likely that Greene had suffered the agonies of conscience he described. He had joined the Church at a youthful age, not fully understanding the demands it might make on him later and yet not protected by the habits that are usually inculcated during childhood. (In a new sense, his childhood was truly lost for it did not assist him in his later spiritual struggles.) And then, perhaps, he found himself trapped in the conflict between faith and desire—by now, a well-known public figure who was identified with a particular organization. How could he back out? Pride was involved, and pride had to struggle against suffering and reason combined. How much easier if, instead of being England's leading novelist, he had been an obscure consular official in Sierra Leone!

This is only a hypothesis, yet how else can we explain the greater appeal of Greene's lovers compared with his religious? He seems to understand the lost souls, the sinners and the damned, so much better than the saved, who are often complacent and unattractive. But more than understanding is involved, one has a sense of approval. At times there is a suspicion that Greene hates his religion as a prisoner hates his cell. His religious never have a satisfactory answer. Perhaps (as is occasionally remarked) they cannot know God's mind and purpose —but why then do they appear to make the effort? Greene is always looking for a sign that never comes. Do any of his characters *love* God? They usually treat Him very much like a prison Governor. Greene admits too much on behalf of his religion. Having made love the highest value, he suddenly thrusts it away and places it beneath a religious feeling that has no arguments. Yes, it is certainly the intellect at work. It is like the man who discards his mistress, whom he genuinely loves, because she is interfering with his career. It would be easier if Greene could take a leaf from F. M. Ford's book and merely *be* a Catholic, not have to appear as one also. But he cannot do this because his Catholicism lives in the brain. His religion has no sound arguments, only sophist ones. It should not be required to live by argument but by illumination. God does not require illumination but the doctrines which are said to be drawn from Him do. But fiction cannot provide this kind of illumination. The experience of art can, but not its explicit content.

Perhaps Greene resembles Byron's Aurora, who loved the 'fallen worship' simply because of its fall. Perhaps he adheres to the Church for dramatic reasons, which could never be supplied by the Anglicans or the Baptists, who have not yet played out afresh the story of Adam's disobedience. I have already said that one attraction of the Church for Greene must have been its refusal to victimize tarts. The impression grows. He is faithful to the Church because of its whiskey priests and Scobies—*not* because they are pardoned, as they would be by a God of love, but because they are damned. I know that Greene said that the priest went to heaven and Scobie to purgatory, but no-one who reads *The Power and the Glory* could be convinced that the priest deserved to go to heaven. One doesn't feel that he should triumph when the unbaptized children go the way of all sinners. Greene is fascinated by sin and his religious thinking and even his Church are tainted by sin. If his Church could adopt a merciful attitude towards the innocent it would be less interesting. There is a stupendous spiritual inversion in Greene's thinking. He preaches mercy and tolerance towards the sinners, which is fine and Christian, but at times one can almost hear his teeth gnashing at those who have omitted to sleep with someone else's wife or husband. The weakness of my case is naturally that this attitude is not explicit. Greene, after all, is not a de Sade. But it is difficult to read Greene's fiction without sensing a contempt for sinlessness.

I am not taking up a moral standpoint. I share his feelings to some extent because there is often a terrifying emptiness about those whose lives are irreproachable. And the attitude can possess its quota of positive good—if that is a concept likely to make Greene writhe, let me hastily change it to charity. When all the godly legions set to work to destroy the reputation of a 'sinner', the latter can usually count on Greene's support. In September 1952 he wrote an open letter to Charlie Chaplin, published in the *New Statesman*. 'Remembering the days of Titus Oates and the terror in England,' he wrote, 'I would like to think that the Catholics of the United States, a powerful body, would give you their sympathy and support.' He is not afraid of hierarchy when he feels injustice is being done. Why did not Cardinal Spellman speak up? He noted with sorrow that McCarthy was a Catholic. 'Have Catholics in the United States not yet suffered enough to stand firmly against this campaign of un-charity?' Some weeks later he contributed 'London Diary' to the same paper. ' "Chaplin can get by Uncle Sam's investigators as regards health. He won't have any difficulty proving he has a sound mind, although his productions have been flops since he deserted comics in favour of 'thought' pieces. When we come to the 'good morals' requirement, we had better draw a curtain over details. We shall simply state that Chaplin has few rivals in the race for top honours in giving Hollywood the reputation for being a moral cesspool." Who is the author of this attack? Crude and illiterate, loose in thought and uncharitable in expression, one easily attributes it to the arch witch-hunter himself. Unfortunately the words were written by a more responsible Catholic, a Catholic priest, in an American Catholic magazine called *The Sign.*' The real point at issue is that this kind of attack might be expected from a Congregation-alist or a Plymouth Brother. One of the main tasks of the Catholic community should be to avoid and discredit such onslaughts. For Greene it is almost its *raison d'être*.

His disloyal duty gives him some uncomfortable moments. Whenever he wants to criticize his Church it is noticeable that he turns to non-Catholic papers such as the *New Statesman*. The unpleasant truth is that the Catholics do not approve of self-criticism. They do not agree that disloyalty can be a duty. Note the tone of appealing hesitancy with which he discusses the Church's shortcomings in his review of Bernard Wall's *Report on the Vatican* (July 1956). He lightheartedly remarks that some serious Protestants are apt to consider it unfair that Catholics should combine an authoritarian Church with freedom of speech and freedom of criticism. There is something disingenuous here, for Greene does not really believe in the existence of such Protestants. No doubt he would like to. When he does draw attention to Catholic faults he treads as nervously as a cat. 'We mustn't let our amusement with the picturesque . . . blind us to the temporary and temporal faults of this huge organization whose only real purpose is the propagation and preservation of Christ's teaching. Because we believe the essential has never been lost, we can be amused up to a point by the faults of conservatism, the elaborations of ceremonial, the small immoralities and dishonesties belonging to any organization.' If that had appeared in *The Tablet* one would have excused its woolliness, just as one had formerly come to expect woolliness, if not to excuse it, in the *Statesman's* treatment of Soviet Russia before Krushchev rendered it unnecessary. In the same review Greene did give some idea of what he considered wrong with the Catholic Church. Justice was not likely to be sold or denied but it could be delayed. 'Some feel it was so delayed in the case of the worker-priests and of the Jesuit teachers of Lyons: others may think the gift of faith may be delayed by the hearty materialism of the Church in North America.' Did Greene really mean that justice was delayed in the case of the worker-priests? Surely it was denied, and if we call such action delay then every injustice is merely a delay on the grounds that all will come right in the unseen future.

I do not wish to detract from Greene's courage when he does venture to criticize the hierarchy. I am only concerned to oppose his claim, never stated with much conviction, that his right to criticize is admitted by his Church. In April 1954 the Vatican announced that Greene had been conferring with Cardinal Griffin, and it was believed that he was trying to reach agreement with the Church, but the subject of negotiation was not disclosed. But the conflict continued. On 16th August in the same year Colette died. She had been twice divorced and had long been out of communion with the Church. Monseigneur Feltin, Cardinal Archbishop of Paris, refused to allow any religious ceremony at her funeral. In an open letter to the Archbishop, printed in Le Figaro Littéraire, Greene wrote: 'It is the right of all who are baptised Catholics to be accompanied to the tomb by a priest. We cannot lose this right—as one can lose the citizenship of a temporal country—by committing a crime or misdemeanour, for no human can judge another. . . . Are two civil marriages so unpardonable? The lives of some of our saints offer even worse examples. True, they repented. But . . . no-one can say what goes through the mind when the spirit is drawn to lucidity by the immediacy of death. . . . Your eminence has given . . . the impression that the Church pursues errors to the other side of the deathbed. . . . Is it to warn your flock of the danger of treating marriage lightly? It would certainly have been better to warn them of the danger of condemning others too easily. . . .' The Archbishop replied that the Church does not wish to impose rites on a person who has voluntarily and freely left the Church, nor did Colette show any signs of repentance before death. There was nothing to stop the offering of private prayers. Apparently letters received by the Archbishop, the editor and Greene himself showed that a majority supported the decision taken.

Yet another cause for complaint came to light when Greene

visited Poland in January 1956 as a correspondent for the *Sunday Times*. The policy of the Vatican, he said, was hard to understand. It seemed directed as much against the Catholic people of Poland as against the Communist Government. No-one in Poland desired the return of the emigré government, yet the Vatican recognized an emigré ambassador. It was comparable to receiving some old Grand Duke as the Russian ambassador. No Pole was prepared to consider the return of Western territories to Germany and yet when the Bishopric of Breslau fell vacant a German cleric was appointed, living in the comfort and security of West Germany. 'Every Catholic in Poland feels a pinprick to his pride when letters to administrators in the Western Territories are addressed by the Roman Curia to "Germania", and prays for the day when the realities of the situation shall be recognized by the Vatican . . .'

Is there, I wonder, any organic relationship between these brushes with the hierarchy and the occasional evidence of troubled faith that may be found in his later work? In his account of opium-smoking ('A Few Pipes', *The London Magazine*, December 1954) Greene records two remarkable dreams. In the first he was present at the birth of Christ and saw the Wise Men offering gifts, but he was puzzled and disturbed because they seemed to be offering them to nothing. In the second he met the Devil on the steps of a club in St James's Street and made a bargain with him. The question of declining faith is given prominence in a recent story, 'A Visit to Morin' (*The London Magazine*, January 1957). An Englishman, Dunlop, calls on an old French novelist, once famous but now disgruntled and half forgotten. Dunlop says he read Morin's books when he was sixteen, and the following conversation takes place:

> 'Oh well, now they are only read by the old—and the pious. Are you pious, Mr Dunlop?'
> 'I'm not a Catholic.'
> 'I'm glad to hear that. Then I shan't offend you.'
> 'Once I thought of becoming one.'
> 'Second thoughts are best.'

Disillusion could scarcely be more explicit.

Morin could easily be identified with Greene. He hits out vigorously at his fellow Catholics. He 'had offended the orthodox Catholics in his own country and pleased the Liberal Catholics abroad; he had pleased, too, the Protestants who believed in God with the same intensity that he seemed to show, and he used to find enthusiastic readers among non-Christians who, when once they had accepted imaginatively his premises, perhaps detected in his work the freedom of speculation which put his fellow-Catholics on their guard'. His critics could find no specific fault yet they disliked the way in which some of his characters accepted a dogma so wholeheartedly that they drew out its implications to the verge of absurdity. (Such as the resurrection of the dead? The possibility of miracles? So now it was not only the Protestants who denied their faith.) Orthodox critics scented heresy but could not locate it. An impatience with theology is expressed. Perhaps Greene's sole venture into the propagation of dogma had had unforeseen results. Morin said you must avoid theology if you want to believe. 'A man can accept anything to do with God until scholars begin to go into the details and the implications. A man can accept the Trinity, but the arguments that follow . . .' Morin complained that he had always had too many priests around him. He had been an exhibit for the faith. He was useful to them, evidence that an intelligent man could believe. First came the Dominicans, who enjoyed literature and good wine; later the Jesuits moved in for they twigged a soul was in danger.

'Perhaps I wrote away my belief like the young man writes away his love. Only it took longer—twenty years and fifteen books,' said Morin. I don't know whether statistics can help—perhaps Greene is waiting for some idiot to take this literally and personally. Still, for what it's worth: *Brighton Rock* to *The Quiet American*, 1938–56. Including *Twenty-One Stories* and *Why Do I Write?*, but excluding the children's books, fourteen titles. One of the most common confessions a priest hears, says Morin, is 'Father, I have lost my faith.' It is worth bearing in mind, for I am not imputing anything sensational to Greene. Nearly every Catholic loses faith at some time or other. But Morin's case has additional interest because of an unfamiliar subtlety. 'I had cut myself off for twenty years from grace and my belief withered as the priests said it would. I don't believe in God and

His Son and His Angels and His Saints, but I know the reason why I don't believe and the reason is—the Church is true and what she taught me is true.' He had lost belief but retained faith. He was afraid to return to the Sacraments for fear he would find them inadequate.

What is the germ that causes Greene to be at odds with so many of his fellow-Catholics? I believe it is his horror of piety, which he regards as a bloodless, formal caricature of devotion. Piety turns so vigorously from the fact of sin that it allows sin to triumph unopposed. Greene has gone to the opposite extreme. His concern with sin has become so intense he finds a life without sin to be devoid of meaning. A knowledge of good and evil is necessary to the complete novelist, he claims. This is certainly true, but the implications are dangerous for it is easy to confuse participation with understanding. There have been good novels where the sense of sin was absent— usually young men's novels such as *Pickwick Papers* and *Sons and Lovers*. Other novels may possess it to a high degree but it will be spurious—Edgar Allan Poe and, among contemporaries, Ray Bradbury exhibit this type of falsity beneath verbal felicity. The result is overpitched and slightly ridiculous. There are also cases where evil intervenes to an unwanted extent, as certainly happened in Huxley's *Point Counter Point*. But for Greene evil must be part of the very essence of the novel, else it will fail to bear a true relation to life. One gets the impression that he actively seeks evil in life, because a writer needs first-hand experience. I believe that he has always tended to this outlook, but that it has been confirmed and strengthened by his theorising. 'Seeking evil' is a sensational phrase; the point to remember is that evil is an elusive quality, and one must look for it (if one wishes to find it) haphazardly as the alchemists sought their life-giving formula. Latterly Greene became friendly with Norman Douglas, and I think he was influenced by Douglas's unashamed search after new experience.

Douglas was fascinated by what the world calls vice. Whether he believed it was vice, and wished to practise it out of devilry, or whether he merely wished to shock the 'pious', I don't know. I have already quoted the phrase, 'the superiority of Hell's constitution', from Greene's youthful poetry. While discussing it I was careful not to dismiss it as adolescent nonsense. Greene's nature was not just like 'anybody else's'. Anyway, it is a slack way of dealing with people to suggest that they all pass through identical phases, although it is a familiar one. Greene has obviously tried his hand at most things which will not bring him into conflict with the law. He has managed to retain a set of values which are superior to those of his critics, e.g., he considers hypocrisy, malice, cruelty and stupidity as infinitely worse habits than adultery, drunkenness, dope-taking and petty lying. He considers it as part of his duty as a novelist to experience all the pleasures—and certainly many of the pains, for he does not spare himself. In 'A Few Pipes' he gives an account of opium-smoking. He does not write of it in any spirit of dare-devilry but quite naturally, as an activity that any man who is fully alive and has the opportunity will sample for himself. He won't withdraw in pious horror, exclaiming 'That's sinful!' Even if it were sinful not even one's religion expects one to avoid sin perpetually. Men live in the world, they can no more avoid sin than they can avoid smuts from chimneys. They must face sin but not be conquered by it. A reviewer in *The Sunday Express* seemed to think that opium should only be used medicinally! We've heard that about brandy. Our inhibiting society produces this type of attitude like carrion produces maggots.[1] At best it will allow a few moments of dare-devilry among the young. But if that is the spirit enveloping an activity one's thoughts will always be of the smug, 'how-wicked-I-am' variety. Greene's attitude is quite different. Smelling the opium as he went up the stairs of the *fumerie*, he wrote, was 'like the first sight of a beautiful woman with whom one realizes a relationship is possible: somebody whose memory will not be dimmed by a night's sleep'. The Saturday night dare-devil sniffs disapprovingly, 'Showing off!'—as it would be for him. Greene tries to restore the almost lost art of performing an action *because* it is in the human range.

A private spy of mine tells me that on Greene's bookshelves is a complete set of Norman Douglas, inscribed by the author. In 1952 he wrote an Introduction to Norman Douglas's *Venus in the*

[1] Greene conducts a running feud with the *Express* papers. In a letter to the *New Statesman* he once explained that the reason why he had not brought libel action against them was because it 'would have brought me in too close contact with an organization which I prefer to keep at a proper distance'.

Kitchen (or *Love's Cookery Book*), a collection of aphrodisiac recipes. Another *bête noire* of the pious, both secular and sacred, and an obvious hunting ground for both Douglas and Greene. Greene called Douglas's life 'consistently open, tolerant, unashamed' and added, ' "Ill-spent" it has been called by the kind of judges whose condemnation is the highest form of praise'. And again, 'he loved life too well to have much patience with puritans or fanatics. He was a gentleman and he disliked a boor'. Poor John Gordon! Perhaps Greene was over-sensitive about Douglas's reputation, as one tends to be when one is in a very small minority. When Harold Nicolson mildly drew attention to Douglas's unorthodoxy after the latter's death, Greene exploded angrily in a letter to *The Spectator*. It was scarcely justified. Nicolson had merely stated that Douglas's private behaviour was distasteful to him. In fact, it was distasteful to most people and Greene should have known better than to attempt to prevent others from making pronouncements about anyone's private life. This is a right claimed by all people who live 'good' and 'decent' lives. Douglas had sought pleasure wherever he could find it, like his beloved Greeks. Greene was of the same mind. Nearly everyone else believes that pleasure is sinful, unless it is so limited that its enjoyment is scarcely noticeable. It is certainly discouraging to find that people who praise charity in their churches have no use for it at all outside, but such things should no longer surprise at the age of forty-eight.

XIX

THE GOD OF THE SOPHISTS

Nineteen Fifty-Three
'The Living Room', 'Essais Catholiques'

The Living Room, a play in two acts, was first presented on 16th April, 1953 at Wyndham's Theatre, with Eric Portman as Father James Browne, and was produced by Peter Glenville with settings by Leslie Hurry. Commercially it was a success, artistically the most false of all Greene's fictions. In an Introduction to the printed edition Glenville stressed that Helen is stupid but not evil and that James, as a priest, is a failure. And that, as usual, seems to be sufficient. The mouth of criticism is to be stopped by the kindly admission that the characters we are concerned with are bad Catholics.

Why is it that Greene's Catholics are always so unsatisfactory? Is it essential to their faith that they should fail? Is a personal idio-syncracy of the author becoming a boring *sine qua non* of spiritual sufficiency? At last one gets tired of hearing it said that God is merciful to these feeble practitioners, with the implication that God loves a sinner because He loves a sin. Might these recurrent failures be due not to the desire of a quaint and unpredictable God but to some-thing much more feasible: faulty doctrine? Perhaps the doctrine makes goodness impossible? Why are we not occasionally shown a priest who can bring comfort? The most they can do is admit their personal shortcomings (who couldn't?) and assume, with barely concealed arrogance, that in some undivulged way their failure is superior to the 'uninstructed' virtues of others. Praise for failure may be acceptable the first time (after all, it panders to the greater part of the human race) but too frequent repetition suggests a groove that has become too comfortable.

We are very quickly intoduced to the illicit love affair that is essential for the formula—for this play is purely and simply formula. Father James makes the expected broadminded remarks about sinners

trusting more in God's mercy than do others, and how valuable it
would be if some of the pious were to commit a big sin. It is when
James comes face to face with the love affair that his failure is
apparent. He advises the lovers to go away, break it off, suffer for a
short time. He does not explain why it would not be better for the
injured wife to suffer for a short time and at least give the lovers the
chance of happiness. It is clear that she will always suffer, whatever
her relations with her husband, Michael, but this is not considered.
When Michael, who is a University Lecturer in Psychology (a sitting
target for Greene, if ever there was one!) uses the word 'neurosis'
James retaliates with a sneer about jargon. His spiritual pride then
gathers force and he exclaims, 'You can't fob off a Catholic with a
registrar's signature and call it a marriage. We do as many wrong
things as you do, but we have the sense to know it.' This smooth,
smug admission of guilt has by now become a commonplace of
'Catholic' literature, and is about as attractive as Uriah Heep's
humility.

The explanation is fairly obvious. Greene is making a desperate
attempt to persuade himself. He knows how cruel, how merciless
and how intellectually dishonest it all is, but he dare not let go. This
'mystery of Christianity', this *'paradoxe du Christianisme'*, are slipped
in to gull the unwary. Where mystery exists let us acknowledge it
and we will readily accept arguments that are as mysterious as the
situation they seek to explain. But where is the mystery here? There
is none. What the Catholic Church has succeeded in doing is to
establish a stupendous mystery of marriage and then give it foundation with sophisms which bewilder with their subtlety. There is a
constant string of nuance and suggestion running through this play
which gives no-one any chance at all—no-one, that is to say, except a
God whose attraction is only for the cunning. A particular kind of
spiritual snobbery is given full play. When Rose believes that
Michael wishes to go away with her (although he is very uneasy) she
tempers her excitement by turning to her uncle and saying, 'Oh,
Uncle, you must think we are very wicked.' James replies, 'No.
Just ignorant. And innocent.' Rose, who is only twenty, says with
pride, 'Not innocent.' She is being made to look a foolish young
girl, who thinks she knows far more about life than she really does.

Girls of that age usually do but it is her creator who puts the pathetically youthful words into her mouth. One feels, behind the words, a hatred for her happiness. It is the subtle, modern way of promising damnation. And almost immediately we get the stage direction about Michael: 'He doesn't look a happy man'. Now this is the author speaking, and no-one else, and it confirms the impression of weighted evidence that the dialogue gives. How on earth could Michael look happy? If he did it would prove he were a villain. But the effect that is being sought is to put into the reader's mind (or the audience's, through producer and actor) that Michael is unhappy because he is sinning. But it is not so simple.

A little later in the same scene we get this passage:

ROSE: . . . It's really awful. Like something in Edgar Allan Poe.

MICHAEL: What a lot of books you've read.

ROSE: You aren't angry about something, are you? I'll do anything you say. Just tell me where to go, and I'll go. Like Ruth. 'Your people shall be my people.' I suppose your people are all psychologists.

MICHAEL: Not all.

ROSE: I've read Freud in Penguin. *The Psychology of Everyday Life*.

MICHAEL: You have, have you?

Oh, Graham, how could you? What chance do you give the girl? In *The Heart of the Matter* you stressed the youth and innocence of Helen, but not to mock her. In that book you were still fighting but now you have surrendered. Did you enjoy the polite, suburban snigger that your killing reference to *The Psychology of Everyday Life* aroused? Not so very long ago you would have writhed at it. Suppose Rattigan had been guilty of it, how you would have flayed him!

Of course, it isn't all false. The odd thing is that when Greene deals with matters of doctrine and religious practice he is invariably feasible and natural. Take this passage, for instance. It is quite unobjectionable. James is reading to Teresa.

JAMES: St John is still talking about the dark night of the soul. It's a bit difficult to understand for me and you who've not got that far. You see it's nearness to God that withers a man up. We are all such a long comfortable distance away. He is trying to describe the black night he found himself in—a night that seemed to be without love or even the power to pray.

TERESA: I pray. Night and morning.

JAMES: Oh, I remember my baby prayers, Teresa. Our Father, Hail Mary, an act of contrition. But I can't meditate for ten minutes without my mind wandering—and as for contemplation it's a whole world away.

He can do this well because his feelings are not touched. That sounds paradoxical, but of course it's the mark of the professional writer. He can write well about things that are remote from his preferences and prejudices. Any articulate person can write well, or at least interestingly, about intimacies—that is why so many people are capable of one good book. But one is not always allowed to write freely about intimacies, or matters of supreme personal concern—and that is why this play fails. Only it is really not a personal failure but the failure of Greene's Church, for it is his Church that has challenged him, interposed itself and conquered the artist in him. This was one situation where disloyalty was put to rout. Greene has come to heel, and he falls back on snobbish clichés to hide doctrinal bankruptcy and dilates on mercy to blank out reality.

One can go on giving examples. In the first Scene of the second Act James tells Helen that they and their house are to blame. 'Blame our dead goodness. Holy books, holy pictures, a subscription to the Altar Society.' If they had asked Rose to make a sacrifice, their own offer would have been pious platitudes. Greene has written before of 'dead goodness', the mark of the pious. But here he turns it to the use of evasion. It is not *he* who is criticizing this time, it is one of the pious themselves, one who knows so well how feeble he is and is so pleased with his own self-criticism. Rose would have sinned if, etc. Where does love come in? If Greene could say that human love doesn't matter, that it is worth sacrificing for the love of God, all would be well—but he doesn't. Perhaps when he is old and the fires burn low he will say something of the kind, and God will know whether to be grateful. But against his own convictions (unless they have changed overnight—and they haven't, see *The Quiet American*) he denies love. It must have felt like Canossa. No effort is made to show how this particular love hurts God. Our attention is drawn to the suffering it causes but nothing is said about the suffering caused by the negation of love. The armies of the pious are gradually manoeuvred into a position where their basic cruelty becomes obvious to all. Even James, a kindly man and not stupid or 'good' in the way detested by Greene, is tainted, for it is he who says to Rose 'I'm glad the hours in Regal Court were so rewarding.' A statement like that at such a time might have destroyed her. She needs help and gets sarcasm.

The true Greene does, however, manage to peep out in one of Roses's speeches. 'Oh, we read about God's successes,' she says. 'We don't read about His failures. His happy failures. Who just don't care much about Him and go on living quietly all the same.' Poor baffled James resorts to his mystery and replies, 'One has to deserve to be a failure.' Greene's failure-wish is a cowardice, but not an obvious one. It is the backwash of his other failure, to find justification for his denial. Rose says what he believes and he is incapable of finding an answer. But as an answer has to be found to enable the play to move forward he resorts to mumbo-jumbo. It is this conflict between author and part which accounts for the occasional tone of cynicism which James surprisingly exhibits. (It is easy to put villainous sentiments into the mouth of a villain; it is horribly difficult to put lies into the mouth of a good man and parade them as truths.) Rose, for instance, challenges James when she announces that 'people run away all the time and are happy'. James replies: 'I've read about them too. And the fairy stories which say, "They lived happily ever afterwards".' His attitude is sheer arrogance. Even if the runaways never completely overcome the pain suffered and passed on to them by their partners, there is no justification for such hatred. The play is weighted, absurdly and unfairly, on the side of dogma. Plays usually are weighted but few people can object to the dramatist's right to set forth his point of view. What makes this play so irritating and unconvincing is the failure of the author to give us his point of view but to give us another in its place, presumably as a penance. It is possible for a man to act brilliantly as his enemy's advocate (as Koestler did in *Darkness at Noon*) but Greene fails miserably. The play ends, punctuated by falsities on nearly every page. Why should Michael's philosophy collapse when it is the pious dogma that has been found wanting—and yet James apparently expects it to? James is allowed to pull one more pompous plum out of his mystery-basket: 'There's one thing I remember from the seminary. I've forgotten nearly all the things they taught me, even the arguments for the existence of God. It comes from some book of devotion. "The more our senses are revolted, uncertain and in despair, the more surely Faith says: 'This is God: all goes well'"'.

Oh, Graham! I have read some of the works of the mystics and although I have not understood I have believed. I also believe I can spot claptrap when I see it. What would you say if you were to read, 'The more Henry James's serpentine sentences confuse me, the more I am certain that he is speaking the truth'? You believe in his truth, but not for that reason. Or if I wrote, 'The more Graham Greene hates his religion the more certain I am that God is good and all is well'. It may be very true but it still doesn't justify a *non sequitur*.[1]

In the same year he published in Paris *Essais Catholiques*. This volume is not spoilt by any of the sophisms that mar *The Living Room*. In the play he is betrayed by his own stridency, the need to announce to unbelievers what he himself does not believe; in the essays he is writing of matters about which he entertains no doubts, and in one instance he is certainly addressing the converted. I will give a brief summary of the views expressed and only pause for comment when there appears to be some relevance to his other work. (Incidentally, 'The Glory of Mary' was reprinted here in translation.) These essays are earlier work and do not belong to the period of emotional-spiritual crisis that produced *The Living Room*.

[1] Fundamentally I am sure Greene still agrees with the statement he made in his contribution to *The Old School*, that marriage is not necessarily and automatically sacred. It would be unfair to quote against any author something he had written twenty years earlier. I merely suggest that the lack of conviction evident in *The Living Room* supports my view that he was writing against the grain.

In the introductory essay, '*Message aux Catholiques Francais*', he says that the eternal enemy believes, and not for the first time, that the final struggle has come. (It will be remembered that he made a similar statement in 'Mary'.) After mentioning the fortifying evidence of miracles, with reference to one he had seen himself, he states that although he is frequently on the edge of sin he feels an incessant call to fidelity. The great tension that had arisen between Christianity and the world at large ceased the moment war was declared. The second essay, '*La Civilisation Chrétienne, Est-Elle en Peril?*' was originally a speech made at the Grand Catholic Conference held at Brussels in 1948. He begins with a few comments on literature—that Mauriac is the greatest living novelist, that English fiction is marked by its materialism. He gets the feeling that he is surrounded by shadows, that Christianity exists elsewhere. These, however, are not the worst years that Europe has known, and he quotes from a document belonging to the reign of Stephen. However desperate the situation appears to be, the crimes are always equalled by the possibility of repentance, and repentance is born in the same moment as the sin. '*Le repentir était né en même temps que le crime: naissances jumelles du péché et du châtiment*'. In English poetry, he says, there is one common note, which he calls 'l'esprit indécis'. I think I am entitled to translate it as 'spirit of mercy' (or of tolerance, the second chance), for later he calls it '*la signature, la sceau de la civilisation chrétienne*'. We can admit our sins and repent them, that is Christian behaviour. (The Nazis, on the other hand, sought justification after defeat by attributing their actions to the rightful obedience of orders.) He then invokes his audience to remember the map of the world and to recognize that Europe alone is not Christianity. He ends with a story of a world state in which Christianity has been eliminated, except for the last Pope. The Chief of Police decides to shoot him personally. The Pope is brought in and '*après avoir offert au Pape une cigarette qu'il refusait et un verre de vin qu'il acceptait*', the Chief tells him of his coming fate. He allows the Pope to pray ('*il avait lu dans un livre que c'était la coutume, mais il ne prenait pas la peine d'écouter la prière*'). He then shoots the Pope but as he bends to finish the job a thought crosses his mind: '*Serait-il possible ce que cet homme croyait fut la vérité?*' A new Christian was born in sorrow.

'*Les Paradoxes du Christianisme*' sounds as though it may give Greene an opportunity to air his unhealed wounds. There is in fact little evidence of bitterness, of human frustration. Perhaps he is hinting at his own troubles when he says that some people adopt the Catholic faith because they imagine it is simple when in fact it is lack of faith that is easy. But the paradoxes he is concerned with are not those of love and marriage. They are as remote and, in a way, as antiseptic as any of Chesterton's had been—which is, of course, not to say that they are untrue. But he does not get worked up about them. He writes calmly, for instance, of a country which bases its life on the absence of paradox, on a simplification (and he does not mean Russia). There is nothing to stir the blood in that, it is as restful as a Euclidean proposition. He refers to '*une ville nordique, l'une des plus belles cités d'Europe*', with its social services, '*le meilleur de la vie*', where the Catholic Church scarcely exists and the Protestant Church is dead. It is to be contrasted with a southern city where there is no security and much vice, yet one hears laughter and feels hope in the air, where in the northern city there had been only indifference. '*Ceci est le millenium et le millenium n'est que ceci.*' It is a return to the mood of *The Lawless Roads*, but quieter, toned down, resigned. Then comes a wistful glance at sin and the statement that where God is, there is His enemy, and where the enemy is not, we despair of finding God. He ends with an account of Stevenson's championship of Father Damien, whose goodness was accompanied by dirty habits and moral shortcomings.

'*Le Paradoxe du Pape*' is of no particular interest, except that Greene makes a mild criticism of Pope Pius XII's literary style and a sterner one of his advisers who were responsible for the banning of Sartre and the worker-priests. He said it was only a passing phase (what he strangely called 'delay' elsewhere),[1] but it was symptomatic of Greene's misgivings about a Church supposedly envied by heretics on account of its tolerance. The original of this essay appeared in *Life* under the title 'The Pope Who Remains a Priest' and in it Greene expresses an emotional appreciation of his Church which is worth a page full of sophisms: 'It was not after all the question—can

[1] By analogy the insistence of the British Government in persisting with H-bomb tests is nothing more serious than delay in abandoning them.

this Thing (Catholicism) survive? It was—how can this Thing ever be defeated?' One is reminded of Morin's rather sour remark: 'If you want to stay a believer keep off theology ...'

In the same year as *The Living Room* there appeared the fourth and last of Greene's children's books. One does not look here for signs of spiritual upheaval, although the effects of it are more likely to colour the whole of his output than would be the case with any other writer. But these stories were proabably all written at about the same time and were released at intervals. In *The Little Steam-roller*, 'a story of Adventure, Mystery and Detection' and again illustrated by Dorothy Craigie, we find that Jim Drover, the bus driver of *It's A Battlefield*, reappears as Bill Driver, the steamroller driver. The plot starts in Africa, one of Greene's adopted continents, and as in the previous book bad men are hunted and caught. There is one moment when a piece of observation is lifted out of the adult novels. At the Customs one of the villains says the toys are for his children. We are told that 'he is looking sideways because he is telling a lie'.

I might as well mention here two stories which in fact appeared in the following year. One of them, 'Special Duties', is not a good story but exhibits a greater degree of cynicism on an aspect of Catholic doctrine than we find anywhere else in his writing. Mr Ferraro employs a special secretary to gain indulgences for him. He finds she has been deceiving him. He had believed that owing to her activities, 36,892 days had been saved from Purgatory. At the same time his wife, who believes herself to be perpetually on the point of death, keeps a resident priest and again there is a tone of contempt in the writing. Apart from the satire on the doctrine of the Treasury of Merit, by which souls can accumulate a balance on a heavenly bank, the author appears to imply that the best way to deprive death of its sting and to avoid Purgatory is to ignore them altogether.

The other story, 'The Destructors', is much better—and (which is presumably significant) is also horrifying and despairing. One house, rather a beautiful one, remains standing while all its neighbours have been destroyed in the blitz. A gang of boys, led by one whose father was an architect who has come down in the world, destroys it completely and very cleverly. What the war didn't do the boys, indirect products of the war's senseless violence, managed to do. 'Destruction after all is a form of creation,' remarks the author. One of his characteristic inverted images is notable for its sense of defeat: 'The grey ash floated above them and fell on their heads like age.' T., the leader, had never been a child, we are told—the lost childhood was no longer a metaphor. One of Greene's special concerns, children without innocence, is the focus of the story. They are brought on the scene as the agents of collapse. There is a poetic truth in this story, as though Greene's subconscious mind had somehow foreseen the damage the corrupted children would do. And the world, in the form of a lorry-driver, remarks, 'You got to admit it's funny' when the house collapses. He is mystified, for he does not understand how it was done. And, true to form, this really shocking incident appears to cause less concern than a rock 'n' roll riot. The story expresses the death that lurks so politely in *The Living Room*.[1]

---

[1] Mr Greene might call this pompous. But he himself made a very revealing comment about this story. It first appeared in *Picture Post* and many readers decided the author must be a cruel man. Greene, we are told, was genuinely sad about this. 'Something must have gone wrong in the writing. I meant it to be funny,' he said. There is not the slightest element of comedy in the story. Similarly, when readers called his religious books depressing, Greene's reply was, 'Not at all. They're most optimistic. They deal with the infinite mercy of God.' But this mercy can only be assumed, we never see any evidence of it. Greene's victims must feel like the dying African native in Kenya, mentioned in one of his letters to *The Times*. As he tried to crawl under the wheels of advancing cars he cried, 'Is there no God?'

XX

PHASES OF INNOCENCE
ALDEN PYLE AND JOHN GORDON

Nineteen Fifty-Five
'Loser Takes All', 'The Quiet American'

T HE world crisis was really a conflict between Communism and Christianity, in Greene's view. As the Catholic Church was the spearhead of Christianity, the conflict was therefore between the Communist Party and the Catholic Church. In Mexico, in Poland and in Malaya Greene has seen events in these terms and during the early nineteen-fifties he sent reports on the struggle from another part of the battlefield to the *Sunday Times*. Some might see the fighting in Indo-China as a contest between East and West, Nationalism and Colonialism, Russia and America—but fundamentally the struggle was religious. If Greene's interpretation was an unusual one, there is no question of his political awareness. The Catholic Church tends to align itself with forces of tradition and reaction. Greene has often been a voice in the wilderness, protesting that the Church's true role lay in supporting the poor and underprivileged. He had the sense to see that only independence could save Vietnam. Despite his admiration of French culture and his hatred of Communism, he knew that the latter must be fought by the people themselves. He did not make the mistake of political innocents in believing that guns can defeat Communism, especially foreign guns. The people must be allowed to take up a position from which Communism will not appear enticing.

The idea of substituting American troops for French was a pipe-dream. It would merely lead to a disastrous temporary peace which would abandon many non-Communists to Vietnam. 'A country one has loved is about to retire behind the curtain,' he wrote sadly. Independence was the last card. But why was it that resistance, dead in so many places, continued in the Catholic areas? The village militia of Thui-Nhai had beaten off nine attacks in four months. The

militia consisted of the whole population, from old men to girls of
twelve. 'They paraded before the church gay with Vietnamese flags
—the small girls carried knives and wore hand-granades on their
belts.' It is impressive, but rather troubling. Is not the militarization
of childhood another form of corruption? Or is the stain removed
in the service of Our Lord?

Greene interviewed Ho Chi Minh. The impressive thing about
Greene's political reporting is his refusal to be misled by his personal
preferences. There is no doubt where his sympathies lay but he
admitted that every Vietnamese welcomed the French defeat at
Dien Bien Phu. The movement was a nationalist one and only
Western clumsiness was compelling it to become Communist. Ho
Chi Minh was a man 'pure as Lucifer', and Greene could not resist
his charm. The Communist leader appealed to the buried relic of
hero-worship in Greene. He resembled the police officer in *The
Power and the Glory*, a sincere man fighting for a cooling universe.
The outstanding fact about the situation in Indo-China was that
never before had the anonymous peasant been treated as an individual. The West talks glibly about individual rights, and thinks of and
acts towards the Eastern peasantry as if it were a vast, undifferenti-
ated mass. The Commissar, preaching collectivism, treats the peasant
as a person. The only man who can challenge him is the Catholic
priest. Greene compared the President of Vietnam with Ho Chi Minh,
and shuddered. 'He has some words in common with Ho Chi Minh,
as Catholicism has some words in common with Communism, but he
is separated from the people by cardinals and police cars with wailing
sirens and foreign advisers droning of global strategy, when he
should be walking in the rice-fields unprotected, learning the hard
way how to be loved and obeyed—the two cannot be separated.
One pictured him there in the Norodom Palace, sitting with his
blank, brown gaze, incorruptible, obstinate, ill-advised, going to his
weekly confession, bolstered up by his belief that God is always on
the Catholic side, waiting for a miracle. The name I would write
under his portrait is the Patriot Ruined by the West.'

Out of this experience came the novel, *The Quiet American*.
Technically it is quite as skilled as any of its predecessors. The old
tricks still succeed, people are etched in by the same old film method

of establishing an environment. ('I shut my eyes and she was again the same as she used to be: she was the hiss of steam, she was a certain hour of the night and the promise of rest'.) The mind that despaired of the West's ever adopting a realistic policy realized with bitterness the futility of much military action. Fowler, the English press correspondent who is the chief character in the novel, goes out with a French patrol. By the time they return their total bag of victims is a mother and child who got in the line of fire. That dead child haunted Fowler. After that, whenever he played dice this war came back to him and with it the dead child. Personally I find it difficult to distinguish between the child dead in a ditch and the children of Thui-Nhai, equipped for action.

From the beginning Fowler insists he is not involved. (It comes like the dim memory of a discussion in that distant novel, *Rumour At Nightfall*.) Fowler was the educated Englishman, rational and Fabianized, a cynical Hogpit who wished everyone well and refused to take sides when each side was so dirty. 'The human condition being what it was, let them fight, let them love, let them murder, I would not be involved.' He preferred to call himself a reporter rather than a correspondent. It is a viewpoint repellent to Greene and some of the falsities of this novel probably derive, once again, from his attempt to write from an alien position. Every novelist must put forward ideas with which he lacks sympathy, but the constant identification with them may prove too great a strain. Some of the strain, on both Fowler and Greene, shows in the former's conversation with Captain Trouin, the Air Force pilot. Trouin detested napalm bombing, partly because no risk is attached to it. Fowler's insistence that he is not involved begins to wear thin. He actually limps from a wound dealt him by the Vietminh forces. However repulsive the war became (and some aspects are hideous), he would not participate. But it is impossible to stay out, says Trouin. Involvement is an emotional matter. You simply don't decide on such things. They decide for themselves. Fowler begins to waver when he realizes that the logical end of non-involvement, the Third Force, is impracticable. It has nothing to fight for. It is an idea from a book. The Third Force which Alden Pyle, of the American Economic Mission, tried to form came from an idea put forward by a 'diplomatic correspondent'

named York Harding. Greene's target is the superior sort of journalist who sets up as an arbiter of the international scene: 'he gets hold
of an idea and then alters every situation to fit the idea'. Pyle tried to
avoid both extremes but nevertheless could not avoid getting mixed
up—but with a cause that had no substance. The last word belongs
to the old Chinese Heng who undertakes to remove Pyle from the
scene: 'sooner or later one has to take sides. If one is to remain
human'.

The novel begins with a touch of disillusion. The age of miracles
is past. The girl's name is Phuong, which means Phœnix, 'but
nothing nowadays is fabulous and nothing rises from its ashes'.
There is a clear distinction between the Roman Catholic French
characters and the agnostic Americans. The French believe in conscience and a sense of guilt, the Americans in economics and the
wickedness of poverty. Fowler, the Englishman, is superficially
closer to the American ethos but in practice he hates the Yanks. One
feels that when he sets down his own views about life and death he is
very close to Greene himself, for there is a distinctly Protestant
element about Greene's Catholicism. When he was wondering
whether to go to Phat Diem or not, he reflected in this manner.
'Always I was afraid of losing happiness. This month, next year,
Phuong would leave me. If not next year, in three years. Death was
the only absolute value in my world. Lose life and one would lose
nothing again for ever. I envied those who could believe in a God
and I distrusted them. I felt they were keeping their courage up with
a fable of the changeless and the permanent. Death was far more certain than God, and with death there would be no longer the daily
possibility of love dying.' Now it would be nonsense to suggest that
these are Greene's permanent views, but I do suspect that they are
the views instilled into his mind from time to time by his dreams.
Greene was a Protestant or agnostic until he entered his twenties, and
during that period certain views and outlooks must obtain so firm a
footing that they can never be driven out altogether. It is another
interpretation of the conflict that is apparent in Greene's work, and
which must in fact trouble all converts, and it helps explain their
occasional stridency. I think we get another hint of the struggle when
Fowler discusses with Pyle who shall have Phuong, only this time the

point of departure is on the religious side of the boundary, i.e., Greene is calling to Fowler, not Fowler to Greene. 'Wouldn't we all do better not trying to understand, accepting the fact that no human being will ever understand another, not a wife a husband, a lover a mistress, nor a parent a child? Perhaps that's why men have invented God—a being capable of understanding.'

The background of sexual desire is as strong as ever. It shows itself in many a casual phrase, crops up unbidden at any hour. 'I wanted a day punctuated by those quick reports that might be car exhausts or might be grenades, I wanted to keep the sight of those silk-trousered figures moving with grace through the hurried noon, I wanted Phuong, and my home had shifted its ground eight thousand miles.' Other matters have caused Greene's powerful sexual drive to be obscured in the discussion of his recent work, but it cannot be over-emphasised. In his development it plays a role similar to Raven's hare-lip and Philip's witness of murder in 'The Basement Room'—that is to say, it is *given* and its influence cannot be ignored nor, much more important, should it be deprecated. Also running true to form is the usual marital difficulty. In England there is a Mrs Fowler—but something had gone wrong, he wasn't sure what. His attitude towards her is one of mingled patience and disinterest, resignation and sudden stabs of hope, something like Scobie's feeling towards Louise. Fowler writes to her, asking to be released, and receives a reply refusing it. It was like a return to the old routine, they were hurting each other again. There is some of the pity and pain expressed in *The Heart of the Matter* and *The End of the Affair*, but with none of the old force. This is not a criticism, for Greene was aiming at a different effect. He is not one of those novelists who is content to rewrite the same novel over and over again in different disguises. There are simply a cry of despair ('If only it were possible to love without injury—fidelity isn't enough') and a conclusion ('The hurt is in the act of possession: we are too small in mind and body to possess another person without pride or to be possessed without humiliation.') It is a part of the human condition, as fundamental as desire itself.

But the over-riding impression one gets from this novel is Greene's intense irritation with the Americans. I have referred to this earlier but since the days of his film-reviewing it had been muted. Now it came to a head—America is the symbol of all that has gone wrong: materialism, godlessness, adult innocence, neutrality. Alden Pyle was the incorrigible 'do-gooder', directing all his energies, all his love even, not to individuals but to a country, a continent, the whole world. (Remember it was the Commissar who was getting at the individual.) It all comes pat, Fowler is 'age and despair', Pyle is 'innocence and goodness', the French are 'conscience and guilt'. But the 'innocence and goodness' are of the wrong kind, they are childlike qualities in an adult mind. Pyle is a 'damned Yankee'. The French policeman has a volume of Pascal on his desk—and it is open. Pyle's bible is York Harding's *The Role of the West*, bloodless clap-trap. Greene cannot restrain his contempt for the college-educated American. 'The Minister had great respect for Pyle—Pyle had taken a good degree in—well, one of those subjects Americans can take degrees in: perhaps public relations or theatrecraft, perhaps even Far Eastern studies (he had read a lot of books).' This has exactly the same tone as Greene's reference to Rose's reading in *The Living Room*. Fowler's American press colleagues were 'big, noisy, boyish and middle-aged, full of sour cracks against the French.' There is a contemptuous account of how, after an engagement, they would go to Hanoi, attend the Commander-in-Chief's conference, stay for a night at a Press Camp (where the barman was the best in Indo-China), fly over the late battlefield at 3000 feet and then return like a school treat to Saigon. Fowler lets fly at the Economic Attaché at one point, he hates everything about the Yanks, their private stores of Coca-Cola, their portable hospitals, their too wide cars, their not quite latest guns. None of them knew what the trouble was about but they fooled around winning the East for democracy.[1]

   This anti-American element is a great splash of emotion and upset a lot of people. I don't think it is true to say that prejudice, even the rankest prejudice, necessarily spoils a novel. There is no reason why the author should not have a viewpoint, and even a crazy view-point does not damn a novel. Who would condemn Poe for his lunacy? The quality of a novel resides in its vitality, not in its

---

[1] This recalls an earlier quotation from a film review: 'What use in pre-tending that with these allies it was ever possible to fight for civilization?'

impartiality. Greene hates Pyle because he sees him as the kind of person who has left our civilization naked and defenceless against its enemies. He knows that his hatred tends to become irrational and on one occasion, after making a comment on one of Pyle's characteristics, he adds, 'I don't write that as a sneer.' Such emotionalism, however, can lead to caricature and caricature is out of place in a realist novel. Pyle undoubtedly does become a caricature. If there are any doubts about this I suggest they are dispelled, once and for all, when Pyle offers Fowler a sandwich. 'Like a sandwich?' he says. 'They're really awfully good. A new sandwich-mixture called Vit-Health. My mother sent it from the States.' Pyle is the earnest American that a large section of the British nation has come progressively to loathe. Swilling gallons of milk and bottles of coke; eating tasteless food preparations with hygienic names; reading digests and going around the world in search of diplomas. In recent years one man in particular has become the representative focus of all this spleen: John Foster Dulles. It is scarcely surprising to read a 'Ballade on a Press Conference' by Greene in the *New Statesman* (June 1956), suggesting that Eisenhower's real sickness is Dulles.

> For thirty feet internally
> Intestines coil, and what we fear
> Is pudding, pie or possibly . . .
> *But what's a Dulles doing here?*

Rex Warner wrote in *The London Magazine* that this was one of Greene's best novels. This suggests it is very good, which it isn't. Perhaps Warner's memory was failing him, or perhaps he rejoiced in the caning of the Yanks. The Americans themselves were puzzled and alarmed. (Incidentally, the pro- or anti-Americanism of this book is not a literary quality but it is bound to be the one that arouses most attention.) They began to search for Greene's motives, for anything that would explain his attack. They could not accept that Greene might genuinely think American policy towards 'the under-privileged' to be mistaken, or that the American way of life was not entirely admirable. After all, there are more refrigerators in the U.S.A. than in the rest of the world put together, aren't there?

They could not be expected to know that in Greene's estimation not even American Catholics came up to scratch. The reviewer in *Newsweek* suggested that Greene was still smarting from the Shirley Temple case, while in *Time* his exclusion from the U.S.A. under the McCarran Act was regarded as a 'possible contributing factor' to his attitude.[1] But putting these pomposities on one side, one must be grateful that the publication of *The Quiet American* stimulated A. J. Liebling to review it for *The New Yorker* (April 1956). Now Liebling is just about the finest journalist writing in English today, although he usually confines his attention to boxers and racehorses.

He discovered that Greene had contrived to make Pyle a perfect specimen of a French author's idea of an Englishman (he speaks bad French, eats tasteless food, is only accidentally and episodically heterosexual, is earnest in an obtuse way and physically brave through lack of imagination). 'Pyle's choice of idiom convinced me that he is a thinly disguised Englishman. But I was impressed by the *toupet* of Mr Greene, sneering down at Pyle from the gastronomic evidence of a soggy crumpet. A British author snooting American food is like the blind twitting the one-eyed'—and Liebling takes the opportunity to mention Marmite. Greene's situation, he says, was familiar to Spengler. 'When England, a French cultural colony, outstripped the homeland after Waterloo and the Industrial Revolution, all that remained for the French to say was, "Nevertheless, you remain nasty, overgrown children". The Italians of the Renaissance said it to the French and I suppose the Greeks said it to the Romans. It is part of the ritual of handing over.' It then occurs to Liebling that Fowler is the 'mock-up of a Hemingway hero—*donc* an American, *donc* One of Us.' He is not a Hemingway hero by Hemingway but the kind of Hemingway hero that crops up in unsolicited manuscripts. Warming to the fun, Liebling gives us an imaginary account of Fowler's boyhood in the States, and his subsequent arrival in Bloomsbury. In short, the book is a second-rate American novel. 'Poor old Greene was in the position of the Javanese politician who

---

[1] While an undergraduate at Oxford Greene had joined the university branch of the Communist Party for four months as 'a prank' in an attempt 'to subvert the subversives'. This was sufficient to prevent his getting a visa to America nearly thirty years later.

told a correspondent he hated the Dutch so specially hard because he could think only in Dutch.'

This is brilliant spoofing. If *The Quiet American* is a good novel, Liebling's article is a better review. Liebling allowed himself a serious moment when he discovered, by a process of reasoning, that Greene held the American State Department responsible for a particularly messy bomb explosion that actually occurred in Saigon. 'There is a difference, after all,' he writes, 'between calling your over-successful offshoot a silly ass and accusing him of murder.' There is a note of cultural snobbery about this novel which, temporarily at least, has replaced the spiritual snobbery I drew attention to before. Greene's development tends to be a process of refining, and there is always the danger of its becoming pseudo-refining. At first only Catholics will pass muster, then American Catholics are excluded, and in time we are left with French Catholics alone. Later he will confine himself to French Catholics who have been purified by the pangs of adultery, and it will probably end with a select circle of adulterous French Catholics who know the Devil personally— only they won't live in France, they will cluster in Equatorial Africa. It is possible, in his enthusiasm for French culture, that Greene has forgotten that most Frenchmen are no longer Catholics and that the French nation in general shows considerable indifference to religious alignments.

To read *The End of the Affair* was to undergo a shattering emotional experience. *The Quiet American* leaves one quite unmoved. Ostensibly the two have so much in common, including the major emotion-stirring factors (a love affair breaking off, frustrated desire), that one is tempted to ask why the effects are so different. This is a question which it is practically impossible to answer in the present state of our knowledge. We simply do not understand the processes by which unhappiness produces tears, and by which the description of unhappiness does the same. Obviously it is a matter of words, their arrangement and order, selection and association—but how do they *act*? We have advanced a little way, we know that concrete expression makes a deeper impact than abstractions, simple indigenous words than latinized symbols—but Greene's writing is always the same in these respects. *The Quiet American* is as direct and actual as

The End of the Affair. Is the difference caused then by the slow build-up of character? Neither Bendrix nor Fowler are pleasant chaps, but perhaps Bendrix is truer than Fowler. His unpleasantness is partly the result of injured decency whereas Fowler's is entirely natural to him. He is a split character who never acts a whole piece. But one must beware of judging a novel by one's opinion of its leading character.

Loser Takes All is a very slight tale which actually appeared before *The Quiet American*, although in the same year. There is no point in dwelling on it for long. There are possibly hints in it of Greene's religious disquiet. In 'Special Duties' he had ridiculed one aspect of Catholic belief. In this novel Cary adheres to a brand of superstition whose code is invented by fate and which could easily be a parody of Catholicism. Its significance is that events are cruel and meaningless (it seems likely that Greene believes this and praises Catholicism for its acceptance of it) and that one's life is just as likely to go wrong because one sees a man with a squint than for any other, more respectable-sounding reason. This given, it becomes clear that one may well be condemned to lifelong misery *because* one has promised to live with a particular woman. Conduct has nothing to do with fate. Cary is really a new edition of Ida Arnold, and her code of superstition has taken the place of Ida's spiritualism. She is alarmingly empty. She keeps saying, 'It's fun not feeling married,' 'I want to live in sin,' and similar phrases. These are jokes to her for she has no awareness of any reality deeper than a passing feeling of excitement. Bertram praises her innocence and calls it Original Innocence, but to us it does not seem far removed from Ida Arnold's vacancy. There is a suggestion that Greene, having fixed his mind too much on the evil that comes from experience, has been trapped by it and is now honouring a vacant mindlessness. Once he had had a horror of vacancy but there are no signs in the writing of this story that he views Cary with anything but complacency.

In a review Neville Braybrooke called this story a 'fairy tale'. The tears it brings will not come from deep, unfathomable places but from shallow pools. It is in the nostalgic key of the non-socialist thirties, the world of Fred Astaire and 'airline tickets to romantic places'. He does not say that the background is still formed by the lower grades of commerce and suburbia, but Greene's sense of realism requires it, if only as a place to jump from. Yet there is an element of nastiness about it, as there is in most of Greene's lighter work. When he doesn't greatly care his writing is tainted with cynicism and triviality. When he takes a grip of himself he inhibits these traits and reveals something much nobler. He has a dangerous talent. If not closely guarded it skates with a sneer on the face of evil, when what it should really be doing is tearing up evil and taking a good look at it. I am reminded of that touching story, 'The Blue Film', which actually belongs to 1954 but was set in the East. Here Greene did succeed in getting beneath the misleading surface appearance, and discovering goodness and beauty where only foulness was visible to the superficial eye. A man takes his wife (at her insistence) to see a 'blue' film and too late he finds it is one in which he participated thirty years ago. His wife was revolted but he could not remember the occasion as revolting. He had loved the girl. It was the only way he could do anything for her (she was paid, of course). It was a great achievement to rid such an incident of its unpleasant associations, to leave the act pure and unsullied. Artists have done as much for industrial scenes that are commonly considered hideous. Baudelaire had done it before but Greene was the first Englishman.

Greene is a difficult person to understand. In nearly everything he does there is an ambivalence. If he seems fascinated by evil one can never be certain whether it is because he knows instinctively that every aspect of evil conceals one of good, or because he is drawn towards the evil itself. All we can be certain of is that he oscillates between the two attitudes. Many of his readers, including some Catholics, are always prepared to believe the worst, as is evident from his dedication of *Loser Takes All* to 'Frere', in which he complains that he is liable to be charged with the encouragement of adultery or the wearing of pyjama tops. I have no views on pyjama tops but I must plead guilty to an occasional conviction that Greene encourages adultery. Not blatantly, of course, but how exciting it is, and how shocking to the innocent! In recent years he has become more and more closely identified with movements to combat prudery and its offspring, censorship mania. In a letter to the *Daily Mirror* in January 1948, concerning its film critic's review of the film

Brighton Rock, he asks whether it is really desirable that all films should be made for the juvenile market. This is at the hub of the argument about censorship and it has been discussed too frequently for it to need any further publicity here. Whatever motives the censor-maniacs believe they possess, the fact remains that if they have their way a large sector of human behaviour (including the most important relationship between men and women, which by its nature requires serious and frank treatment instead of the nudges and sniggers it sometimes receives) will be excluded from literary and artistic expression.[1]

Mr John Gordon, a columnist on *The Sunday Express*, is normally associated with these views. Like Alden Pyle, he is a modern innocent (the most pathetic type of innocent, in Greene's view, the adult), but he is not a fictitious character. Nevertheless, his very existence rouses Greene's antagonism as violently as Harold Nicolson's comments on Norman Douglas's private life. Although he never states them directly (he is fearfully rhetorical in his plain-man style) Mr Gordon's views can be summarized as follows; sex is disgusting; literary references to sex as a normal activity are likewise disgusting; the proper attitude to sex is one of sniggering and hooting (this is implied, for it is beyond human resource to ignore the subject completely); a small measure of control is possible by insisting that, if people must be disgusting, they should all be disgusting in the same way. Greene opposes these views and finally, in a fit of exasperation or pity, I am not clear which, proposed the founding of a Society for the protection of John Gordon. The John Gordon Society, as it was called, came into existence at a private meeting held on 6th March, 1956. Those present included, besides Graham Greene, John Sutro, A. S. Frere of Heinemann, Mr Birch (editor of *Picture Post*), Chris Chataway, Peter Brook, Lord Kinross, Angus Wilson, T. O'Keefe of Hutchinson, Professor A. J. Ayer, Peter Wildeblood, Ronald Duncan and Christopher Isherwood.

One feels rather sorry for Mr Gordon, a helpless old bumbler, when opposed by this formidable array (not that he was there in

[1] There is, in fact, great freedom today in the discussion of sex. The point at issue, however, is that a writer always feels constrained when he knows that limitations exist, even if they are limitations he does not wish to transcend.

person). However, it was his susceptibilities they were planning to protect and he, least of all, had any cause for complaint. Greene was elected President and suggested that the makers of the game Scrabble should be asked to include a pledge for purchasers to sign, that no words that were not used in the Oxford Concise Dictionary should be used. (The aim of this provision was that human beings should learn Bad Words at the age of sixteen, not twelve.) Mr Frere suggested that publishers might be asked to submit proofs to the Society, and to put bands round their books stating that they were 'Banned by the John Gordon Society'. Mr O'Keefe said he would press Hutchinsons to follow suit. (This was to save adults time, trouble and annoyance in selecting adult books.) Mr O'Keefe also urged a special meeting to be held on the anniversary of Dr Bowdler and an expurgated version of Bowdler's Shakespeare to be prepared. (This would have many advantages. It would, for instance, keep expectant mothers entirely ignorant of the nature of a Caesarian operation, so that if they had to undergo one it would come as a pleasant surprise.) A lady suggested a safety pin as a suitable emblem. (This was rude, for one does not mention nappies in polite society. Or was she thinking of Nietzsche's statement, 'To prick a swollen one in the belly I call good sport'?) The subscription was fixed at half a guinea, with a small charge at meetings for 'comestibles'— Ovaltine and biscuits. (There is something vulgar about the word 'food'.) A member of Jesus College asked that there should be a special rate for schoolchildren, that the rot might be stopped at its source. The title Vice-Chairman was naturally changed to Second or Deputy Chairman. Greene sent the members away with a Thought, being a quotation from a work by a Mr John Styles in 1806 condemning Shakespeare for his lewdness. It was a pity Mr Gordon was not there. He would have been proud.

Spoofing apart, the many-sided Mr Greene has worked hard in the last few years to maintain a rather precarious position against the adolescents and the puritans, the cranks and the unco guid, the pious and the pompous. These are always enemies of artists, and they are the more dangerous because there are some inferior artists who are taken in by them or even share their characteristics. If an artist is tainted in any way by these attitudes, his work will be the worse for it. A mentally arrested writer will never be able to write convincingly of the relationship between the sexes, an over-pious writer will fail to understand a very large part of his material. It is a problem that concerns the English more than any other European race. The immaturity of most English authors during the last hundred years has been too obvious to be dismissed as accidental. It means that naturally gifted writers such as Kipling and Barrie have in fact produced work of the utmost falsity. There is falsity in Greene, but it does not come through lack of understanding. If a writer lacks human understanding he ought to give up and take to commerce. It is similar to a carpenter's failure to understand wood. A carpenter may fail in design, and a writer undergoes similar occupational hazards. Greene himself writes falsely when he is not quite sure of what he believes; sometimes he believes one thing and seems to be writing in defence of its opposite. But with people and their behaviour his touch is usually sure. He has refused the attractively easy outlooks of Pyle and Gordon (text-book maxims) and has observed people even when they were behaving *monstrously*. I italicize the word because there is no space left to discuss what is monstrous. I dare say, to get his information, Greene has also behaved *monstrously*. If only John Gordon would, the sales of *The Sunday Express* would drop and he'd be worth reading. I'm a snob, too.

Reviewing Charles Carrington's *Rudyard Kipling: His Life and Work* in *The London Magazine* (March 1956), Greene showed a special understanding of that immature genius. 'The overpowering shyness of the schoolboy intellectual who doesn't want to admit to the hearties of the prefect's room that he really takes literature seriously', Greene wrote, meaning Kipling, but it would do for himself. For Kipling wrote best when he wrote out of hate (not worst, as Kingsmill imagined) and some of Greene's best work comes from hate too. There are rights and wrongs in life, but none in literary excellence. Kipling was the worthy successor of those tortured men, Dryden and Pope, and perhaps Greene felt that he came from the same stock, that Rudyard Kipling was a distant cousin who came home at about the age when Greene set out for the East.

XXI

DREAMS COME TRUE

Mʀ Pʀʏᴄᴇ-Jᴏɴᴇꜱ says the Entertainments are 'stripped of religion'. Knowing the damage done to Greene's reputation by religious garments, one is tempted to shout for joy. 'The heroes of the entertainments generally make their disavowal of religious interest quite explicit.' I fear the shadow falls between the concept and the deed. Public avowals and disavowals make not the slightest difference to the true content of Greene's work. He is always writing about the same things. What we call religious issues are always with us but we react to them in a variety of ways. One of my main assertions is that the critics have, in general, paid far too much attention to the theology expressed by author and characters—a theology that is, under the circumstances, superficial. Take away the theological discussion and you are left with exactly the same as you started with: let's be sensibly vague and call it man's condition. *Our Man in Havana* is an entertainment. Greene by now finds it improper to write a book without Catholics, just as he has to play with his Carters and Davises. But here he is cunning, he puts the load on to Milly. It is an excellent idea, he quiets his conscience and he gives the book a start in life which it makes use of with gusto. Wormold doesn't care two hoots about religion, but Milly has been brought up as a Catholic because of a promise made to her divorced mother. This doesn't make the novel a mere triviality. It is one of the most professional pieces of writing Greene has given us, it moves with the speed and precision of a battleship, and it manages to pass comments on life which are central to Greene's thinking. All of this is done without any self-conscious concern with what the Church will think. The novel is triumphant, religion is put in its proper place. There is only one occasion when the familiar Catholic compulsion that disturbed the balance of so much work in the past is allowed to interfere. This is when Captain Segura is said to have an objection to a direct lie and the novelist comments, 'he might be a good Catholic'. Any other novelist could get away with such a harmless statement, but as soon as it is uttered by Greene we look suspiciously for the long body of the serpent of which this is the tipped fang.

There is a constant flow of *bons mots* and imagist felicities. Greene is at his most fluent and controlled. This is the best of the entertainments, and it ranks high in the novels taken as a whole. One must resist the temptation to dismiss it as of no account because it moves in James Bond territory. The territory doesn't matter; the pathos does. In this novel Greeneland is at last revealed as our own world, a conclusion we have previously never been able to accept. But at last the two have merged. The dream has become reality, reality is possibly a dream. When the new safe is opened a dead mouse is found inside. This was a moment of truth, a moment not merely for this one novel but for Greene's whole career. There are still falsities, but they are few. Just as the Catholic compulsion peeps out once so, I think, does the dream-reality syndrome falter twice. First the night club song: it is the kind of song an intellectual would write, not the kind that is sung. And then there is the duel with Carter: 'it's a fair duel, he told himself, he's more accustomed to killing than I am, the chances are equal enough'. Carter cannot stand this sudden precipitation into the role of the professional killer. I would swear that Carter had never killed anyone in his life. No-one can feel surprise when Wormold kills. He is sick afterwards but it was his first. The important thing is that he wasn't sick first.

But it is the growing insistence that life resembles a dream, that our dreams may be our inner convictions, that dream logic is the significant logic, that makes this novel stand out. Truth is expressed through the tragic figure of Hasselbacher who says, 'You should dream more, Mr Wormold. Reality in our century is not something to be faced'. The theme is reverted to constantly. In the bank Wormold realises that he cannot expect to be honoured and admired while his overdraft is only fifty dollars. We are taught by moralists and parents not to owe money, always to pay our way, but later you discover that debts bring power. Which is real, which is dream? He felt reality in the evening hour when he talked with Milly and realised how much he needed her. Such states may be felt to be tenuous—we even use the term 'unreal'—while the 'real' world contained governments, police stations, atom bombs and political leaders writing notes to each other. Hasselbacher, who in many ways contains the key to this novel, teases a tourist, challenging him to prove he exists—and the tourist, with a 'hint of tears', cites his real-estate business, his wife and kids in Miami, his airflight, the very Scotch he is drinking. Finally the terrifying invention of a person who turns out to exist. *If* only the subconscious can pierce to the heart of this particular matter, and *as* we still know nothing about the mechanics of the subconscious, *so* we are driven to an awareness of responsibility. No-one dreams another's dreams.

I pointed out in an earlier chapter, and other writers have commented on the same thing, that Greene has a minor obsession with dreams. There are no dreams in this book. This is merely an acknowledgment of the fact that dream and reality have merged. Facts are perceived and events are lived which were formerly dreamed. Hasselbacher (again) had his work destoyed because 'I wanted to dream'. That was how he lived, and the implication is that all decent people must live in this way. 'Reality in our century is not something to be faced.' The governments and the police stations, the atom bombs and the political leaders writing notes to each other, oppose this identification, but they represent the past, a bad old past, one that is immensely strong but which must lose. Decent, ordinary people will oppose them and will eventually compel them to forsake the horrible reality they have imposed upon the world.

I have also shown how names are buoys on the sea of Greene's subconscious. Carter, who had previously been sinister and unpleasant, appears as a murderer (with Nucleaners). On the very next page Carter asks Wormold if he knew a fellow named (guess-who) Davis. There is something very mysterious here and one day a computer will get to the bottom of it. And there's Savage. He makes his fourth appearance as an off-stage member of Hawthorne's spy-ring.

Returning to reality . . . We assume in normal daily life that what we can see and touch and hear is real. Quality is left out. So is intelligence. No matter how idiotic and shocking our perceptions are, they are real because they are perceived. The abused mind dreams its own reality, and because this is a response to some kind of horror it is a more agreeable reality. And so, if we are to be sane, this dreamed reality must become lived reality. That is what it amounts to. Greene had been groping towards a statement of this for some time but had never said it so plainly as here. Theology got in his way, and few critics realised that Greene has an important social message. Once, when goaded by Wormold, Beatrice made a list of real jobs which should be unreal: 'designing a new plastic soapbox, making pokerwork jokes for public houses, writing advertisement slogans, being an M.P., talking to UNESCO conferences'. But the money was real. Money was a bridge between the two states. A long line of writers has agreed that you are entitled to take their money. After all, to call it 'their' money is only a figure of speech. It is ours. You have to play cunning with cunning and you tell lies where they will help. Greene has always maintained that a white lie is one of society's major protections. Human beings cannot bear the brutality of truth and should not be expected to. Beatrice, who had a talent for imagery, declares that the world is modelled on popular magazines these days. How could it not be? How could magazines be popular if they did not reflect very faithfully either the world that exists or the world that they have called into existence. (This is simpler in the long run.) The kind of crazy world they were playing with was *Boy's Own Paper* or the *Sunday Mirror*. Her husband came out of *Encounter*.

Dreams and childhood: these are the two promontories in his work. Adulthood is so often an illusion, as in the case of Hawthorne. He worked for the governments and powers, he was important, he and his kind made headlines—yet he belonged essentially to the world of childhood. 'Cruel and inexplicable,' Greene calls it, and the same comment is made when Hasselbacher's flat is broken up: 'it was as though a malevolent child had been at work . . .' Back in London the Chief had a pale blue glass eye which might have come out of a doll which said 'Mama'. This is the world we have entered often before, where the children are mystified and the grown-ups are playing a stupid and dangerous game. In this novel it is what we call 'real' life that is the dream and the adults who are the children. There is an assertion of crossed wires and false values. It needs no theological interpretation and it is not weakened by being called an Entertainment.

In *A Burnt-Out Case* the dreams are back. They are bad ones. The story Querry tells to Marie Rycker is also an extended dream. My theory of the dream in Greene's work would suggest that he is a prey to unease, that the composure he exhibits in *Our Man* (he, not society) has been broken. There is little doubt of this. It reads like an unhappy *novel*, which is not at all the same thing as a novel about unhappy people.[1] Minor technical points emphasise the mood—for instance, the constant use of the addressee's surname heightens the effect of doom knocking and fate calling. The old genius for a telling phrase is still there, but it serves the new master as efficiently as it served the previous one. 'The pouches under his eyes were like purses that contained the smuggled memories of a disappointing life.' The novel itself has pouches under its eyes. And yet—how odd! Professor Evans says, in his Introduction to *Graham Greene: Some Special Considerations*, that this is the first of Greene's books which suggests salvation in this world. Previously there had been a tendency to suicide.[2] In fact, the Superior stated that it was 'really quite a happy ending'. Greene himself, in an interview, attributed much of the new mood to Teilhard de Chardin's *The Phenomenon of Man*, which influenced him greatly during the writing. Does this sound contradictory? I don't think so. As I have said in the earlier chapters of this book, Greene has spent the greater part of his life struggling with a view of life that he finds uncongenial. At last, in this novel, he admits it. It is a painful admission for any man to make. This explains why a book that is superficially optimistic is fundamentally a cry of despair.[3]

[1] When the book first appeared I was astonished by the insensitivity to this quality shown by nearly all reviewers. The only review I read that caught this tone was in the *Spectator*, I think by Alan Brien. I felt I was speaking against the stream when I reviewed it on Radio Omdurman. Yet when his *In Search of a Character* came out everyone immediately seized on his loss of confidence as its main subject. It had been obvious much earlier.

[2] Revived, incidentally, in all the plays: one in *The Living Room*, two attempts in *The Potting Shed*, the suspicion of one in *The Complaisant Lover* and a threat in *Carving a Statue*.

[3] Or 'fundamentally optimistic is superficially a cry of despair'. I don't know. One needs a longer perspective than I have to answer that one.

Deformity and mutilation become the dominant symbols—to be frightfully bright and modern, they are the check-points between our world and others. (There is no merger in this novel.) The dreams are back; there are no children (unless we except Marie Rycker, the emphasis on the childlikeness of some of the priests), but there is the primitive. We know enough of Greene's private symbolism now to know what we are in for. The quotation from Wardekar on the fly-leaf, in which he draws attention to the disgust felt by men for deformity and its effect on their personalities, throws the mind back to an earlier hare lip. We are now among the toeless and fingerless. But Querry is also one of the mutilated, as he admits himself. Dr Colin agrees although his mutilation is outside his sphere. Querry is a burnt-out case, but it is his heart that is burnt out. He is a hollow man.

He has come to the end of desire and the end of vocation. It seemed difficult not to believe that this was the author speaking. And with the author, along with the dreams, came the Catholic conflicts. But (pardon the repetition) these are flowers of discontent. The real subject of this novel is a profound disillusion with European civilisation. Africa pinpoints his agony. Africans have every right, he feels, to fear European cruelty. After all, Europeans themselves have every right to do the same. And when he quotes some of the cruelties they are the more recent and lesser ones. 'These people here are all dying,' says Dr Colin, and adds hastily, 'oh, I don't mean of leprosy, I mean of us.'

But an unhappy novel never runs smooth. The human intercourse, the give and take of people, is unsure. In the past Greene used to administer tiny shocks to the reader by studied gaucheries. In this book they are far too common, as if he is afraid we are not really paying attention. (And wasn't he right? How many people originally read this novel with attention? Perhaps modern conditions proscribe attention, but that's another story.) But Greene has to express his deep unease more positively than by technical tricks. He is compelled to do something that he had flirted with before but never quite dared to tackle baldheaded. It's not that the Church is wrong—that cannot be. But perhaps the priests don't always get the message right. Right up to *The Living Room* priests transmit the wisdom of the Church, although they often do it ineffectively. But what about the Superior at the leproserie?

The Superior said, 'I do not tell you to do good things for the love of God. That is very hard. Too hard for most of us. It is much easier to show mercy because a child weeps or to love because a girl or a young man pleases your eye. That's not wrong, that's good. Only remember that the love you feel and the mercy you show were made in you by God. You must go on using them and perhaps if you pray Klistian prayers it makes it easier for you to show mercy a second time and a third time . . .'

'And to love a second and a third girl,' Querry said.

'Why not?' the doctor asked.

'Mercy . . . love . . .' Querry said. 'Hasn't he ever known people to kill with love and kill with mercy? When a priest speaks those words they sound as though they had no meaning outside the vestry and the guild-meetings.'

It is in the conversations with eager, innocent Father Thomas that the mood gets its best expression. It is useless for Querry to explain that he is not a 'good' man, that he has not only lost faith but is not even looking for faith, that he is (as Querry puts it) cured! Cured of belief! The idea is so preposterous Father Thomas cannot grasp its meaning.

The view of God and religion we are given here is nihilist, or at least tends to nihilism. The final, brutal act of rejection does not occur nor can we expect it. But a lot of ground has been covered when Greene tells us, in effect, that if religion has a value, or if it is to realise its value, it must be persuasive as well as redemptive. In this book it has lost its function. Dr Colin is the High Priest, the others group round him hoping they can find something useful to do. The dilemma of post-Renaissance religion, so well analysed in Auden's middle and later verse, is spread before us. Father Thomas, odd man out, feels that a layman may sometimes have more capacity for understanding than a priest. There is symbolism in his move from the leproserie to a seminary in the bush from which he hoped to obtain a teacher for a new class. Here was a situation where sin did not matter and none of the priests pretended it mattered. Moral theology was the last thing they were concerned with; Father

Thomas's doubts and scruples were the final twistings of an out-moded system. A catechist who had lost nose, fingers and toes fathered a baby on to a woman who could only crawl on the ground dragging her crippled legs behind her. The child was taken to the Church and baptised Emmanuel. The question of marriage was not raised. But how many other people, in how many other countries, living graciously amid cocktails and *Time-Life Magazine*, are in situations equally desperate? After nearly two thousand years of advice, torture and pleading, has anything been done for them? Can we continue to accept the approach? Is there not a major irrelevance?

Querry is not a pleasant fellow and his tone pervades the book. He hates himself and inevitably hates everything else. He drama-tises his own predicament by insisting on being non-dramatic—for an element of drama is native to the human condition. The theme of Catholic apology is raised by his convenient lack of faith. It is a perverse novel for there is a tendency to state opinions and pref-erences through their opposites. He tells Father Thomas that he no longer believes and he no longer loves. 'Father, if I must speak plainly, I don't believe at all. Not at all. I've worked it out of my system—like women.' And he adds grimly that he has no desire to convert others to disbelief, which sets him aside from the humanist, positivist tradition of modern times. Of course, a man cannot set aside a lifetime of faith like an old shirt. Dr Colin saw this and told him that he was too troubled by his lack of faith. He kept fingering it like a sore he wished to be rid of. But this is not a victory for the faith. A man who has given up smoking or alcohol feels the same irritation. Parallel with the loss of faith ran the loss of vocation; perhaps they did more than run parallel, perhaps they were of the same essence. There was also a positive mutilation, success. Success mutilates the natural man, causes him to be stared at and sought out, to be written about. He cannot be himself again, not even if he retires into the jungle.

An unhappy book and a very courageous one. 'This is my body and this is my blood,' muses Querry. 'Now when I read that passage it seems so obviously symbolic, but how can you expect a lot of poor fishermen to recognise symbols?' But this is not an occasion for smug Protestant grins, for Greene's view of the other world, the non-Catholic world, remains unchanged. Parkinson stands before us, the best creation of its type since Ida Arnold. He had the allure of corruption, virtue had died in him long ago, nothing could hurt him but failure. Greene's fascination with failure can be graded; Parkinson is an ugly specimen of the type compared with, say, Scobie. And yet even for Parkinson he exhibits a kind of grudging admiration, the kind you have for a smelly old dog who has won all his battles even if they were not worth the winning. That is Parkinson, Ida Arnold, George Bernard Shaw, the liberal humanist world, the secular state, the policeman: failures in a framework they cannot see, let alone understand.

Of the four stories in *A Sense of Reality*, one had already appeared and has been mentioned earlier. ('A Visit to Morin'.) The impression one gets from this book is that Greene had finally become fully conscious and decided to face his internal dilemmas head-on. (I mean by this that much of the significance in a creative writer's work is an unconscious product.) These stories, except for the Morin one, which belongs to the earlier, religious phase, are ostensibly concerned with reality. They therefore do not resemble his other stories, which were never about reality but about real things. After reading these stories one gets the feeling that a Professor of English Literature has condescended to tell us what life means. As a result, they lack the hallucinatory atmosphere which the earlier stories usually possessed and which these need badly. Puzzles are planted in the text, illustrations are included, and there is a severe rash of fiction's most dangerous disease: ponderosity. Naturally, an attempt is made to hide it but it is much too heavy for the apparatus which conceals it.

Again there is a sense of unhappiness, particularly of loss. In 'Under the Garden' (the most important of the three), Wilditch is obsessed by a dream from his childhood, the only one he remembered. But was it a dream? Or was it an imagination, or a game he had played? Could it possibly have happened? At this point we reach the familiar entrepot in Greeneland, where dream and reality merge. Was it no more than a fantasy which he had written for his school magazine, much to the dismay of his Fabian mother? (We may ask ourselves, at this point, whether the fantasy, which is reprinted, does not bear a close resemblance to the story told by Querry to Marie Rycker in *A Burnt-Out Case*.) After reading it, Wilditch got into bed and wondered how he he had come to construct such a trivial little day-dream. It must have been a dream, yet a dream was itself an experience.

As usual, dreaming and childhood belong to the same world. In the introductory section to this story the plight of childhood is forced upon us. As Wilditch walks away from his doctor's, where he has been delicately told that he probably has little life left in him, he hears a child behind him whimpering, 'But it hurt', and the mother replying, 'You make a fuss about nothing'. Children are hurt and adults show little sympathy. Conversely, adults are hurt and children do not understand. There is a great deal of Greene in this parallelism. Wilditch has a child, a mysterious child . . . in Africa . . . or Asia . . . he has seen little of it. The child has a disability, a wound; it is coloured. When Wilditch decides to return to his childhood home, a last pilgrimage, while there is still time, he knows he will hurt himself. Like Querry, he must finger his sore. But with the calmness of mind that the knowledge of approaching death brings, he is aware that his own wound is his most precious possession. We are formed by our wounds. Edmund Wilson had said it more explicitly.

On this occasion the return to the world of childhood uses the technique of the children's author. There are echoes of E. Nesbit, whom Greene showed a liking for in *Journey Without Maps*. Down the tunnel brings back *Alice in Wonderland*, as does the tendency to pun on the part of Javitt. Even stylistically there is a nod to Stevenson: 'I had expected him to wake with a howl of rage and even in my fear some of the pride Jack must have experienced at outwitting the giant'. But the techniques are being used for a very different purpose. This story is not meant for children. It is about children.

It is like a summary of what has gone before. Javitt is very talkative on the subject of names. You have several, he says. There was one used by the midwife, one by your parents, one by your tribe, another by strangers. The latter was the only one that had no power. The really powerful one was the first. Metaphorically, Greene has always given us the strangers' name. Throughout his work there is a reluctance to speak out, to reveal himself completely. Javitt told him that his duty to the human race was to be disloyal, advice which Greene has passed on to his readers and, especially, his fellow-writers. All that has been said before, particularly implied before, is said again, rather arcanely, but it's too deliberate. The symbolism is blurred to the extent that we can never be sure whether an object is an object or a symbol. For instance, there is a chamber pot. Now a chamber pot is a necessary piece of furniture in Greeneland, and it carries with it its special aura, but there is a possibility that the aura is here out of place, because it has been introduced too pointedly. There is a possibility that the only function of the chamber pot is to prove that it all really happened.

I said at the beginning that this book exudes a sense of loss. The things that are lost are, in order, a myth, a faith, integrity and an ancestry. Of these, there is the suggestion that the myth has been rediscovered. But what comfort we are to get from this it is hard to say. Perhaps no more than that while the myth is recoverable there is still hope. The Christian consolations have been found wanting. So long as we keep contact with the myths of childhood we may yet find redemption.

In Search of a Character contains two journals, one of which, 'Convoy to West Africa', had appeared in a periodical several years before and has been referred to earlier in this book. 'Congo Journal' is the kind of document critics will give their eyes for. It belongs to the period when Greene was finding material for *A Burnt-Out Case*. Not only are the parallels obvious, they are stated without any inhibitions whatsoever. In a footnote to one entry he says 'I was already beginning to live in the skin of Querry, a man who had turned at bay'. There is an air of depression (again) and he speaks of his own spiritual poverty compared with Conrad, who had made a similar journey. If poverty is betrayed by a fragmentary response to life, then here we have poverty. One should not condemn on the evidence of a notebook, whose strength might well be that it is a collection of first-hand impressions, unrelated. But the lack of cohesion is not new, there has been a kind of disinterest at the heart of his recent writings. The insistence of the average critic on taking the theologising seriously has ricocheted on the novelist. Here we see him naked, a man at bay, in a way that would never be allowable in a novel. For Greene is a novelist to his finger-tips and in this journal the finger-tips are working ten to a dozen. The religious discussion is and was a patina, and should never have deceived the alert mind. Yet at one point Greene makes a strange statement: 'am I beginning to plot, to succumb to that abiding temptation to tell a good story?' he asks. Has he finally deceived himself? Doesn't the novelist, if he is a novelist and not a masquerading philosopher, always seek to tell a good story? Isn't one of the weaknesses of much modern fiction been that it works from a preconceived moral?

I said earlier that the dreams had come back in *A Burnt-Out Case*. Greene is aware of them, wants to use them. A whole day was dominated by a dream about a single person—he remarks ironically, 'How strange it is that for more than a hundred years Africa has been recommended as a cure for the sick heart'. He wonders if there is a way in which he can use the dreams of X, who was to become Querry. A strange question, when you consider how, throughout his career as a writer, he has used dreams. In a later footnote he recognises this preoccupation and attributes his interest in dreams to the psychoanalysis he went through at the age of sixteen. He tells us that one of Querry's dreams was in fact dreamt by himself, and at the very moment when he needed it. He wrote it in next morning. *It's a Battlefield*, he says, originated in a dream. In Africa he encountered a persistent faith in magic, which he equated with dreaming, and commented on the failure of primitives and children to distinguish between dream and reality. Many of the views expressed in *Journey Without Maps* recur here. Sociologically the most perceptive is his fear that Africa will step in one stride from tribal magic to American gadgetry. This is happening. The hope that Africa would reveal her personality through the freedom and independence movements of our time is rapidly dying. 'Congo Journal' is a valuable commentary on a cultural mess.

When the first edition of this book was published Greene had had one play produced. I have already written about this and there is nothing to add on a re-reading except (a) when, in Act I Scene 2 Michael explains how he first met Rose 'she was like a landscape you see from a train and you want to stop just there', one winces because this is novelist's language and shouldn't be put into anyone's mouth, but this is a first play and one expects a few such gaucheries; (b) in the first scene of Act II the play finds itself, i.e., becomes sincere, probably because here Greene is dealing with the passions unqualified, having discarded temporarily the religious commentary and reaction which was uphill work; and (c) I note that Peter Glenville in his Introduction urges the cast and director not to concern themselves with Catholic belief.

The next play was *The Potting Shed*, dramatically a considerable advance. Jacob H. Adler, in an essay entitled 'Graham Greene's Plays' in the Kentucky University volume, says that the gardener's name, Potter, brings the *Rubaiyat* to the mind of any literate Englishman. It is probable that Greene intended such an association, for not only does he choose names carefully (or they choose themselves carefully) but the linking of Potter with Potting Shed is too obvious to ignore. The play appears to have been written during 1957, and God is still with us. Again it is the religious references, with their pointed significance, that are hardest to swallow. There is a reference to Lazarus (Act II Scene 1) which is so embarrassing that it suggests the author's own lack of ease, about which there is by this stage no doubt. The whiskey priest of *The Power and the Glory* is back under the name of Father Callifer. One feels that Greene is far happier with him than with the priest in *The Living Room*, whose vices were merely negative. Callifer doesn't even believe. He goes through the motions. 'I have to say Mass in the morning. I abide by the rules. It's the least I can do.' One feels that this is an eminently satisfying situation. Of course, he had believed, especially when the miracle happened. Back of the lost faith lies a tragedy, perhaps a personal working-out of the cosmic tragedy on which J. H. Newman based his faith. Father Callifer gave his faith in return for James's life, just as Sarah had sacrificed her love for Bendrix's life. This is quite acceptable, as it was in *The End of the Affair*. The theme of this play holds the attention and requires no abuse of one's own private loyalties; it is the minor touches, often sounding like petulant little gobbets of pique, that detract from the sincerity. Isn't this the pert monstrosity:

JOHN: Why should He do a miracle for you?

JAMES: If I knew I wouldn't believe in him. I couldn't believe in a God I could understand.

In Act III there is a conversation between James and Sarah that comes direct from the glibber Entertainments, of which this is representative:

SARAH: I don't want eternity. I hate big things—Everest and the Empire State Building.

JAMES: Everest exists.

Aside from these proprietorial lapses, and a few mechanical gaucheries that remind the reader that the author is still virtually a newcomer to the form (see the summoning of Mrs Potter by Anne in Act II Scene 1), Greeneland holds its spell. The psychological emptiness of James is movingly described and presented. He is Pile, he is Querry, each with a difference, but most of all he is the little boy from the Basement Room who has now grown up. We were told in the story what he would be like and here he is. James has discovered that love doesn't last; such statements are usually to be interpreted spiritually but there is a suspicion that in this case physical love is at least partly intended. One remembers the author again, and Querry. When love has gone one is a burnt-out case. But one can never be sure. In *In Search of a Character* Greene tells us how desire is smothered by surfeit—then feels something quicken at the unexpected sight of a beautiful African girl.

During his heyday I think of Greene as a man who loved love and thought he ought to love God. Later, when the machine is running down, he loses faith in both. It is when he is tempted to philosophise from the losses of his later years that one feels he is getting out of touch. He rejoices in parallels, seems to have a conviction (surely magical) that the mere existence of parallelism is a powerful proof of the ideas that run together. 'Boredom is not a good reason for changing a profession or a marriage', says the dreadful Victor in *The Complaisant Lover*. This is the negative assault which Greene resorts to so often, and it is repeated again and again. Robin, the child, calls and Victor says: 'You'd better go to him.' 'I'll have to go,' says wife Mary. Root, the lover, calls and Victor says she must go to him. 'I'll have to go,' says Mary.

What is he saying here? Not much, and we can't expect much. If he is saying that the only difference between a husband and a lover is that the first suffers from the disadvantage of an impossible situation, which is monotony, it is hard not to agree. This is a comedy of manners and a welcome essay on Greene's part. I'll stick my neck out and say that this is as vital as many of the Restoration comedies which are still presented from time to time. The present period suffers from no lack of social comedy in the theatre, but few have the authority and maturity of this one. It is written by a man who has no natural bent for comedy (there was *Loser Takes All* and there was *Our Man in Havana*, a tragicomedy), so that the comedy does not come from natural gaiety, as it does with O'Casey, but entirely from the situation. And here Greene is on firm ground, for he has always been a master of situation. The wryer the situation, the more he likes it. Dramatic irony is native to him, and in the last scene we have enough to send any West End audience home gurgling with delight. The comparison with Coward also presents itself; Greene is less witty but a good bit more penetrating—of the psychological layers, that is. And not since Middleton has so much fun been squeezed out of a man for being Dutch.

What makes this comedy superior to most of its contemporaries is that Greene cannot help letting a strain of seriousness creep in. The utter, hundred per cent, uncomplicated comedy makes us roar with laughter for an act, and then we stop all of a sudden because the vacuity makes itself felt. The best comedy, the lasting comedy, gives us more; by confronting us from time to time with the uncomic we keep our perspectives and amusement is fortified by conviction.[1] The character of Victor Rhodes in this play is so completely Greenesque, our response is bound to be more than a laugh. To begin with, Rhodes is a dentist, and in Greeneland a dentist is a symbol of pain, of emptiness and indifference. With his execrable jokes, his self-conscious 'sense of humour' and his utter insensitivity,

[1] Which is why an O'Casey tragedy is more comic than a Veman Sylvaine farce. (Greene once praised Sylvaine for her stage craft).

Rhodes is impossible—and yet Greene has done as much as anyone to teach us that the impossible is among us, to portray his immense pathos. It is a pity that Rhodes goes out of character towards the end. We know that strong emotion and suffering can mature a mind, but they cannot revolutionise a vocabulary in a couple of minutes.

The last play to date, *Carving a Statue*, is a new departure. Here Greene is consciously tapping a strain of fantasy in a way he had rarely done before—in his early work only in *The Bear Fell Free* and a few stories and, more recently, in *A Sense of Reality*. It was bound to upset the orthodox, apart from what may be the nearest thing the public theatre has yet seen to on-stage sexual intercourse. The first Act is a perfect dialogue in itself—innocence and wonder talking to wonder and innocence, only divided by a chasm of years. One could not expect such a level to be maintained throughout three acts.

The Father is obsessed. The Boy is imprisoned by his Father's obsession. He tries to discover freedom first through sex, then through love, but he is robbed of both. Feebly the mystery of childhood returns and nags him. Something about his mother . . . 'Where were you when mother died?' he asks his Father. We discover that he ran away, literally ran away. And he has been running away for the rest of his life. The great man, the man who is recreating God, has never been able to face life. Life is too pressing, too real, he would rather take the easy way and reduce it to an Idea. When the Idea of God the Father becomes too much for him he can exchange it for the Idea of Lucifer.

This play is a hopeful sign. We may see in it Greene's first approach to a territory which probably exists but which so far has not been settled: that lying between the better West End production, to which Greene's earlier plays belong, and the Royal Court-Theatre Workshop new wave. With great courage and tenacity he has succeeded in a new medium when he felt that his powers had deserted him in the old. But he has brought to the new field many of his familiar beliefs, characteristics and prejudices. In his *Epitaph* (the play was supposedly killed, but it will rise again) he implied that it should have been written for fun but wasn't. Writing for fun is something that Greene must find enormously difficult, but at least he can write as he pleases. He has always shown a hankering after anonymity, despite the fact that this leads to charges of 'Kafka!' being flung at him. In this play only one character has a name. The theme is given the sense of universality he is seeking. I feel that the Boy speaks for the author and for many of his creations when he says: 'I wanted to be a sailor once. You've seen how good I am at knots. I had dreams of ports like Valparaiso. But all I want now is a borrowed bed and a room over the petrol pumps'. It would be unfair to let loose the symbolists over such passages, but one thinks of the Nigerian Navy, the love tangles and the Catholic Church. And Davies (with an e) appears as a murderer, leaning over Brighton Pier. Perhaps this play was too personal, too much a distillation of the author's career, to come to terms with the reality of the living theatre. It remains a dream. And the interpretation of this dream is going to be one of the merriest hunting grounds for literary journalists since James Joyce was worked over.